Anestis Keselopoulos

Lessons From a Greek Island

From the "Saint of Greek Letters," Alexandros Papadiamandis

(previously *Greece's Dostoevsky: The Theological Vision
of Alexandros Papadiamandis*)

PROTECTING VEIL

Acknowledgements:

The translator would like to thank George and Judith Middleton, Sally Anna Boyle, Yvonne Hyma, Philip Navarro, Aaron Taylor, Constantinos Koutoumbas, Denise Harvey et al., Father Gregory Edwards, Owen White, Dr. Constantine Cavarnos, Dr. Christopher Veniamin, Bishop Basil (Essey), Patrick Barnes, and many others for their assistance with the preparation and promotion of this text, without whom this work would have never come to completion.

Editor: Sally Anna Boyle
Graphic Design/Layout: Yvonne Hyma

PROTECTING VEIL
www.ProtectingVeil.com
www.Facebook.com/ProtectingVeil
Info@ProtectingVeil.com

ISBN-13: 978-1500268633
ISBN-10: 1500268631

Inside book photos (used with permission) by:
Edwards, Fr. Gregory: 169
Harvey, Denise et al: Map of Skiathos on 234-235
Koutoumbas, Constantinos: 26, 118
Middleton, Herman A.: 33, 35, 40, 43, 52, 60, 63, 66, 77, 78, 81, 90, 93, 95, 115, 120
Perov, Vassili Grigorovich (Wikimedia Commons): 29
Stieler, Joseph Karl (Wikimedia Commons): 165
Uncut Mountain Supply: 58
Cover Image: Boyan Dimitrov/BigStockPhoto.Com

Anestis Keselopoulos

Lessons From a Greek Island

From the "Saint of Greek Letters," Alexandros Papadiamandis

(previously *Greece's Dostoevsky: The Theological Vision of Alexandros Papadiamandis*)

Foreword by Hieromonk Alexis (Trader)

Translated from the Greek, compiled, edited, and with an introduction, notes, and glossary

by

Herman A. Middleton

PROTECTING VEIL

Author's Dedication:

This book is dedicated to the memory of those
who lived the liturgical tradition of the Orthodox Church,
and for the love of those who continue to live it.

CONTENTS

TRANSLATOR'S INTRODUCTION

A Note on the New Edition

About a month ago, I sent out the following message to the Protecting Veil newsletter:

"It has become clear that our latest book, *Greece's Dostoevsky: The Theological Vision of Alexandros Papadiamandis*, needs a new title. Why is this? The feedback I have received is that the title makes the book sound overly academic and abstract (which the book is not!) One of our bishops purchased 60 copies (one for each of his priests!) because he believes that the book is a practical guide for parish life."

I asked for the assistance of our readers to re-title the book, and we went with the most popular title. When I originally decided to translate the book I did so because I was struck by how Dr. Keselopoulos brings theology to life through the lives of Papadiamandis's characters. This book is the opposite of abstract: it is a vibrant witness to the practical and loving approach the Church takes to the everyday struggles of the faithful. Dr. Keselopoulos reveals how Papadiamandis, through his stories, provides practical "spiritual lessons," for the faithful. He takes the theology of the Church and reveals how it relates to everyday life.

Papadiamandis is greatly beloved in Greece, and among Orthodox faithful all over the world, as the "Saint of Greek Letters" (he was also affectionately referred to as a "Kosmokalogeros" - a "monk living in the world"). While Papadiamandis was by no means perfect, he had a profound and abiding love for the Church, for the pious traditions and life of the Greek people, and for the Saints (such as St. Nicholas Planas, for whom Papadiamandis served as chanter). He also had a rare literary gift, which he used in his service to the Church. I personally have a great love for

Papadiamandis and I sincerely hope that this new edition will enable many more in the west to meet and be edified by this most wonderful of Christians.

- Los Angeles, California. Ascension, 2014.

Original Translator's Introduction

The question of the relationship between art and the spiritual life of Orthodox Christians is a topic that is both ancient and contemporary. The publication of *Lessons From a Greek Island* provides an opportunity to revisit this question, for Alexandros Papadiamandis is an example of a faithful churchman who was also a dedicated artist.

Orthodox thinkers have not thoroughly addressed this important issue, which affects Orthodox throughout the world, especially those living in a modern Western society increasingly influenced and informed by art. In addressing this question, it is important to note that we all come to this issue with certain preconceptions, which are largely the product of our distinctly Western education. C. S. Lewis notes that modern Western culture tends to confuse the artistic with the spiritual. He points out that at some point during the nineteenth century the English word "spiritual" began to take on a broader meaning.[i] Rather than being exclusively used in conjunction with religious life, it began to be used as a way of describing art. Artistic pursuits began to be described as "spiritual" pursuits. One could also note the misuse of other closely related words such as "sublime" and "ineffable" that were once used exclusively to describe religious experience, and which began to be used to describe art. Lewis rightly decries this adulteration of meaning, yet we are heirs to this tradition. Orthodoxy, on the other hand, does not romanticize art and artists, but insists on a realistic approach to life. The artistic pursuit is no more spiritual than cleaning the house, although both may be prayerfully done to the glory of God.

The confusion arises at least partially because man's creative

[i] Lewis thought that it might have first appeared as an idea in print through the pen of the poet and cultural critic Matthew Arnold.

impulse is (rightly) perceived as a product of his creation in the image and likeness of God, and as a continuation of Adam's creative vocation (naming the animals, tending to the garden, and so on). However, rather than being particularly spiritual in their own right, these functions are part of what it means to be human—part of our vocation as humans is to use and develop our God-given gifts. When art is considered to be a spiritual pursuit in and of itself it takes on a diabolical aspect. In this case, art ceases to be the means to an end (the glory of God), and it becomes the end itself and thus, an idol. All good things may be perverted and art is certainly not immune.

We should be quick to note, however, that as with all positive aspects of man, Orthodoxy affirms the artistic impulse. The Church's tradition provides many healthy examples of the proper use of man's artistic gifts. The description of Solomon's temple in 1 Kings 6 gives clear witness to the propriety of using the costliest materials and the most beautiful art to glorify God. In the world of language and literature, the Fathers often use an allegorical interpretation of Scripture, which makes sense as Christ Himself employed allegory in His use of parables. Large portions of the Old Testament are poetic and aim at teaching through images and story. Many Fathers wrote poetry, having found normal language inadequate for describing their spiritual experience. They found poetic language, if still insufficient, at any rate more adequate.

The Church's tradition provides countless examples of its use of art, and Church history provides countless examples of the power of art, both liturgical and non-liturgical, to change hearts and to inspire faith. It was the sublimity of the services combined with the artistic beauty of the church of the Holy Wisdom in Constantinople that convinced the emissaries of Prince Vladimir of Kiev that Orthodox Christianity revealed the true worship of God. The artistic achievements of Byzantium and Orthodox Russia, in particular, continue to give witness to the presence of God among men. In modern times, many have found faith in God through the works of writers such as Fyodor Dostoevsky and Alexandros Papadiamandis.[ii] There can be no question that art, both liturgical and non-liturgical, can bear wonderful fruit.

Having considered some of the positive aspects of art in the life of the Church, we now consider artistic creation in relation to the spiritual life. For, while the Church does not reject the positive aspects of the artistic impulse, its approach is realistic and its main criterion for judgment is the effect something has on the spiritual life. The spiritual experience of the Church has shown that the active cultivation of one's artistic impulse almost inevitably comes into conflict, eventually, with one's spiritual life. In the words of Archimandrite Sophrony, "Pride strengthens the action of the imagination, whereas humility suspends it. Pride bristles with desire to create its own world, whereas humility is quick to receive life from God."[iii] Earlier in the same text Archimandrite Sophrony provides a succinct and profound discussion of human creativity as it relates to man's creation in the image and likeness of God:

> Whereas the creative thought of God becomes a reality and is materialized in the world, the free movement of the created being follows the reverse route, relinquishing things created and seeking God Himself, since in Him lie the ultimate end and meaning of man's existence. The world is not self-sufficient. It does not exist of and for itself. Its purpose is the final transfiguration of the creature through knowledge of the Creator....
>
> Hesychastic prayer is neither artistic creation nor scientific investigation; neither philosophic research and speculation nor abstract intellectual theology. The spiritual life does not mean satisfying our emotional desires, as do the arts, for instance. All these activities, some noble, some less so, relate to the sphere of the imagination which must be overcome if one is to attain perfect prayer, true theology, and a life verily pleasing to God.... God creates the world, and this creation

[ii]As Fr. Alexis Trader notes in the Foreword, "More than one soul has turned to Orthodoxy on account of the good seed sown by Dostoevsky's works," (see p. 29).
[iii]*Saint Silouan the Athonite*, 167.

is a con-descension. But man's movement towards God is an ascension. In rising from the created world towards God, the ascetic does not deny the reality and value of the creation. All he does is not to regard it as an absolute, not to deify it or consider it an end and a value in itself. God did not create the world in order that He Himself might live the life of the creature. He created it in order to associate man with His own Divine Life. And when man does not arrive at deification, which cannot be achieved without his own collaboration, the very meaning of his existence disappears.... In God there is accomplishment, having no need of incarnation.[iv]

While Archimandrite Sophrony does not reject art, he describes the authentic Orthodox approach towards art, "the ascetic does not deny the reality and value of the creation. All he does is not to regard it as an absolute." These words provide a very clear vision of the place of art, and all secular pursuits, in the lives of Orthodox Christians. All of life can be used to the glory of God, but when any aspect of creation is absolutized, it becomes an idol.

What, then, are some of the hallmarks of an artist who is also self-avowedly Orthodox? From Dr. Keselopoulos's book, we can discern a number of things that characterize the art of Alexandros Papadiamandis.

1) Christian art is characterized by its realism; it is honest about life—about tragedy as well as joy. The artist identifies with people's pain and joy and never loses sight of the possibility of life's redemption and transformation.

Papadiamandis refuses to romanticize any aspect of life or the Church. In stories such as "The Visit of the Holy Bishop," and "The Monk" he addresses serious problems in the Church with sincerity and directness.

2) Christian art makes use of the "language" of Christianity: Christian symbolism, language, music, history, and so on. The Christian artist uses art as a way of interpreting and elucidating

[iv]Ibid., 156-158.

Christian truth. In the case of Papadiamandis, he was immersed in the life of the Church from an early age, he understood Her language intuitively and lived the Gospel as the Church lives the Gospel: experientially. "Papadiamandis knows that an intellectual acceptance of the tradition does not suffice. For this reason, he chose a different path for himself: to live humbly within this tradition. Thus, his own life also became a part of this tradition, along with his work."

3) Christian art is not afraid of asking difficult questions and of interpreting world history in light of Christian revelation. This is especially true with those traditions (pagan, Jewish, etc.) that influenced Christianity. Truth is revealed in unity and agreement, not in opposition, and Christian art should strive to find this unity in life, in history, in language. "Those who complain about the presence of pagan elements or hidden pagan tendencies in his work forget that Papadiamandis does not express the fragmentary and particular, but the unified and the whole. The center of his life, the Church, incorporates and transforms everything, which is why, in his thought and writing, these two seemingly contradictory traditions find continuity and unity within each other."

4) While Christian art often reveals Christian truth in an indirect way, when appropriate it does not shy away from describing religious subjects. It does not have to (and should not) idealize what it describes, but it should attempt to provide the whole picture: human weakness and struggle as well as divine presence.

Much more could be written on this topic. Our purpose here was to introduce some of the ideas and themes involved in the conversation. We also wanted to "prime the pump" so that as you work your way through *Lessons From a Greek Island*, you will be inspired to engage these issues.

TRANSLATOR'S NOTES

I used as my benchmark the transliteration chart of the Library of Congress. Certain changes were made when usability factors outweighed faithfulness to the chart. While the titles of most Modern Greek sources in the endnotes were transliterated, some references to ancient Greek sources were translated for texts for which English translations exist. In all cases usefulness to the scholar and general reader was chosen over faithfulness to established conventions.

The translations of Papadiamandis's texts are mainly my own and are also taken from the recently published collection of his short stories, *The Boundless Garden*, Volume I (Limni, Greece: Denise Harvey, 2007) and are indicated accordingly in the endnotes. The translation in the Appendix of the story "A Village Easter" is from Volume I of *The Boundless Garden* and that of "Without a Wedding Crown" is from Volume II (forthcoming); the map of Skiathos is from the same publication. I am grateful to the publisher for permission to use these translations and reproduce the map.

Unless otherwise noted, footnotes were added by me. Most of the endnotes are from Dr. Keselopoulos, unless followed by [Tr.] indicating that they were my addition.

Biblical quotations are from the NKJV.

Words included in the *Glossary* are marked with a † on their initial occurrence in the text.

FOREWORD

A Unique Witness to a Unique Opportunity

Hieromonk Alexis (Trader)

America is known worldwide as a land of great opportunity, but every American must discover this opportunity for himself and, once he has found it, must seize it in order to make it his own. The Holy Orthodox Faith is not simply an opportunity. It is the great opportunity for every man that comes into the world. It involves the opportunity to be healed of the harmful desires and deceptive thoughts that cripple the life of proud and selfish man. It includes the opportunity to become a new creation in Christ Jesus guided by humility and selfless love. It contains the opportunity to become a vessel of the Holy Spirit ceaselessly united with Christ in the heart. It encompasses the opportunity to truly become Christ-like by grace and, in turn, to humbly embrace all of creation with His boundless love. The Church is truly a land of opportunity. The "great cloud of witnesses" — the Saints throughout the ages — give testimony to the fact that this land of opportunity really exists, but every believer must still find his way into that promised land and make its great opportunity his own. This wonderful book on Alexandros Papadiamandis by Dr. Anestis Keselopoulos provides a map for this very quest.

Papadiamandis was not a bishop. He was not priest. He was not a monk. He was a simple yet genuinely Orthodox layman who observed those who seized upon the great opportunity and those who failed to do so. His observations, in turn, became the heart of his fictional, but not fictitious, writings. As a layman and as an artist, he had the freedom to explore the great opportunity from every angle and the boldness to point out the obstacles to that opportunity, which are created when the misguided misunderstand the eucharistic and liturgical aspect of ecclesial life that makes that opportunity possible and act on that misunderstanding. Dr. Keselopoulos makes it quite clear that Papadiamandis's profound understanding of what liturgy is and what liturgy can do enable Papadiamandis to initiate others through his writings into the mystery of this great opportunity. *Lessons From a Greek Island* will be, for many, the first step across the threshold of this mystery.

Liturgical renewal is not a new theme for Christians in the land of opportunity. Orthodox Christians in America are well aware of the importance of liturgical texts, sacred icons, and participation by the faithful in the divine services. Nevertheless, Papadiamandis opens another window by letting us see how the liturgy flowers, in all its manifestations, under the right conditions such as those that were present on his native island of Skiathos, and how it withers when fallen human interests deprive it of its proper soil and care. What makes this vision of Papadiamandis so compelling is that he does not merely offer us another philosophy of the liturgy or a new ideology for conservative or liberal reform. Instead, he offers us human examples taken from the experience of day-to-day life in Christ. His priests and lay folk are people with whom we can identify and to whom we can turn for guidance as we enter the same struggle to offer God the worship He is due.

This makes *Lessons From a Greek Island* far more than a description of theological teachings contained within the literature of an important writer in modern Greece. It is a catechism. In fact, it is not only a catechism for those who know little about Orthodox liturgy and faith — it can also act as a compass for those who have some knowledge about Orthodox prayer and doctrine but are in need of criteria for evaluating authentic liturgical life today. In other words, this gift to America is both a catechism and a strategy for Orthodox evangelism that begins with the pulse of the heart of Orthodoxy—the liturgical life of the faithful. As a catechism, *Lessons From a Greek Island* provides instruction on the ideal conditions that enable the grace of God to sanctify and transfigure the faithful in the eucharistic gathering. As a strategy, it warns those serving the Church of the pitfalls that prevent those conditions from being established and, by extension, prevent conversion and transformation of the faithful as well.

Liturgical Art and Life: East and West

Non-Orthodox readers might well be mystified by the importance of hymnography, architecture, iconography, and ecclesiastical music as sources of life and wisdom for Papadiamandis. They may be tempted to view Papadiamandis as a mystic or, even worse, as a religious fanatic.[i] Such a view would greatly diminish the value of Papadiamandis's observations and could not be further from the truth. Papadiamandis was a normal, healthy Orthodox Christian. He was a realist and, one could say, an empiricist. By experience, he knew the transfiguring power of the ecclesiastical arts in the Orthodox Church, and the wisdom he gained therefrom entered his fiction in a most natural way.

Nevertheless, if those who are unfamiliar with the Orthodox Church are puzzled by his source of inspiration, they are certainly justified. Today in the West, Roman Catholics and Protestants are primarily instructed by listening to sermons, attending Bible studies, and reading theological works. Although some of these Western Christians consider the ecclesiastical arts to be praiseworthy expressions of individual creativity and piety, these arts remain external forms of only relative value and secondary importance. These arts can be easily altered or replaced by other quite different artistic forms without compromising the worship service whose essence is

[i]One is, in fact, reminded of Dostoevsky's hero in *The Brothers Karamazov*. "I must explain that this young man Alexei, or Alyosha, as we fondly call him, was not a fanatic, and in my opinion, at least was not even a mystic." Fyodor Dostoevsky, *The Brothers Karamazov*, Book I, chapter 4, The Third Son (Signet Classic: New York: 1999) 29.

as nebulous as its changing forms. In fact, in terms of the elevating emotions evoked by art, the difference between an aria and the settings for a mass or between a religious painting and a secular masterpiece is relatively insignificant.

Other analogies are necessary in order to understand the fundamental role that art plays in the Orthodox East. Art is used to instruct the believer in a concrete Orthodox Christian approach to life in its manifold dimensions. The modern term for this ancient teaching technique would be the "multimedia experience," with visual, musical, linguistic, and even olfactory dimensions. Each sense receives impressions that direct the entire soul to glorify God and repent for its own estrangement from the divine beauty that envelopes the soul during divine worship. Art is used not merely to educate the mind but, more importantly, to shape the heart and redirect its desires and ambitions.

In other words, the liturgical arts are the time-tested tools that the Church uses to heal the faithful and direct them to Christ. In Orthodoxy, the arts are not intended to provide religious entertainment for the senses but to purify them.[ii] The theological essence of Orthodoxy is quite precise, and the forms that protect the essence are necessarily precise as well. Those who attained to union with Christ either produced the liturgical arts or affirmed the fact that their use helps lead others to that same union. These artistic creations are the precious fruits of life in the Holy Spirit that lead those willing to be led to the spiritual life of Paradise. They have the purpose not only of opening the heavenly world of God's glory to the believer, but also of opening up the believer's own inner world so that he can see his passions and deceitful desires and, by God's grace, defeat them. One hymn in the veritable sea of liturgical texts has the faithful chant (and thus confess), "many times when I am chanting hymns I am also committing sins; for while my mouth utters songs of praise, my soul is pondering unseemly things."[iii] Even the modern psychologist would agree

[ii] In the first ode of the canon for Holy Pascha, Orthodox Christians are exhorted, "let us purify our senses and we shall see Christ in the unapproachable light of the resurrection." This purification is the necessary first step towards the vision of Christ in glory, the stage of perfection or theosis.

[iii] Taken from the Tuesday Matins Aposticha in the third tone (*Octoechoes*).

that this brutal honesty about our fallenness and recognition of our hypocrisy is the first step to overcoming them both.

Another aspect of Papadiamandis's vision that may seem strange in the West is the absolute centrality of the Church as experience. The liturgical life consists of more than a Protestant Sunday worship service or even a Roman Catholic daily mass. It is the oxygen that infuses the atmosphere of the believer's entire life, enabling him to breathe. The texts from the divine services are what help him make basic decisions in his daily dealings with others. The liturgical life gives meaning to the most basic aspect of created life – time, the coming of day in Matins and the coming of night at Vespers. Simultaneously, it takes the believer beyond time in the Divine Liturgy to the uncreated reality of the glory of the Holy Trinity. Each day in the liturgical cycle is a unique gift of God, a unique opportunity to approach Him in thanksgiving and repentance. This is also reflected by the central icon of the Saint whose memory is celebrated on any particular day as well as by the liturgical texts that change with the hour, the day, and the season.

In the Orthodox Church, worship is a source of joyful sadness that clears the mind and heart with a sober optimism. It is also a real struggle of body and soul. This athletic aspect of Orthodox liturgical life may also perplex the non-Orthodox reader. Although the importance of pilgrimage is a common theme in the religious texts of Western Christendom, the importance of vigils, which are also associated with pilgrimage, may not be so readily apparent. Vigils enable the believer to give his entire self over to the liturgical life of the Church for an extended period of time. The night hours during which visibility is lessened enable the believer to focus on turning inward. By devoting these hours of darkness to prayer, although they are the customary time for sleep, the believer offers a small sacrifice to God. In spite of the real struggles a vigil requires, the believer who turns to God for such an extended period of time does not feel as though he is offering God anything of particular significance, but that he is the fortunate recipient of mercy from God. The many blessed hours at prayer humble the soul, soften it, make it less selfish, and thus open it up to the grace of the Holy Spirit. There is nothing gloomy about these vigils. They are illumined by another light and quite naturally become a source of great joy; for, through such vigils, man can find his true self by finding the God of his heart.

Religious Fiction and Greece's Dostoevsky

Throughout the ages, fiction has been used to convey ideas and experiences of ultimate import. In the West, there is a long literary tradition of addressing religious topics or using religious practices as a backdrop for fiction even before Chaucer's *Canterbury Tales*. In the modern era, George Bernanos's *Diary of A Country Priest* comes to mind as a Western counterpart to some of Papadiamandis's literary explorations. The closest parallel to Papadiamandis's short stories and novels, however, is found in large sections of Fyodor Dostoevsky's *The Brothers Karamazov*, which are likewise saturated with Orthodox teaching taken, in many instances, from texts read during the liturgical services. While these sections in *The Brothers Karamazov* can be read without an in-depth knowledge of Orthodox spirituality and liturgical life, they only reverberate properly within that context. Only within the context of life in the Orthodox Church can the significance of many gestures be appreciated and the many subtleties distinguishing the exaggerated from the conventional be perceived. This same remark could be made of Papadiamandis and is, in itself, justification for Dr. Keselopoulos's study. Like Dostoevsky, Papadiamandis looked deep into the human soul and found that its beauty and nobility depend not on the power of its intellect, or on the intensity of its desire, but on its genuine relationship with God.

There is, however, an important difference between Dostoevsky and his Greek counterpart. A book like *The Brothers Karamazov* explores the vast extremes of the human soul, from the most vulgar and sensual to the most refined and holy. Many who read *The Brothers Karamazov* in the educated West take more of an interest in Ivan, the intellectual, than in the devout Alyosha, the would-be monk, even though Alyosha is declared to be the story's hero by the narrator himself. This shift in focus has made it possible for many, including such prominent figures as Freud and Sartre, to read and admire *The Brothers Karamazov* and completely miss its true import — that the Christ-like experience of transfiguration brought about by humble love and holiness within the Orthodox Church is the rebuttal to the atheist's most brilliant philosophical arguments and the sensualist's uncontrolled desires. From Dr. Keselopoulos's descriptions of Papadiamandis's sketches, it is clear that such a misinterpretation of the significance of Papadiamandis's work would be much more difficult, and Professor Keselopoulos's analysis of these sketches makes this misinterpretation well-nigh impossible. The analogy with Dostoevsky hinges on the realization that what is most precious in Dostoevsky is neither the tormented personality, nor conflicts with the subconscious, but Orthodoxy itself.

Although Papadiamandis is a well-known literary figure in modern Greece, his sizeable corpus remains relatively unknown in the West, where knowledge of Modern Greek literature hardly extends beyond the novels of Nikos Kazantzakis. In a secular age given to blasphemy, Papadiamandis's works seem by comparison out of step. Nevertheless, what gives his works their strength is not the trendy doubts and passions of contemporary man, but the perennial possibility of transcending every doubt and passion by union with God. It is hoped that Dr. Keselopoulos's study will initiate an interest in Papadiamandis as a literary figure, initially among Orthodox Christian readers, and lead to the translation and wider dissemination of Papadiamandis's own works among the English-speaking public at large. Good literature is capable of leaving a mark on people's choices and people's lives. More than one soul has turned to Orthodoxy on account of the good seed sown by Dostoevsky's works. The same can surely take place through Greece's Dostoevsky as well. Professor Keselopoulos's book is meant to ready that seed for sowing.

Some Significant Themes for Orthodoxy in America

Many of the themes covered in *Lessons From a Greek Island* can be found scattered throughout Orthodox ascetic literature and lives of the Saints. What makes Papadiamandis's treatment of these themes unique, apart from the use of the modern novel and short story as a medium, is that his vision is formed by the truly praiseworthy, though much-maligned, *Kollyvádes* fathers. These modern fathers, devoted to the tradition of the *Philokalia*, refused to separate liturgical practice from dogma and spiritual endeavor for the sake of secondary expediencies of convenience or practicality. They understood that the true goal of liturgy, dogma, and spiritual endeavor is union with Christ. All the details in the rich tapestry of Orthodoxy must serve that goal, or they fray into an incoherent tangled mass of strands leading nowhere at all. The *Kollyvádes* fathers were Papadiamandis's teachers, and by experience he knew the benefits of following their guidance. Even a cursory glance at some of this guidance, gleaned by Dr. Keselopoulos from the writings of Papadiamandis, intimates what a blessing this unified vision of the spiritual life and authentic liturgical experience will be for Orthodox Christians in America and for all people whose lives are marked by the fractured and compartmentalized nature of society at large.

For Papadiamandis, the way the divine services are conducted and the texts and actions called for by these services form a unity. In particular, humility rather than ostentation is the guide for how the priest should serve, how the chanters should chant, and how the Church should be adorned. This humility is not a forced posturing but the natural outcome of serving the Eucharist with awareness that Christ is the One offering and being offered.[iv] Papadiamandis's characters demonstrate that the beginning of humility is honesty with themselves, by admitting that they are sinners "and the chief of them," and honesty with God. Their refreshing simplicity and forthrightness springs from their unified life in the Church nourished by liturgical texts, which encourage frankness in the believer's approach to himself and to God.

Can an American living in such a complex society with people traumatized by a diversity of psychological disorders gain this

---

[iv]In the silent prayer before the Cherubic hymn, the priest says, "For Thou art the Offerer and the Offered," meaning that Christ is the true Celebrant of the mysteries and the Mystery being celebrated. In humility and the fear of God, the priest simply lends his hands and his mouth to Christ.

honesty, simplicity, and humility? If he has the opportunity to immerse himself fully in the life of the Church and if the wise precepts of the fathers for the liturgical life and the life in Christ are implemented, all things are clearly possible through the grace of Christ. In fact, the point of Papadiamandis's narratives is that the downtrodden, wounded, and despised can be transfigured into the glorious people of God through the Church's divine worship.

Humility in liturgical celebrations enables the priest to be shepherded with his flock by Christ, the One True Shepherd. Humility enables the priest to console the suffering. Humility encourages the priest to be dedicated to the divine services and to celebrate them with the fear of God and precision [akriveia]. This precision and fear of God in serving the services as the typicon and sacred canons prescribe, in turn, sanctify the priest, crowning him with the wisdom and understanding needed to be a good physician to the souls under his care.

Of course, the issue of being precise or strict [akriveia] in contrast to making adjustments [economy] is highly debated by Orthodox Christians in America. Dr. Keselopoulos's treatment of Papadiamandis makes it clear that strict adherence to the canons and typicon need not be legalistic. The canons and typicon are fruits of worship imbued with the grace of the Holy Spirit, and they aim at enabling each generation to enter into that same worship. Entering fully into this worship makes the pious fisherman of every age most wise through the grace of the Holy Spirit.[v] It enabled the "uneducated" priests of Skiathos to become illumined and full of understanding; it can do the same for the humble priests of America. When, however, the canons are disregarded, the Church cannot function properly. Economy serves the same aim as the strict application of the canons; it is not a *carte blanche* for changes or exceptions that fail to take into account the therapeutic aim of canon law. It should be noted that the faithful and careful celebration of the divine services

[v]Apolytikion for Pentecost, "Blessed art Thou, O Christ our God, for Thou hast shown the fishermen to be most wise by sending down to them the Holy Spirit."

gives the priest the understanding necessary to apply the canons appropriately in each situation that arises. In particular, the attentive reading of the priestly prayers kindles the priest's zeal to do good. Unwavering obedience to the instructions for celebrating the divine services together with humility and self-reproach before the holy altar accustoms the priest to doing good according to the will of God. Together these blessed habits ingrain in him a patristic mindset and, more importantly, a receptivity to divine grace that provides the illumination necessary for the canons to be applied in a God-pleasing way. "God is not unjust and does not close the door against those who knock with humility."[vi] The faithful and careful celebration of the divine services is among the most important ways in which the priest learns how to knock at the door of God's tender mercy.

An issue related to the subject of liturgical precision is that of full-length monastic services. Orthodoxy in America is currently blessed with a flowering of monastic endeavor. This flowering, however, raises questions about the relationship between the services in parishes and in monasteries as well as the relationship between the monastic typicon and the so-called parish typicon. On this issue, Papadiamandis is particularly clear. The monastic services provide a model and serve as an inspiration that the parishes should strive to imitate as much as possible given the requirements of life in the world. "Angels are a light for monks, and the monastic life is a light for all men."[vii] There is no reason why monks should be the only Orthodox Christians to enjoy the sweetness of vigils that last throughout the entire night. There is no reason why the monks alone should feast on the plentiful banquet of divine services, while those in the world should be content with only a few crumbs from the Master's table. Papadiamandis's examples reveal that all-night vigils full of compunction and humility concluding with the Divine Liturgy are not only feasible for believers in a parish but can become as

[vi]Saint John Climacus, *The Ladder of Divine Ascent*, Step 26:118 (Holy Transfiguration Monastery: Brookline, 1979), 179.
[vii]Ibid., Step 26:31, 167.

much their joy and source of strength as they are for any monk in a monastic community. In Orthodoxy, there is not one spirituality for the laity and another spirituality for the monastics. There is one unifying goal in the Church — union with Christ. The surest way to that goal is through the cultivation of a genuine liturgical ethos of repentance and thanksgiving. Since this ethos is directly dependant on the length of time spent at genuine prayer, the length and form of the services celebrated in the monasteries provide those living in the world with a concrete and detailed model for how this ethos can become their own.

In recent years, the patristic analogy of the Church as a hospital has been rightly stressed. There is a tendency, however, to view the priests exclusively as physicians and the laity exclusively as patients. Papadiamandis offers an important corrective to this tendency through his emphasis on lay ministry. First of all, everyone including the priest is a patient in this hospital under the care of Christ the Great Physician. Although the priest has a fundamental role as a physician, the staff, which includes nurses and technicians of various kinds, is also absolutely necessary. That staff, for Papadiamandis, is the laity, whose pastoral labors extend beyond the space of the Church building and time of the Church services.

On the other hand, Papadiamandis notes the dangers of laity assuming responsibility when they are infected with the spiritual diseases of vanity, vainglory, and acquisitiveness. Wardens or parish councils without an ecclesial and Eucharistic mindset can act like tyrants and sabotage the very work of the Church. Their relation to the ecclesial body and respect for the position of the ordained is also crucial for the unity of the Church.

In an age of plastic, disposable, virtual reality, Americans thirst for what is solid, enduring, and real. In a fractured, compartmentalized society, they long for unity and wholeness with God, with their fellow man, and with themselves. In *Lessons From a Greek Island*, the American Orthodox Christian will not only be given a glass of water to quench this thirst, but he will also be directed to that fount of living water in the genuine and faithful liturgical tradition of the Orthodox Church.

A vigil in the ruins of the church of the Panagia of Prekla

Papadiamandis's works bear witness to the fact that the solid, the enduring, and the real that unite all creation are ultimately found in the experience of Christ, nurtured in the Orthodox Church, the same yesterday, today, and forever. This is the great opportunity that Dr. Keselopoulos illuminates through Papadiamandis's writings. May we all make this opportunity our own.

Father Alexis (Trader)
The Sacred Monastery of Karakallou
The Holy Mountain of Athos

INTRODUCTION

People yearn to experience true worship, which is the conscious living of the mystery of the Church. Orthodox worship, and particularly the Divine Liturgy, is the Church's eternal self-revelation. The path of the Christian leads through worship to the Church and, through the Church, to worship. The Church's approach to life is revealed through Her communal experience of worship. True Christian spiritual life revolves around the cultivation of a genuine liturgical ethos during and after worship.

True Christian worship is the rational worship,[1] in the Spirit, of the people of God. The faithful follow what the Apostle Paul says, "I will pray with the spirit, and I will pray with the understanding also: I will sing with the spirit, and I will sing with the understanding also."[2] If the rational aspect is absent, there is a danger that worship will take on a magical character. But worship is also above rationality; as a mystery, it is primarily the work of God. This is the meaning of the liturgical expression, "It is time for the Lord to act."[i] As a work of God, worship is a mystery concealing an exceptional power that cannot be judged or fathomed by human means. As an action of the body of Christ, the Church, it is primarily the action of the Holy Spirit; according to the prayer of the anaphora in the Liturgy of St. Basil, the Holy Spirit strengthens all noetic and rational creation so that it may be able to worship God and offer an eternal doxology to Him.

---

[i] With this expression, the deacon summons the priest to begin the Divine Liturgy. The priest responds with "Blessed is the kingdom."

In the world of Greek literature, Alexandros Papadiamandis is widely acknowledged as the most important theological figure of the nineteenth century, and yet theologians have not properly examined his work. If his work has a particular theological value, it is because it has the Church and her liturgical tradition at its center and as its starting point. In articles published in newspapers on the occasion of large feasts of the liturgical year, Papadiamandis addresses and confirms the primary need for worship to have a rational nature. Knowing that the Church's services were formed in earlier times and that the liturgical texts were written in a form of Greek that is no longer spoken, he presents the liturgical ethos of the Church in terms that the public can understand. By interpreting liturgical services and prayers and analyzing hymns and forms of worship, he attempts to reveal the liturgical wealth of the Orthodox Church, which, in the minds of many Greeks in the early twentieth century, had become a museum artifact without any substantive value.

While working to illustrate the value and relevance of Orthodox worship to his contemporaries, Papadiamandis reveals the dynamic dimension of worship enlivened by the Holy Spirit. Through his short stories in particular, he boldly presents a theological anatomy of the spiritual life of the Orthodox Greek world and leaves his unique mark on the liturgical tradition and the eucharistic ethos of his people. The theology hidden in his works is, in the final analysis, a theology of the Transfiguration — for it depicts the transformation both of a group of people into the body of Christ, and the simple piety of the humble and rejected into worship, spiritual glory, and truth.

Living thousands of miles to the north of Greece, Papadiamandis's contemporary, the Orthodox Russian Fyodor Dostoevsky, provided his people with a similar witness. Although his Orthodoxy is perhaps more veiled, Dostoevsky describes the internal spiritual life of the Orthodox Russian world. His works similarly give witness to the Transfiguration and the possibility of man and society's spiritual transformation and redemption. As with Papadiamandis, Dostoevsky's works themselves become authentic expressions of the faith of the Church: artistic expressions whose source is the Church and Her liturgical tradition.

A portrait of Fyodor Dostoevsky
by Vassili Grigorovich Perov, 1872

Despite the importance of Papadiamandis to Orthodoxy in modern Greece, no treatise or study in the field of theology, of which we are aware, has dealt with the theological and liturgical tradition as recorded in his writings. Papadiamandis's prolific and profound literary corpus gave rise to the present undertaking. The present work does not constitute an even partial repayment of the common debt toward Papadiamandis, nor a counterweight for all he and his legacy have suffered at the hands of so-called academic theology. The goal of this study is not to attempt to provide the scholarship that Papadiamandis's work deserves, but primarily to reveal the abundant riches of his work—a treasure that offers sustenance to a world of the spiritually impoverished.

In the pages that follow, we show how the eucharistic ethos in the works of Alexandros Papadiamandis is an extension and consequence of his experience of the liturgical life. Before we deal with his theology in detail, we first consider the life of Papadiamandis and his ecclesiastical and literary world. In the first chapter we introduce some of the issues and debates concerning both his literary talent and the authenticity of his Orthodox faith. We also consider the question of Greek ecclesiastical language and its translation as it relates to Papadiamandis. This is an issue that has been and continues to be a source of heated debate in Greece, in whose rich linguistic heritage the New Testament, the canons of the Church, and most patristic texts belong. In the chapters that follow, we deal in more detail with the liturgical tradition in the works of our storyteller.

The second chapter considers clerics in the liturgical life of the Church and their broader pastoral service. In Papadiamandis's Skiathan stories, the priests come forth from the people of God. Although those in power during the Bavarian Occupation of Greece[ii] attempted, in the days of our writer, to forcefully distance the clergy from social life, the clergy continued to be an integral

[ii]When government was first established in Greece after the First Greek War of Independence, an attempt to establish a monarchy was made using royalty imported from Germany.

part of Greek society. The close participation of the clergy in the lives of the people is a given, both in the celebration of their joys and in the consolation of their woes and trials. In contrast to the ecclesiastical situation of Athens, the pastoral care of the simple priests of Skiathos is administered with great sensitivity and, above all, with a real connection to the liturgical life. In the final section of the chapter, reference is made to Papadiamandis's constructive, albeit harsh, criticism of some of the problems besetting the clergy, which he notes mainly in the behavior, practices, and methods of pastoral care of certain bishops of his period.

In the third chapter, we focus on the place of the laity in the Church, emphasizing the unity of clergy and laity. We observe that the priests of Papadiamandis's stories are aware that they are performing a ministry and service that does not exclude, but rather encourages, lay ministry and service. The clergy's acceptance and cultivation of the ministries of laypeople is shown to be necessary for the healthy operation of the ecclesiastical body. In Papadiamandis's writings, not only are laymen called concelebrants[iii][†] but they also truly act in this capacity. The chapter closes with a discussion of Papadiamandis's attitude toward the first appearances of the Greek religious brotherhoods[iv] and the relationship of the Church to the world, the State, and politics.

The fourth chapter concentrates on the meaning and content of ecclesiastical tradition and shows how it is the spring from which flows the Papadiamandian corpus. This becomes apparent through Papadiamandis's many references to Holy Scripture, patristic texts, the canons, the hymnology of the Church, and the hagiographic and synaxarian[v][†] tradition. Through Papadiamandis's writings, we see how the tradition of the Church is protected by its catholicity and, at the same

[iii]One that serves (celebrates) the Liturgy together with the priest.

[iv]This is a reference to para-ecclesial organizations that began appearing in Greece under Protestant influence at the turn of the twentieth century.

[v]The *Synaxarion* is a collection of the lives of the Saints, arranged according to the day their memory is celebrated during the ecclesiastical year.

time, how its catholicity is realized in its tradition.[vi] Tradition is possible only within the bounds of genuine ecclesiastical community and cannot survive outside of it. Finally, we present the diachronicity of tradition, as understood by our author, and underline how inextricable Hellenism and Byzantium remain in his thought and life.

In the fifth chapter, we attempt to discern and express Papadiamandis's understanding of the form and essence of worship. We present his stance regarding the liturgical order and the typicon[vii†] of the Church and identify the influences of the monastic typicon on the liturgical typicon of his native island of Skiathos. From this discussion we assert that, for Papadiamandis, maintaining a common liturgical typicon, ecclesiastical music, psalmody, and reading is an essential presupposition for ensuring the unity of the liturgical tradition. Finally, we conclude by revealing the great mystery depicted in Papadiamandis's writing: the transfiguration of people and society that takes place in the eucharistic gathering, in the human-divine communion.

As the whole of Papadiamandis's art has an ecclesiastical character and liturgical orientation, it inevitably includes commentary on the contemporary state of the Church's liturgical art. In the sixth chapter, we consider how Papadiamandis presents churches and icons. His writings greatly surpass simple descriptions, and themselves become representations, poems, and melodies that express the tradition. These expositions not only reflect on the history and technique of the icons but also confirm the personal and substantial relationship that the faithful can have with them. Papadiamandis's position regarding the exploitation of icons and the conversion of icons

[vi]The Church's tradition is protected by the universal affirmation and the living of these traditions by Orthodox Christians throughout the world and throughout the centuries. At the same time, the universal bond shared by Orthodox Christians throughout the world and throughout the centuries is protected and strengthened by the shared affirmation and living of the Church's tradition.

[vii]Typicon: In this case the term refers to the rules/directions governing how a liturgical service is to be celebrated.

The country chapel of St. Elissaios
(previously the chapel of the Prophet Elijah),
which was renovated during the 1980's

and liturgical vessels into museum pieces is also discussed, as are his opinions regarding the debasement of all ecclesiastical arts, particularly music, when they follow Western fads.

THE LIFE AND WORK OF
ALEXANDROS PAPADIAMANDIS

A Short Biography of Alexandros Papadiamandis

Alexandros Papadiamandis was born on the Greek island of Skiathos on March 4, 1851, "the second Sunday of Lent and the feast day of Gregory Palamas, while they were singing the *triadiká*[i] in church" (as we are informed by his fellow countryman Papa-George Rigas,[ii] distinguished scholar of folk traditions and specialist of the liturgical typicon). While this first intimation of God's favor appeared during Papadiamandis's birth, the second took place during his Baptism:

He was baptized on the Monday of Bright Week and named Alexandros. Something unusual happened while the priest, Papa-Nicholas, performed the Baptism; as he poured the oil in the baptismal font, the oil immediately made the form of the cross on the water. Papa-Nicholas interpreted this strange phenomenon, saying, "This child will be great."[1]

His father was the pious priest Adamantios Emmanuel. Papadiamandis writes that he was "a beneficent guide in all ecclesiastical questions and a sublime adornment of ecclesiastical celebrations"[2] in the church of the Three Hierarchs and in the

[i]Triadiká: A series of hymns sung in honor of the Holy Trinity.
[ii]Papa: A diminutive for a priest, used before his first name. It is often used as a term of endearment.

The chanter's stand where Papadiamandis chanted,
in the church of the Three Hierarchs in Skiathos.

country chapels of Skiathos.[iii] From an early age, Alexandros followed his father around the island helping him, sometimes in the altar and sometimes at the lectern as chanter. With his exceptional sensitivity, Alexandros treasured his experiences of sharing this liturgical service with his father. His heart was filled with and his *nous*[iv]†was instructed by images from the priestly life and the Church's services. He was so influenced by them that most of the scenes he chose to paint as a child were taken from the life of the Church. Reflecting on this time, he writes in his autobiographical memoir, "When I was young I would paint Saints, or I would write [hymnographical] verse."[3]

[iii]It is a common practice in Greece for the faithful to build small chapels throughout the countryside, often in gratitude for miraculous interventions by Christ, the Mother of God, or the Saints. The tiny island of Patmos, for example, has 365 chapels and churches. The chapels serve as places of prayer and pilgrimage and are the focus of worship on the feast day of the Saint or event for which the chapel is named.

[iv]The word *nous* has been translated as "reason" or "intellect," but used in the patristic sense, as it is here, it refers to man's spiritual faculty rather than his logical ability.

From his childhood years, Alexandros had the opportunity to live the tradition of the *Kollyvádes*[v]† fathers (those Athonite fathers involved in the eighteenth century movement that inspired spiritual renewal and a return to more traditional liturgical and spiritual practices).[4] This tradition had been preserved on Skiathos through the presence of a monastery built by the *Kollyvádes*, the Monastery of the Annunciation. Although the monastery was in decline during Papadiamandis's later years, the diligently preserved kollyvadian tradition remained alive in the inhabitants of the island. He would later write, "In this small monastery [of the Panagia[vi]† of Kounistras in Skiathos] at the end of the eighteenth and beginning of the nineteenth century, six of my relatives were priest-monks."[5] Papadiamandis gives an account of the monastery's spiritual life and foundation on Skiathos:

> Papa-Gregory...the ascetic, descended from the heights of Athos[vii]† together with his elder, Papa-Niphon, and thirty other monks. They sailed to the island of Gregory's birth [Skiathos], and there, in the gorge of Angallianous, they built a beautiful, awe-inspiring monastery—patriarchal, Stavropegic,[viii]† and coenobitic[ix]†—with an exquisite, very

[v]The name *Kollyvádes* is derived from the Greek word *kóllyva*, the boiled wheat prepared by the faithful to be blessed in church in memory of the reposed. The use of wheat as a Christian symbol for the soul is rooted in Christ's words in John 12:24. The name *Kollyvádes* was derisively given to this movement of spiritual renewal because one of the issues addressed was the performance of memorial services for the reposed on Sundays. The kollyvadian fathers were opposed to this innovation, as it was not in accordance with the traditional resurrectional character of Sunday.

[vi]Panagia: This is perhaps the most popular term of endearment for Mary the Mother of God in the Greek language.

[vii]Mount Athos: A monastic republic in northern Greece, on a peninsula surrounded by the Aegean Sea.

[viii]A Stavropegic monastery is one that falls under the direct supervision of the most senior bishop in any given Church jurisdiction. In the case of large parts of Greece, a Stavropegic monastery would fall directly under the supervision of the Patriarch of Constantinople. In the same way, the monasteries of Mount Athos are also Stavropegic and enjoy a similar spiritual independence from the local bishop.

[ix]Coenobitic literally means "common life" and refers to a monastery where all members of the community share monastic life: in prayer, worship, and work. This is the most common form of monastic life.

fine church, built with great care. It was so beautiful that during those years, at the beginning of the nineteenth century, it was famous and enjoyed great respect among the monasteries of Athos. These ascetics...were the so-called *Kollyvádes*, who were under persecution on the Holy Mountain, as they insisted on precision[x†] (regarding frequent communion), and on many other things.[6]

The renowned Elder Dionysios was a distinguished spiritual father and learned priest-monk who lived on Skiathos, whose roots were in the kollyvadian tradition. Papadiamandis knew him personally and did not hide his admiration for him.[7] He was "the inspired spiritual father in the small monastery of the Prophet Elijah."[8] Papadiamandis had such monks and monasteries in mind when he wrote, "the rule of prayer should be complete, following all the old typicons, with the vigils[xi†] and pre-dawn Matins, with all the appointed verses and readings from the Psalter."[9]

Papadiamandis was initiated into this kollyvadian—the genuine Orthodox—tradition, in his own home by his father, Papa-Adamantios, and by the broader world of the Church in Skiathos. In an unsigned obituary for his father, he wrote that

Papa-Adamantios, like all of the older priests of the island, was taught how to celebrate the Mysteries[xii†] by those venerable *Kollyvádes*, who, at the end of the last century,

[x]Within ecclesiastical vocabulary, precision [*akríveia*] generally denotes the precise keeping of the Church's traditions (canonical, liturgical, etc.) as opposed to the use of Economy—understood as a loosening of these traditions at a certain time, for a certain person (or persons), when precision obstructs the path to salvation.

[xi]The Greek word for vigil (*agrypnía*) refers both to one's own private vigil in prayer as well as to the long night services (particularly for Church feasts) celebrated in the Orthodox Church. An Athonite monastery has an average of thirty-five vigils a year. A standard vigil lasts between nine and ten hours, while patronal vigils can last between twelve and seventeen hours.

[xii]The Greek word *mystírion* is translated throughout this work as "Mystery" rather than as "sacrament," as it corresponds more closely to the theological meaning of the word. It is capitalized so as to differentiate it from the common meaning of the word.

established the Monastery of the Annunciation...which became a seedbed of humble priests for our island, priests who were lovers of the divine services. Simple and virtuous, they enjoyed the love and respect of the inhabitants, having no affectations or hypocrisy, and displaying no vanity as they lived their lives as priests.[10]

Seeds of spiritual struggle that had been planted in Papadiamandis during his childhood and adolescence at home and in the wider environment of Skiathos were brought to fruition when he went on a pilgrimage to the Holy Mountain[xiii†] for a few months at the age of twenty-one. In one of his stories, we read about some of the events of his visit, mainly at the Skete[xiv†] of Xenophontos, and we perceive how the charm of the Holy Mountain was an inspiration for him. While there, he met many ascetics and hesychasts[xv†] and became familiar with the liturgical life of the monks. He was enthralled by the vigils of the monastics and recorded in his heart not only the strict typicon and the Byzantine melodies but also the spirit that governed it all. In this way, Athos and its traditions affected the path his life took and enriched it with unforgettable memories.

Given his rich spiritual upbringing, experiences, and heritage, it is only natural that Papadiamandis would choose to spend his life within this rich Orthodox tradition, preserving the Orthodox liturgical ethos through his writings and life. The critics of his age believed that there was little value in a detailed description of "how a village priest went to celebrate the liturgy in a country chapel for a little community of peasants or shepherds, who and how many took part in the festival, and what their customs were like."[11] Papadiamandis, however, did not regard the celebrations

---

[xiii]Also known as Mount Athos, see above.

[xiv]The most common type of skete is a type of monastic organization somewhere between a coenobitic monastery and a hermitage. In a skete, a group of small monastic dwellings are located around a central church.

[xv]Hesychasts are monastics that undertake the ascetic practice of hesychia, meaning "stillness." It is an ancient spiritual tradition that helps the ascetic remain constantly in prayer.

as mere holidays, but himself lived the events and the life of the Church as the center and foundation of all events and all life.

Papadiamandis moved within this ecclesiastical environment and within the wider Greek tradition. He lived both aspects of this tradition, Ancient and Byzantine, in a diachronic unity, which spanned the ages. He had utter integrity, both as a person and as a Greek, within whose Hellenism was Byzantium and in whose love for Byzantium might be discerned Hellenism. In his texts, Ancient Greece resembles a flower that, wilting from its desire for the truth, then bears great fruit in the warmth of the Sun of Righteousness [Christ]. When history is viewed as a progression toward the discovery of the fullness of the truth of Orthodoxy, tradition truly lives, and history is kept from being fragmented. Photios Kontoglou[xvi] and, even more so, Nikos Gabriel Pentzikis[xvii] would act from this perspective later on, with both their pens and their brushes. Together with our author, they are regarded as solid links in this tradition.

God favored Papadiamandis with many gifts, and he struggled to use them in a way that would bear the most God-pleasing fruit. The reverent and liturgical ethos expressed through Papadiamandis's writings and life bear witness to the successful cultivation of his gifts. His desire to glorify God is shown even more in the way he ended his life and in his attitude toward death. In a prayer he offered at the end of a poem entitled, "To the Little Panagia in the Turret," he beseeches her, "comfort me, as well, my Panagia, before / I depart and will be no more."[12] In a letter written by Papa-George Rigas, we learn about the last moments of Papadiamandis's life on earth:

His repose took place as follows: He became ill on the 29th of November 1910. On the third day of his illness,

[xvi]Photios Kontoglou (1895-1965): A writer, artist, and iconographer. He is best known for his study of Byzantine iconography and his great struggle to reintroduce traditional iconography into modern Greece.

[xvii]Nikos Gabriel Pentzikis (1908-1993): A novelist, artist, and pharmacist whose pharmacy in Thessalonica became a refuge for poets and painters in the mid-twentieth century. He is buried at the women's monastery of Ormylia in Halkidiki.

Papadiamandis's tomb in the cemetery in Skiathos

he fainted. When he revived, he asked, "What happened to me?" "It's nothing, a small fainting spell," his three brothers who were at his side told him. "I haven't fainted," Alexandros said, "in so many years; doesn't it seem that it's a prelude to my repose? Get the priest immediately and don't delay."... Soon after, having been called [by his brothers], the priest and the doctor arrived at the same time. Papadiamandis was, above all things...a pious Christian. So, as soon as he saw the doctor, he asked him, "What are you doing here?" "I came to see you," the doctor told him. "Keep quiet," the sick man told him. "I will first follow the ecclesiastical path [and call upon the help of God], and then you can come later."... He had control of his faculties until the end and wanted to write a story. Until the end, his mind was dedicated to God. On his own, a few hours before his repose, he called for the priest to come so he could partake of Holy Communion. "Perhaps later on I won't be able to swallow!" he explained. It was the eve of his repose and, as irony would have it, it was the day they told him that he would receive the medal of the Cross of the Savior. On the eve of his repose, the second of January, he said, "Light a candle [and] bring me an [ecclesiastical] book." The candle was lit. The book was about to be brought. However, Papadiamandis wearily said, "Don't worry about the book; tonight I will sing whatever I remember by heart." And he began to chant in a trembling voice, "Thy Hand Touching" [a troparion from the Hours of the eve of Theophany].[13]

Papadiamandis sang this final hymn and, as day broke between the second and third of January of his sixtieth year, he wearily fell asleep. After passing through the furnace of pain and trials and tasting many of the bitter dregs of life while faithfully living the liturgical life of the Church, he now stretched out his strong wings to fly to the upper chapel of the angels, toward which he had oriented his whole life. It snowed on the following day and, like Uncle Yiannios in the story, "Love in the Snow," Papadiamandis lay down his worn-out body, presenting himself, his life, and his work before the Judge, the Ancient of Days, the Thrice-Holy. This was, finally, the only judgment with which he was concerned as he passed through life. Though his life and struggle in this world have ended, his work will continue to give witness to his devotion to the liturgical tradition of the Orthodox Church for generations to come.

Papadiamandis's Life and Work in the Context of Modern Greek Literature

Papadiamandis's life echoes the life of every genuine disciple of Christ: there were those who accepted Papadiamandis and those who rejected him, "destined for the fall and rising of many... and for a sign which will be spoken against."[14] For example, the ambitious and rationalistic generation of the thirties in Greece, if judged by its chief theorists, was motivated by a desire to discredit and question all the ideas that had come before it. These scholars casually brushed Papadiamandis aside, who had spent his life in honest poverty, wearing his worn-out pea coat. With a few bright exceptions, when the era's theorists did not speak negatively of his work, they were indifferent or condescending toward it. The most uncharitable of Papadiamandis's critics was the influential literary theorist of the period, Constantine Dimaras who, though unquestionably competent to study the Enlightenment, was completely unable to approach the world of Papadiamandis.[15] Unfortunately, Demetrios Balanos, professor of Patrology at the Theological School of the University of Athens, also belonged to those who could not, or did not want to, understand Papadiamandis. In a special issue of *Néa Estía* dedicated to Papadiamandis in 1941, Balanos wrote a very negative article about the honoree. With the desire to express "objective criticism," he argued that "the great admiration for Papadiamandis has given rise to exaggerations, attributing to him and his work a much wider scope than reality allows."[16]

In opposition to the criticism and haughtiness of academic Philology and Theology, the poets, including Zisimos Lorentzatos, Odysseus Elitis, Angelos Sikelianos, and Miltiadis Malakasis, provide an unshakeable witness for our author. Lorentzatos once wrote, "Among Greek poets up until today...only Solomos passes without question; as for novelists, only Papadiamandis passes."[17] He added that he could bear witness for both, from personal experience. Odysseus Elitis, the poet and denizen of the Aegean, writes the following in "It is Truly Meet":

> Wherever evil finds you, brothers,
> Wherever your nous becomes blurred
> Bring to mind Dionysios Solomos
> And bring to mind Alexandros Papadiamandis.
> The voice unacquainted with lying
> Will give rest to the martyred.[18]

Angelos Sikelianos speaks of Papadiamandis passing his life "quietly humming through his teeth" while resting "upon

Papadiamandis's reliquary,
preserved in the church of the Panagia of Limnia

the tables of the taverna."[19] Finally, Miltiadis Malakasi, who was older than the other poets and an actual acquaintance of Papadiamandis, described our author's world with particular clarity in the four verses written in 1908, entitled, "To the Image of Papadiamandis."

> Your every meditation,
> Song of songs;
> In your world,
> Every creation a world.[20]

Transcending criticism and praise, Papadiamandis's writing speaks for itself. If, from a literary or philological perspective, the foundation of his creation was put into question or thought to be occasionally ambiguous, his works were always true to experience and theologically clear. Few authors have displayed the consistency and interdependence between personal life and literary creation that Papadiamandis did. He and his circle of contemporaries sensed "an inexpressible joy and sweetness" when they found themselves in the tabernacle of the Lord of hosts.[21] His own experience of the Church's liturgical life, as well as his beliefs concerning the things of the world, are expressed through the mouths of the heroes of his stories and govern their actions.[22]

He lived and viewed his entire life as the worship of Christ that unifies all things; so, in his writing he inevitably views all aspects of life and the world (including material things, the physical environment, and Greek traditions) in relation to that divine worship. Few authors have so clearly expressed in writing their faith in this unity: "For my part, as long as I live and breathe and am of sound mind, I will never cease, especially during these resplendent days, to praise and adore Christ, to depict nature lovingly, and to represent with affection those customs which are authentically Greek."[23] Elsewhere, he again affirms, "I am a genuine child of the Orthodox Church."[24] He stamps himself with these words and defines his identity. After all, it would be unnatural for one who, in his own life and writing, could not bear to leave even a small stone unturned and in obscurity to be indifferent to or unaware of his own identity. From whatever perspective one begins to approach him, one is forced to ponder Papadiamandis's unapologetic identity as an Orthodox Christian.

It is obvious that Papadiamandis's writing is formed by a life that is watered from the spiritual tradition of his people. Even his language has the liturgical spontaneity and impact of the *símantron*[xviii]† of Papa-Dianelos in "Easter Chanter," which is sometimes sounded in trochean meter (*ton Adám, Adám, Adám*) and sometimes in iambic meter (*to tá-lanton, to tá-lanton*) calling the sleepy shepherds to the resurrectional Liturgy.[25] Papadiamandis was in constant contact with the language of the *Synaxarion*, the Church's hymns, and other liturgical and patristic texts. He lived according to them, so he understood the value of these texts and their language and was able to convey this in his descriptions. Some readers might have been predisposed to regard this language as gloomy rhetoric, as stiff Sunday clothing. In the sincere hands of Papadiamandis, however, the language of the Church has the impact of a heartfelt speech. His writings are both living and life-giving, not only to people of years past but also to moderns.

Many today, especially the young, criticize the formality of this form of Greek and consider it to be the greatest obstacle to approaching both Papadiamandis and the worship of the Church.[xix] This is not a new problem. Tellos Agras[xx] referred to it in 1936: "Sometimes, I read pages from Papadiamandis to [young people].

[xviii]*Símantron*: Most commonly, a long and slender piece of wood struck rhythmically with a mallet. They are usually used in monasteries to call the community to services, although some parish churches also use them. According to a tradition of the Church, the use of the *símantron* dates from the time of Noah, who used the *símantron* to call the animals into the ark in pairs. Similarly, the *símantron* is used to call the "rational flock," the faithful, into the ark of salvation, which is the Church.

[xix]Dr. Keselopoulos is referring to the debate, which is not peculiar to Greece, concerning the translation of liturgical services into modern languages. This debate is particularly heated in Greece, as the Church's services are celebrated there in the liturgical Greek in which they were originally written.

[xx]Tellos Agras (1899-1944): A renowned Greek poet and philologist of the early twentieth century.

I see that they now find him bewildering...and I am afraid that one of the joys of which tomorrow's young person will be deprived is reading Papadiamandis."[26] His prediction has largely come true in our days, and his assertion that the *Katharévousa*[xxi†] of our author makes interaction with his work difficult is not without foundation. However, we are also obliged to accept that, "beyond the small or large obstacles that Papadiamandis's language places before us, we find the substance and lessons revealed through this language to be the real stumbling block."[27]

The spoken liturgical language of the Church, which has a unique place within the broader symbolic scope of language, presents similar difficulties. Within the Church's life and world, there are liturgical actions and movements, architecture, painting, and music that exist apart from the spoken word that constitute the "language," in the broader meaning of the word, of the Divine Liturgy. Papadiamandis incorporates the richness of this language and of this world into his texts, which often creates difficulties for the modern reader.

> It is not so much unknown words that keep us from Papadiamandis as ignorance, and often the insistent rejection, of his world. The "All-Night Vigil at St. Elisha" by Gerasimos Vokos...sketches with clarity the world where Papadiamandis, even while drifting about as an exile from Skiathos, found consolation. What meaning does such a vigil have for most people in our incredibly bustling age? Most likely, none at all. This is why the reading of Papadiamandis becomes increasingly difficult.[28]

All complaints concerning Papadiamandis's language diminish in light of the true understanding of the language of the Divine Liturgy, which gives witness to the liturgical ethos and life of the Orthodox tradition. Though he sees this tradition lying dormant or forgotten in his society, Papadiamandis has a thorough

---

[xxi]A form of Modern Greek based on the literary tradition. It is considerably more complex than Modern *Demotic* Greek. It is also sometimes called *Purist Greek*, which is how we will subsequently refer to it.

understanding of the ailment and a clear recommendation for the course of action to cure this condition. He is confident that the Orthodox tradition can bring forth abundant fruit again if society returns to the truth of communal life preserved by the Church. He clearly points out the ancient imperative: that the Church lives the reality of the eucharistic gathering, the liturgical gathering of the parish in each locale, which incarnates Christ as the mystical union of the many with Christ. This is the tradition of the Church, where the Holy Eucharist, the fundamental Mystery of communion, is realized during the Divine Liturgy.

If Papadiamandis's life both expresses and is expressed most fully by the Orthodox liturgical ethos, it is because he does not limit himself to a typical, common participation in the Divine Liturgy or in certain ecclesiastical services and ceremonies. Instead, his participation in the worship and life of the Church extends beyond the dismissal of the church services and into the other liturgy—that of life. His relationship to the Church and Her worship is neither half-hearted nor legalistic: "To my mind, the *libres penseurs* [free thinkers] in Western Europe, those who have simply and clearly broken every connection and relationship with the Church, are more sensible than we who continue to mimic Christian worship without faith and without the clear conscience of a virtuous life."[29]

2

THE CLERGY

Pastoral Service

The Church is a mystery of divine-human communion in Christ. The Apostle Paul's well-known image of the Church as the body of Christ expresses the indissoluble relation and communal union of its members. It is a "communion of Saints" made up of clergy and lay Christians, having the communion of the three Persons of the Trinitarian God as its prototype. The clergy are given the duty and the gift to "guide the people,"[1] not because they possess their own priesthood, but because they put on the priesthood of Christ within the Church.[2] The clergy, "clothed in the grace of the priesthood" of Christ[3] during the liturgical gathering of the community, stand together with the community before the holy altar and officiate the Immaculate Body and the Precious Blood of Christ. According to the synodal spirit that has permeated the whole life of the Church since the apostolic period, the people encourage eligible candidates toward the priesthood. "Synod"[i] and "synodal spirit" refer to a procession, the common path of the members of the Church—clergy and laity—toward the Kingdom of God. The clergy have the charisma[ii] to lead this procession and show the way. They are neither outside nor above the procession. As pastors, they must not dominate or master; rather, they should serve the unity of their flock. Traveling this path to God's kingdom in unity, the clergy and laity together

[i]The Greek word is made up of the two words "together" and "way."
[ii]This word may also be translated "gift," in the sense of a spiritual gift.

reveal the communal character of the Church, and, "in concord and unified love, their hymns honor Jesus Christ."[4]

In studying the writings of Alexandros Papadiamandis, especially those set on his island of Skiathos, one begins to see the unity of the ecclesiastical and liturgical community as the body of Christ. The priests are chosen from among the people and have united their lives with the lives of the people. In Papadiamandis's day, the Bavarian-controlled political and ecclesiastical powers of Greece made systematic attempts to secularize the Church and its clerics, but the priests of Skiathos would not give in to this pressure. They pastor their rational sheep, while they are pastored by the Head, and essentially the *only*, Shepherd—Christ. Thus, the priests are constantly aware that the sheep they pastor are not their own but Christ's. "Feed my sheep," Christ commands Peter.[5] Despite their own human weaknesses and imperfections, the priests of Skiathos pastor their flocks in a way that confirms Christ's words, "I know my sheep, and am known by My own."[6]

Papadiamandis's priests are characterized by their humility before the greatness of God and before the struggles and yearnings of the people. They have an acute sense of their own sinfulness, so self-assertion and arrogance have no place in their lives. Contrary to the model of clergy-laity relations that the Bavarians were then attempting to impose,[7] the priests of Skiathos are not given to wielding power. In their unassuming humility, they are able to console those who are despairing, grieved by their passions, and rejected by their communities. In the story "The Unchurched," Papa-Garophalos remains an eloquent model of the shepherd who has true love and genuine pastoral concern. When he finds Uncle Kolia, "the unchurched one," having lived distant from the people and villages of their island for about thirty years, the priest does not reject him as one cut off from the Church, nor does he consider him a sinner. Instead, he sees Kolia as one who has been neglected. Papa-Garophalos looks upon him as a member of the Church who has received the grace of Holy Baptism, which is why he calls Kolia by his baptismal name—Nicholas—and appeals to his patron Saint. He approaches him with brotherly love and fatherly tenderness and implores him to stay for the

ἐγώ μέν βαπτίζω ἡμᾶς ἐν ὕδατι εἰς μετάνοιαν, ὁ δέ ὀπίσω μου ἐρχόμενος, ἰσχυρότερός μου ἐστιν, οὗ οὐκ εἰμί ἱκανός τά ὑποδήματα βαστάσαι· αὐτός ὑμᾶς βαπτίσει ἐν πνεύματι ἁγίῳ καί πυρί:~

"He who is coming after me...will baptize you with the Holy Spirit and fire"

celebration of the Resurrection. This gives him the opportunity to taste the joy of the gathering and of the communion with the faithful that help him overcome loneliness and death. Here, the simple Levite[iii] embodies the ineffable joy and love of the Church, beseeching Nicholas to share in this joy and love:

> May you have the blessing of Christ, my child! Come now!...
> Come and receive a blessing!...Let your soul radiate fragrance!
> Come and delight in the joy of our Christ! Don't neglect
> yourself! Don't fulfill the desires of the enemy!...Trample
> on the temptation! Come on, Kolia! Come now, Nicholas;
> come blessed Nicholas! May St. Nicholas enlighten you![8]

These wonderful words, from the lips of an uneducated country priest, are reminiscent of the Easter sermon of St. John Chrysostom read in church on the night of the Easter service. The holy father writes, "So come into the joy of our Lord....Let everyone enjoy the feast of faith."[9] Here the Skiathan priest,

---

[iii]Levite: In this context, Dr. Keselopoulos is referring to the fact that in the Old Testament the Levites performed the priestly functions on behalf of the people of God. The priests of the Christian Church are the ones who continue this priestly service.

with the same emotion, repeats the words of the Saint, "Come and delight in the joy of our Christ." St. John Chrysostom unhesitatingly calls the neglectful to experience the joy of the Lord. Papa-Garophalos shows a similar boldness, calling blessed the one who some describe as a true werewolf.

The priests' attitude of service and love toward their fellow men is not a type of feigned humility. It reveals their true humility, which is based on their genuine eucharistic and liturgical ethos. It flows forth from their awareness that, as they lend Christ their hands and mouths in the Holy Eucharist, they also forgive the suffering and sinful during the Mystery of Confession without taking the place of Christ, the ultimate source of grace. It is important to note that the priests of Skiathos live within the Orthodox tradition, which never knew the presumptuous authoritarianism of Roman Catholicism, expressed (among other ways) through their use of the phrase *ego te absolvo* ("I [the priest] forgive you"). These priests live in awareness of the complete sovereignty of Christ and learn to forgive in his name.

Papadiamandis's works are full of accounts of the priests' spiritual solidarity with and service to the simple faithful. At the beginning of the story, "A Village Easter," he speaks of Papa-Vangelis, a priest-monk and parish priest, who is also the abbot and only monk of the little Monastery of St. Athanasios. Four times a year, during every long fasting period and despite unfavorable weather, he goes to spiritually encourage and hear the confessions of some Christians who live in isolated spots along the coast opposite Skiathos, people who are characterized as "hill-people" and "mountain-scarecrows" by the villagers of Skiathos.[10] In the stories "Easter Chanter," "A Pilgrimage to the Kastro," "The Unchurched," and many others, we sense the same pastoral attitude in the clergy and their awareness that they share a common path with the laity. In this spirit of unbroken unity with the people, the clergy regard them as members of the ecclesiastical body and the liturgical community. They do not forget about those few goat-herding families who live in the parts of the island that are most difficult to reach. It is their conviction that those families should not be separated from the Church's

View of the Skiathos shoreline from the gate of the Castle

services, especially on the great feasts of the Church year. They travel such distances and in such difficult conditions so that these families might also share in the joy of Christmas, Easter, and the rest of the Church's liturgical feasts.

Just as the priests are with the people of God during the Church feasts and celebrations, they also share their sorrows, troubles, and trials, practicing St. Paul's injunction to "rejoice with those who rejoice, and weep with those who weep."[11] Many of Papadiamandis's stories describe the support that the priests show during difficult circumstances and trials in the lives of the people. The married village priest Papa-Vangelis goes up the mountain in the snow to baptize a newborn child who is in danger of death.[12] For him, it does not suffice to send holy water and to read the necessary prayers of churching from a distance, as the child's godmother suggests. He feels the need to support, with his presence, those people living isolated on the mountain. In another story, for "more than three months [the priest of the church of the Panagia of Kechrea] read prayers" over a young woman who stuttered and gave out inarticulate screams.[13]

The priests approach the community's outcasts and sinners with the same sense of pastoral responsibility as they approach the pious. Papa-Pantelis in Athens does not hesitate to enter and perform the blessing of waters in the houses of prostitutes or to celebrate the Liturgy in country chapels at the summons of Mrs. Spiridoulas, a woman whom her neighbors judge because she rents rooms to women of ill repute.[14] When her good neighbors are scandalized and some are bold enough to demand a justification from the priest, he simply answers that Christ did not come to call the righteous, but sinners, to repentance. Naturally, Papadiamandis does not pardon Mrs. Spiridoulas, nor does he accept the business in which she engages. He does, however, want to highlight how this priest shrugs off the judgment of the wider Athenian society, one that lacks a true worshipping community like that found on Skiathos.[15]

Reading Papadiamandis's stories—especially those set in the microcosm of his island—one discovers that the priests are at the center of society's life, not on the edge. They move comfortably among their parishioners performing whatever job requires literacy, even though they do not have formal higher education. In the society in which they live, they are regarded as the most educated. "Come to re-read the letter, Papa," Stephen says, summoning his parish priest to read a letter from his son, Athanasios, living in South America.[16]

While the priests are recognized for their knowledge of letters, this is not the main reason for the admiration with which their communities regard them. They are most appreciated for their liturgical ethos and pastoral sensitivity, which inspire the love and trust of their flocks. When Aunt Achtitsas's son writes a letter home from Panama, where he has spent years as a migrant worker, he sends it to his parish priest, Papa-Demetrios, because the priest is able to read it to his illiterate parents. Beyond this, however, he shows his trust in the priest by sending a check in his name. If Aunt Achtitsa and her husband have died, their son asks the priest to distribute the money to his siblings, nieces, and nephews, and to the other poor children of the island. He closes by telling the priest, "Father, if my parents are dead, please reserve part of the money for the forty liturgies in their memory."[iv][17]

The pastoral responsibility of Papadiamandis's priests is also revealed in the way they verbally teach the people. Papadiamandis places the theology of the Orthodox Church in the mouths of the priests of Skiathos, who express it in a simple and discerning way. In "Easter Chanter," Papa-Dianelos talks to a simple parishioner about the nature of God's miracles, the memorial services, and the offerings of the people:

> "[T]he point was not to demonstrate God's power, which is proved by countless miracles," answered the priest, "but simply to show the power of memorials and of the offerings made for the dead, and that nothing that a person sacrifices, nothing that he offers up to God or to the poor, no good deed, no virtue, no patience, no tribulation, no tear, nothing is wasted. They all fall on fertile ground, like the corn of wheat, as the Lord said, which if it fall into the ground and die (like *kóllyva*, and like the dead) it bringeth forth much fruit."[18]

Christ the Sower

These words of Papa-Dianelos suggest the biblical and patristic position concerning the goal of miracles in the life of the Christian. Miracles do not aim at impressing people but at the edification

---

[iv]The serving of forty liturgies in a row is not unusual after the repose of a Christian, as well as during fast periods and in other times of particular need. The liturgies are not paid for, but it is common to make an offering to the priest who, during the period Papadiamandis was writing, would not have received a salary from the Church. In order to serve forty liturgies in a row, a priest would have been forced to take time off from the job that provided the income for his family.

and salvation of man. His comments are reminiscent of verses from the Psalms[19] as well as sections of ecclesiastical hymnody.[20] The Skiathan priest also echoes Christ's words, "Most assuredly, I say to you, unless a grain of wheat falls into the ground and dies, it remains alone; but if it dies, it produces much grain."[21] He translates these words for his simple parishioners in a pastoral way. "[W]hen we bury a dead person who has lived a virtuous life in Christ, it's as though we're planting a grain of corn in the ground. . . and the Lord will raise him up on the last day, as he himself graciously promised us."[22]

The same pastoral responsibility and wisdom distinguish Papa-Phrangoulis in the story, "A Pilgrimage to the Kastro." His parishioner Panagos teasingly asks him an innocent question: "Why doesn't Christ give us good weather, Father, if He wants the people to [be able to] go participate in His feast?" Papa-Phrangoulis replies:

> Ah, Panagos, my friend, I see that we don't really know what we are talking about, do we?...Who are we to understand these things!...What's generally true is one thing and what's true in a particular time and place, Panagos, is another....The heavy winter comes for the good, for the earth's fertility and even for our health. Christ has no need for people to go and celebrate the liturgy for him...but where there is a little good will, and one has a debt to pay, and maybe even if there is a risk involved, where it has to do with helping others, as in our case here, there God comes to our side, even in the case of bad weather and a thousand obstacles....There God keeps us company, easing the way, working a miracle even.[23]

It is characteristic that this teaching does not refer only to the love of the Christian toward God but also toward other people. According to this teaching, the vertical relationship with God precedes the horizontal relationship with others, revealing our author's faith in Orthodox patristic teaching. He knows that one must love God before one can have true love for others. As St. Gregory of Nyssa writes, "It is necessary to understand the order of love."[24]

Papadiamandis's views on the education of the clergy are expressed indirectly through his stories, as in the preceding examples, and more directly and extensively in his article, "Priests of the Cities and Priests of the Villages."

> When they speak of the education of the clergy, what do they mean by education? Don't they mean book learning? The priests of the generation before this one were often undereducated. They weren't formally educated, but they were well rounded and educated through their work. They were respected and virtuous. But they weren't able to give sermons, you say? So much the better for them and for the faithful; they taught by their example....They would speak little, say few things, but make a deep impression.[25]

Papadiamandis does not, of course, praise the illiteracy of the clergy but, rather, their simplicity and virtue. He does not reject religious education or "any attempt made from good intentions."[26] However, he does not separate the question of clerical education from the person of the cleric. He does not believe that knowledge can, by itself, change a reprobate or incapable cleric. For this reason, he accords education "only relative worth,"[27] while in another text he states that "it is better to be unschooled than full of oneself."[28] The type of education he considers most important is that possessed by the old, thoroughly practical priests, those priests deeply imbued with the liturgical life and praxis of the Church, despite the fact that they were called uneducated by university graduates of Papadiamandis's time. These priests knew how to celebrate the Divine Liturgy, the Mysteries, and the Church's other services with precision because they had within themselves a spring of devotion for, and fear of, God. He contrasts them to the "swarm of priests, many [spiritually] unrefined and uncultivated men, whose ordinations were imposed by corrupt politics upon the eminent hierarchs."[29] Because they have "badly served or, rather, done badly in neglecting the typicon and rejecting the Church's order of the services, they are incapable of true Orthodox pastoral care, which must be centered on worship."[30]

Papadiamandis knew that during the period of the Turkish occupation priests or monks undertook responsibility for the education of the people. Although many intellectuals influenced by Western ideas criticized them and their *kollyvográmmata*[v] as supposedly simple, these priests and monks kept the *Romyoí*[vi†] within the Orthodox tradition, teaching the people a sense of philanthropy and shaping them in the fear of God. In Papadiamandis's day, as well, there were priests who, though nearly illiterate, were virtuous in their simplicity and educated the people through their example.[31] One of these, who made a deep impression on Papadiamandis and on all who came to know him, was Papa-Nicholas Planas, who was formally glorified by the Church as a Saint.

> I know a priest in Athens. He is the humblest of priests and the simplest of men. If you give him a drachma, or fifty cents, or ten cents,[vii] he will do any *ieropraxía*[viii] you want. If you don't give him anything, he won't ask. For three drachmas, he will do a complete all-night vigil—Compline, Vespers, Matins, Hours, Liturgy. The whole thing lasts nine hours. If you give him two drachmas, he won't complain.[ix]

[v]*Kollyvográmmata*: This is a term that refers to spiritual and intellectual formation by the *Kollyvádes*. This education was usually undertaken secretly in underground schools, as the Turkish occupiers forbade the Greeks to learn their native language, traditions, and faith.

[vi]The term *Romyoí* or simply, Roman, is arguably the most accurate way of referring to Orthodox Christians within the area and tradition of what is today known as the Byzantine Empire. For more on this issue, see the works of Fr. John Romanidis.

[vii]Greek currency. Before being replaced by the Euro, the exchange rate was about 365 drachmas to the American dollar. The drachma, in turn, was made up of 100 cents.

[viii]In addition to the Mysteries of the Church, this word includes every ecclesiastical service a priest undertakes.

[ix]At the time Papadiamandis was writing, priests were dependent on income from parishioners. The situation was particularly difficult for priests in the cities, where they did not have the opportunity to cultivate a garden or provide for themselves in some other traditional way.

St. Nicholas Planas, "I know a priest in Athens.
He is the humblest of priests and the simplest of men"

Once you give it to him, he keeps every prayer list,[x] bearing the names of the reposed to be commemorated, forever. For two, three, four, five years, he continues to commemorate the names for the twenty cents you had once given him. In every preparation of the gifts,[xi] he remembers two or three thousand names. He never gets troubled. When he does the preparation of the gifts, it takes two hours. The Liturgy takes another two hours. At the dismissal of the Liturgy, he distributes whatever bits of bread he has in the altar, from the altar bread[xii] or from the *artoklasía*,[xiii] to those

[x]Paper containing the names of those (living and dead) for whom intercessory prayers are to be made by the priest.

[xi]The preparation of the elements of bread and wine before the Liturgy.

[xii]The altar bread is leavened and made with wheat flour and is used for the Eucharist. It is common in Greece for the faithful to bake these loaves and bring them to the priest along with a list of names to be commemorated during the Liturgy. Usually the number of loaves far exceeds the number necessary for the Eucharist, so they are either kept by the priest or distributed to the faithful at the end of the Liturgy.

[xiii]The Vespers Service for an important feast includes *artoklasía*, or the blessing of the five loaves, which are distributed to the faithful at the end of the service.

who happen to be there. He holds onto nearly nothing. One time, he owed a small sum of money and wanted to pay his debt; he had ten or fifteen drachmas, all in coins, which he counted for two hours, but he couldn't figure out how much it was. Finally, a Christian man helped him undertake the counting....The mistakes he makes while reading in church are often humorous. Despite this, however, among all those listening, among the entire congregation, not one of us laughs. Why? We have gotten used to him, and we like it. He is loveable. He is simple and virtuous. He is worthy of the first of the Savior's Beatitudes.[xiv][32]

The liturgical and worshipful ethos of Papadiamandis's priests serves as the proper foundation and orientation for their pastoral service. The celebrants actively participate in what they perform and proclaim liturgically. They accept the gentle correction that the Divine Liturgy and all the Church's services bring about in their everyday lives. With eagerness and a servant's spirit, they pastor the people whom God has entrusted to them, for the altar, and the experiences it provides, are at the core of their pastoral care. It is where they live the mystery of the Church as the Body of Christ. They implement the words of the Apostle Peter in their everyday actions: "Shepherd the flock of God which is among you, serving as overseers, not by compulsion but willingly, not for dishonest gain but eagerly; nor as being lords over those entrusted to you, but being examples to the flock."[33] The priests, being lovers of the services, implement and realize within their own lives that for which the Church prays during the ordination service: "Give to him love for the beauty of Thy house, to stand before the gates of the temple of Thy holiness, to light the lamp of the glory of Thy tabernacle."[34] The priests of Skiathos serve vigils, Divine Liturgies, Matins, and Vespers in the two parish churches in town, the Three Hierarchs and Panagia Limnia, and at the many country churches around the

[xiv]"Blessed are the poor in spirit, for theirs is the kingdom of heaven." Matthew 5:3.

Church of the Nativity of the Theotokos: The Panagia of Limnia
The church was built in 1837

island. They are in church daily, "celebrating the apportioned holy public services and rites, throughout the Church year, as defined by the ecclesiastical governance."[35]

When performing other sanctifying actions outside of the church, Papadiamandis's priests display the same liturgical ethos and pastoral responsibility as they do when celebrating the Mysteries. Though they have not studied the theology of worship at a university, they attempt to preserve the precision and meaning of what is being done during their daily services. In this way, the seriousness and ethos of the Church's services are preserved. In the story, "The Wedding of Karahmet," which takes place in the pre-1821[xv] Skiathos of the Castle,[xvi] Papa-Stamelos is a fine example of the seriousness with which the priests of Skiathos treat the services of the Church. Papa-Stamelos is tricked by Koumbi Nicholas, "one of the first among the dignitaries of the village,"[36]

[xv] In 1821 the Greek revolution began at Kalavrita in the Peloponnese.

[xvi] A period during which the Greeks of the island lived in the island's castle, so as to protect themselves from the Turkish occupiers.

who has good relations with the Turks "and a great talent for coercing people."[37] The priest is summoned to the flagship of the Pasha[xvii] to perform the blessing of the waters, but, upon arrival, he is instead asked to perform a wedding—the marriage of Koumbi, who has abandoned his wife, to the guileless Lelouda. Papa-Stamelos is initially frightened and hesitant. He thinks of resisting but, finally, decides to perform the service for a second marriage. When the Greek (Phanariot)[xviii]† secretary of Captain Pasha intervenes and orders him to perform the service for a first marriage "as they do at the Phanar," the Skiathan priest insists, "I don't know what happens at the Phanar. I'm going to read the service for a second marriage." The Pasha's secretary threatens to hang the priest from the mast of the flagship, but finally gives in before the priest's insistence.[38]

For reasons of pastoral responsibility and liturgical consistency, the simple Levite believes that the service of crowning for a second marriage must be read. When he understands the whole situation, he knows it is necessary for the prayers of repentance and forgiveness included in that service to be heard. He believes there is an unbreakable unity between what is said in the service and what is lived before and after the service. He cannot in good conscience chant the hymn, "Lord, our God, crown them with glory and honor,"[xix] since Koumbi has left his lawful wife. It does not matter that "the bride is a virgin and is entering into a first marriage," as the Pasha's secretary argues. Papa-Stamelos is obviously more interested in the truth than in pleasing powerful people. The story makes it clear that the priest has no more room to resist than he does and that further resistance would be futile and dangerous. Still, with the position he takes, he asserts that the Church must not yield to the pressure of worldly or political expediencies.

[xvii]Pasha: This was a title bestowed upon high-ranking members of Ottoman Turkish society. It may be compared with the title "Lord" in Britain.

[xviii]It is the name given to one who is from the Phanar, which is the section of Constantinople (Istanbul) where the Patriarchate is located.

[xix]This is a prayer from the Orthodox service of a first marriage.

Despite his many favorable depictions of the clergy, the great respect that Papadiamandis has for clerics does not tempt him to idealize them or cause him to overlook their human character and their daily problems. He notes several important issues that weaken the clergy and thus dilute and harm the true ethos of the Church. He uses his stories as a vehicle for shedding light on these problems and, often, to suggest a solution that exemplifies the Church's genuine ethos.

Many of these problems develop from the difficult economic situation in which the priests find themselves. In the story "A Village Easter," Papadiamandis describes the temptation Papa-Kyriakos has concerning his co-priest, Papa-Thodori Sphontilas. Papa-Kyriakos believes that he is being treated unfairly by Papa-Thodori as regards the gifts given to the clergy.[xx] These thoughts incite the passion of anger within him. He reaches the point of throwing off his vestments, which he is wearing to celebrate the Resurrection, and leaving the church and parishioners to run and demand an account from his co-priest. In his stories, Papadiamandis refers to the economic problems experienced by the clerics of his time and gives his personal opinion about their situation. He points out that "married priests are usually out of pocket and out of luck, and, being forever burdened by the need to feed their offspring, they can appear to be grasping individuals, who do not even trust their own colleagues fully."[39] Concerning the way the world views the gifts given to the clerics, we hear through the mouth of Papa-Thodori Sphontilas that "'On the rare day,' he said, 'that we actually get something in the collection box, everyone has plenty to say about it — but they never stop to consider all the weeks and months that go by without harvest!'"[40]

Papadiamandis is aware that some Christians are easily scandalized. "[There are] gossips with nothing better to think

---

[xx]These are money, gifts, etc. given by parishioners to help the priests and their families survive.

The ruins of the church of the Panagia of Prekla in the Castle

about, who might otherwise kick up a fuss,"[41] about the money the priests supposedly receive, because economic questions have always been a sensitive spot in the body of the Church. This does not keep Papadiamandis from referring often, and in a simple and natural manner, to the offerings of the faithful and the administration of ecclesiastical things. An example of this may be seen in the story "Reverie of the Fifteenth of August," where many families, individuals, pilgrims, and festivalgoers from the villages of Skiathos attend the feast of the private church[xxi] of the Panagia of Prekla on the fifteenth of August. Papa-Nicholas, related by marriage to the owner of the church, Phrangoulis Phrangoulas, went to serve the vigil. "Phrangoulas gave Papa-Nicholas a five drachma piece, more than what he [Papa-Nicholas]

[xxi]It is not uncommon in Greece and in other traditionally Orthodox countries for the faithful to build chapels next to their homes.

received from the ten-cent pieces he received from the women...
for the prayer lists! All the other things—altar breads, *artoklasía*,
sale of candles, etc., Phrangoulas kept...."[42]

Papadiamandis's Skiathan priests do not hesitate to go about
"on the eve of the feast of lights,[xxii] with their lanterns, blessing
homes, streets, and stores,"[43] for which they receive "blessings"
in the form of loaves of bread stamped with the sign of the
Cross that the women parishioners offer during the forty days
of Christmas.[44] Papadiamandis does not hesitate to describe the
offerings of the people to God. He does not regard it as mistaken
piety or an indication of exploitation and social injustice when
shack-dwelling women and shepherdesses go to the country
chapels "bearing huge baskets filled with flowers, tall candles,
tapers, jars of oil, loaves of bread, and small bottles of wine for
consecration."[45]

In some of his stories set in Athens, Papadiamandis does take
a negative stance regarding the gifts offered to the clergy by
the faithful. He is not against these gifts in and of themselves,
especially since the priests did not receive a salary from the
government at that time, and the gifts from their parishioners
were their only source of income. Rather, he gets upset when
priests have more concern for these gifts than pastoral concern
for the faithful and exploit their flocks to receive more. As an
example, Papadiamandis describes four priests in an Athenian
church who remain at the chanters stand during Vespers and
glance back at the door occasionally in case some parishioner has
entered to get a blessing.

> [I]f he happened to be responsible for the area of the parish
> in which the woman lived, [the priest who was serving] was
> quite capable of interrupting Vespers in order to make sure
> that he was the one to give her the blessing, fearful that the
> other three might "steal" his parishioner. And after Vespers,
> when they started arguing about the share-out of the candle

[xxii]That is, Theophany, January 6.

money, accusing each other of greed and grubbing, then the church would become not so much like a monastic lavra, but (God, forgive me) a rowdy *havra*.[xxiii][46]

As part of the solution to clerics' economic difficulties, Papadiamandis suggests that the wealth of abandoned monasteries, rather than being confiscated by the government, should be used to finance the preservation of these monasteries and, if anything is left over, be put in the common purse of the Church "to help indigent and sick priests and monks."[47]

The Relationship Between Monastics and the Parish

Papadiamandis is very clear in his position regarding another issue affecting the clergy of his time—that of unmarried priests serving parishes in the world. He considers the pastoral care exercised by these clerics and their undertaking of permanent priestly responsibilities in parishes in Athens as dubious and uncanonical. "Priest-monks or archimandrites need to enter their monasteries and leave the parishes of the city to the married clerics, to whom alone these [parishes] belong."[48] Papadiamandis also regards the permanent presence of monastics in the world and the assumption of service in the parishes by a number of them— for economic or missionary reasons—to be against the tradition of the Orthodox Church and of Eastern monasticism.[49]

Papadiamandis, however, does not propose the complete absence of unmarried clerics, and particularly of charismatic monastic figures, from the pastoral work of the Church, so long as it is undertaken with discernment and has the monastery as its center. In his story "The Death Agony," Papadiamandis describes the extent to which people sought these figures as spiritual fathers. Captain Georgakis "was just forty-five years old, and had been successful in his business dealings," but "he had passed so many years without confession. His conscience was still laden

The country chapel of the Prophet Elias

with all the sins of his youth, the fleshly passions, and all the rest."[50] When he came to Skiathos after a trip, he decided to go "to confess with the spiritual father, who lived as a monk and on his own in a desert place (for decades, without ever entering into the city)."[51] This spiritual father was Fr. Jeremiah, who lived in the *hesychastírion*[xxiv] of the Prophet Elijah. Many aspects of Papadiamandis's character Fr. Jeremiah are based upon Elder Dionysios, who Papadiamandis characterizes as "the inspired spiritual father of the small Monastery of the Prophet Elijah."[52]

Fr. Dionysios was one of the last representatives of the *Kollyvádes* movement, which impacted monasticism and the Church and preserved the authenticity of the Orthodox tradition. Papadiamandis had especial reverence for the *Kollyvádes*, and he wrote an obituary for Elder Dionysios upon his death:

> Dionysios belonged to that most ancient order of monastics, the so-called *Kollyvádes*, of which he was nearly its final

[xxiv]A place dedicated to the spiritual ascetic effort of the preservation of hesychia (stillness).

representative.... What this community of *Kollyvádes* monks was, it's not for the present to discuss.... I note here only that this derisive nickname was unfairly given to them by worldly people ill-disposed toward the monastic life...and that, among the *Kollyvádes*, were the old erudite fathers, Makarios Notaras of Corinth, honored as a Saint, Athanasios of Paros and Nikodemos the prolific writer, Cyril, Elijah, Arsenios, as well as other virtuous men.[53]

The impression this charismatic elder, Fr. Dionysios, left on people was enormous, and his pastoral presence and relation to them was dynamic. As Papadiamandis recounts in this same text, the life of the Elder was a continuous spiritual struggle: his pains were virtues, and his entire life was an epic story. In the islands of the Aegean—particularly on Hydra and Syros, where he found himself exiled and an immigrant—and on the island of his birth, Skiathos, "his fame as a spiritual father was universal; so great was the attraction to the Elder that his words were as though prophecies."[54]

Karoulia: the desert of the Holy Mountain

The monasteries, at their height, were poles of attraction for the faithful and places of spiritual replenishment for the married priests of the parishes. The Monastery of the Annunciation on Skiathos, which *Kollyvádes* monks from the Skete of St. Basil on the Holy Mountain had established, affirmed this truth during the period of its spiritual height up until the end of the nineteenth century. The priests of Skiathos were spiritually formed at this monastery and here they received the education necessary for their service. Among them was Papa-Adamantios, the father of Alexandros Papadiamandis.

As all of the older priests of the island, [Papa-Adamantios] was taught how to celebrate the Mysteries by those venerable *Kollyvádes* who, at the end of the last century, had established the Monastery of the Annunciation on the island, which became a seedbed of humble priests for our island—priests that were lovers of the divine services, simple and virtuous. They enjoyed the love and respect of the inhabitants, having no affectations or hypocrisy, nor displaying vanity as they lived their lives as priests.[55]

Bishops

Particularly disparaging and pointed is Papadiamandis's criticism of the behavior and actions of the bishops of his age, especially in his stories "The Monk" and "The Visit of the Holy Bishop." His criticism does not have an anti-ecclesiastical or anti-clerical spirit because it is voiced within the Church, out of love for the Church and in true distress for Her. Papadiamandis himself avows that he is and remains Her genuine child: "We hasten to add that with these thoughts we do not strike at the authority of the Church," as one eventually would who desired to "improve" the things of the Church without being truly interested in Her, "but simply express our sorrow at the state of affairs."[56] In "The Visit of the Holy Bishop," he describes a bishop who has forgotten that he is a bishop; he gives the impression of being a director and legislator more than a spiritual father and shepherd. Both the clerics and the people view him as a supervisor who comes to reprimand, rather than a father who cares for, teaches, and guides his children.[57]

It seems that this situation was particularly common among the bishops in his days—which does not, of course, mean that it is unknown or infrequent in our own days. If it appeared to be an epidemic sickness in his day, it is because of the particularly difficult historical conditions and situations through which the Church in Greece passed at that time. A characteristic example from the years immediately following this period is the mentality that prevailed among the bishops of the so-called New Lands[xxv] during the liberation of their dioceses from Turkish control, a mentality that appears in the synod they convened to study the new situation. Through the unification of their areas with the

[xxv]This refers to those parts of Greece that were liberated during the Greek War of Independence.

rest of the Greek governmental structure, these bishops lost many of their legislative, economic, judicial, and educational responsibilities and began to be concerned about how they would spend their time. They seemed to have forgotten that they were bishops, shepherds with Christ as their model, and that their main work was the guidance and spiritual pasturing of the people. They had become comfortable in their legislative roles and felt better suited to them than to their proper role of pastoral care.[xxvi][58]

Papadiamandis has particularly caustic criticism for the unorthodox and worldly means by which the bishops get themselves elected and select their priests, and he indicates the depth of the bishops' responsibility for this aberration. His criticism is borne of the conviction that the election and ordination of the Church's priests and bishops is a very important issue, and that the presuppositions and requirements that the Orthodox Church posits for this process are of primary importance to the Church. Papadiamandis regards this topic as one of the most fundamental, both as regards the Church's essence as well as in relation to the realization of Her mission in the world. The way in which shepherds are chosen has momentous consequences for the very substance, nature, and character of this sacred body and for the spiritual growth of the people of God.

In his story "The Little Star" Papadiamandis illustrates the erosion of ethos that may be caused by adopting questionable criteria for choosing clerics. He presents a certain Dimos Barodimos, who spends all his time at bars and tells completely unseemly jokes. At the same time, he proudly gloats at the prospect of becoming a deacon. Papadiamandis records the dialogue:

"Have you learned the news, Alexi?"
"What's happening, Dimos?"
"I'm going to become a deacon."

[xxvi]During the Ottoman captivity of Greece the Church was the one institution that bound the Greek people together. The Ottomans assigned the Church's hierarchs worldly responsibilities, and regarded the Patriarch of Constantinople as the political leader of the Greek people. With the establishment of the modern Greek state the influence of the Church was once more restricted to Her spiritual ministry.

"A deacon? Really?"

"Yes, now I'm waiting for the Bishop to come. I'm collecting referrals. Tell me, Alexi, you would know...how much money do I need to give the Bishop?"

"I don't know, Dimos."[59]

He completes his thought a bit later: "The newly ordained bishop had recently come on a tour to this place for the first time and had, as many people complained, established a price list for the ordinations of clerics. He himself had told them, they said, that he had to pay for all he had spent on the gifts given to the guests at his ordination."[60] With the phrases, "as many people complained" and "they said," Papadiamandis keeps a distance from the rumors of the particular situation without, of course, denying them. Unfortunately, simony, opportunism, and corruption were common situations among the higher orders of ecclesiastics in his day. Bishops opportunistically violated their relationship with their flocks and misused the office of bishop in order to acquire material goods and an easy life. In the story "The Promiscuous One," he notes that, "with two lobster tails and a big flask of Muscat wine, the question could be happily solved at the seat of the bishopric...."[61] The "question" mentioned was the granting of permission for marriage when there were obstacles due to kinship.

All these things, however, express a more fundamental ailment of ecclesiastical life—secularism. Papadiamandis believes that the special ministry of clerics—and especially that of the bishops— does not include the exercise of power and oppression; these are the attributes that characterize the authority of Caesar. This is not just an idealistic position that Papadiamandis holds; it is the reversal of the worldly mentality towards power, which Christ puts forth in the Gospel. A true shepherd and bishop of the Church "is first" and "bears power" according to the Gospel's definition of these things, not the world's.[62]

Papadiamandis believes that the clergy, and particularly bishops, should have a continuous experience of the living presence of Christ in the life of the Church, His Body. In light of this position, one may understand the views that appear in his works[63] concerning the place of the bishop in the ecclesiastical body, as a service rendered to guide the Church of Christ. On this point, he rightly divides the word of truth,[64] since, in the Biblical and patristic tradition, the bishop, despite his foundational position in the life of the Church, is not understood as a substitute or representative who replaces the absent Christ—as is believed in the Roman Catholic Church—but as making present, with his person and presence, the Christ Who is "invisibly present with us."[65] The lofty but practical ecclesiology of St. John Chrysostom teaches that the Holy Eucharist is offered not only by the celebrant but also by the whole liturgical community that he leads. At the same time, the sanctification of this offering, of these gifts, "is not an accomplishment of human nature,...but the grace of the Holy Spirit present and hovering over everything forms that mystical sacrifice."[66] The celebrant simply "lends his tongue and offers his hand" to God.[67] Bishops and all clerics are called to pastor the sheep of Christ,[68] not as lords or rulers, but as Christ-like bearers of liturgical grace.

Liturgical Life: The Center of Pastoral Care

In his novels and his Athenian stories, Papadiamandis mentions the exploitation of the piety of the faithful by pastors and monastics. In his novel, *Merchants of the Nations*, he presents the abbess of St. Cosmas, Mother Philikiti, who, "with Fathers Marthonos and Vincent, divide among themselves the offerings of piety" given by Mouchras's pious wife.[69] Papadiamandis does not usually intrude into the private lives of the clergy, as the center of his thought is not pietistic or moralistic, but liturgical and ecclesiological. For this reason, in his writings he charges the clergy with the responsibility of "ministering the worship."[70] Worship is the center of pastoral care and, more generally, of the life of the Church. This is why it is primarily on the level of worship that true shepherds are distinguished from "professional priests." When Papadiamandis found himself in Athens, the "New Babylon," he was especially grieved when he saw many priests who were not true shepherds: they did not care for the people of God and were not interested in the proper performance of worship.[71] Such priests are like the Levite and the priest in the parable of the Good Samaritan. Although they have ostensibly dedicated their lives to offer help, they ignore the needs of the people that appear before them with wounds from the various "thieves" of daily life, in a "half-dead" state. Only some priests, such as Papa-Nicholas Planas, are good Samaritans and have mercy on them. Papadiamandis recognizes that the people's greatest hunger is for good shepherds—shepherds who imitate Christ, Who, "when He saw the multitudes, He was moved with compassion for them, because they were weary and scattered, like sheep having no shepherd."[72] When "professional priests" neglect the liturgical life and abolish the Church's order of services, they are incapable of true Orthodox pastoral care, the heart of which is the life of worship.[73] The absence of true pastoral care on the part of the shepherds is a cause of doctrinal divergence, delusion, and heresy.

[S]ince the majority of people thirst for religious instruction and those responsible and competent do little to meet this need by drawing on pure and orthodox sources rather than foreign and distorted ones, it was only to be expected that many pious and well-intentioned people would be misled, in good faith, on hearing the Christian doctrine, albeit adulterated, wherever this is preached, because when the springs and fountains grow cloudy, with those in authority concealing the clear spring waters, men and beasts, dying of thirst, will prefer to drink from the cloudy stream, finding some slight hope of deliverance in this, rather than die of thirst....[74]

3

THE ROLE OF THE LAITY

Clergy-Laity Relations

A layman is one who belongs to the people of God and is a member of the Church. All Christians, clergy and laity, are essentially "laity" in that they belong to the *laós*, or people, of God.[i] Unfortunately, the laity is often wrongly considered to be the lower section of the Church, with the clergy regarded as the upper section. However, the laity is not just a part of the Church, but makes up the whole Church. In the patristic tradition there is no class distinction between the clergy and laity, as all are members of the one Body of Christ. Even the division of the faithful into sheep and shepherds, which is particularly common in our days, is completely conventional and human, since, as St. John Chrysostom explains, "according to God, all are sheep; both sheep and shepherds are led by the One Shepherd, the Shepherd from on high."[1] The unity of the Body does not allow worldly distinctions between lords and vassals. "The Church is not the place for the conceit of rulers nor the slavish spirit of vassals, but it is a spiritual place and has this advantage [from the spiritual perspective]: that we ask for more struggles and not more honor."[2] John Karmiris, a contemporary theologian, has correctly noted that the laity, "on the basis of the common Baptism, are equal members of the Body of Christ with the clergy—all called to

---

[i] The Greek word for layman, *laikós*, is derived from the Greek word for people, *laós*.

service in the Church but each one to a different extent, in a different place, and a different service."[3]

If there is some difference between clergy and laity, it is in their offering of labor and the type of ministration and service required of them. There are gifts, ministrations, and services for all members of the Church. During the apostolic period, people who believed the Christian preaching were baptized and received the Holy Spirit. However, because the Holy Spirit is invisible, all who received Him were given a tangible and visible sign of His working—the gift of speaking in tongues, of prophecy, or of miracle working.[ii]

The priesthood is a gift that is realized in a particular ministration. Although this ministration is a foundation of the Church, the importance of the priesthood does not overshadow the importance of lay gifts and ministrations.[4] Patristic texts from the first years of Christianity bear witness to the way in which all the members of the Church lived and prayed together, when relationships were not based on an administrative structure but on the gifts exercised by each of the faithful. As St. Clement of Rome explains:

> Every one of us, brethren, in the same battalion, should please God in good conscience, not straying from the specific rule of his ministration, but in modesty. For the bishops have been given identical ministrations. To the priests, the same places have been given, and, to the Levites, equivalent ministries have been given; but the layman is bound by lay rules.[5]

The work to which each member of the Church was called was determined by the gifts given to them by the Holy Spirit, and each member was accountable to the rules and duties of his specific calling.

[ii]Although the signs or gifts given to present-day Christians may not be as obvious, the gifts bestowed by the Holy Spirit are often revealed in the specific ministrations and spiritual services to which the faithful are called. Some receive the gift and calling of the priesthood, while others are given the ability to serve as chanters, theologians, teachers, and so on.

Alexandros Papadiamandis testifies to the same truth nearly eighteen centuries later. In his texts the Church—as the Body of Christ—appears as an organic, not an ideological, unity. The priests of his stories realize that they are undertaking a ministration and service that does not preclude the contribution of gifts and services by laymen. Rather, they know that the ministrations of the laymen are vital to the life of the Church. For these priests, every feudal or tyrannical conception of the priesthood is incomprehensible. Their unified vision reveals a basic ecclesiological truth—that the differentiation of spiritual service and ministration within the body of the Church does not preclude the equal regard for all members before the Head of the Church. Priest and layman, together, live and function within the Church according to the words of the Apostle Paul: "For as we have many members in one body, but all the members do not have the same function, so we, being many, are one body in Christ, and individually members of one another."[6] In the words of St. Gregory the Theologian, "in Church, all things become one body, which is made up of different parts."[7] The priests come from the people and live in close relationship with them, and together they make up the worshipping community. In Papadiamandis's stories, those who attend the festal celebrations for Skiathos's country chapels, who make the food and other preparations for the celebrations, and all the simple pilgrims attending the Church's festal services are not an audience or mere decoration: they are the basic foundation of an active church community.

In the adventurous excursion depicted in "A Pilgrimage to the Kastro," Papadiamandis describes the crowded boat used to travel to the feast and the spiritual depth of the members of the Church in Skiathos. Uncle Stephen, his seventeen-year-old son (who pilots the boat), Aunt Malamos, Alexandros the chanter, three feast-goers, and four lady pilgrims find themselves together in a boat—and together later in the liturgical gathering—with Papa-Phrangoulis, his wife, their eldest daughter, and their young son. At the last moment, a sixteenth person is added. The presence of the priest is, of course, crucially important in this worshipping community, but the active participation of all of the other lay members is also unquestionably essential. When rough waters and the overcrowding of the boat put the group in danger of capsizing, the quality and *phrónima*[iii]† of the group is revealed. "All the usual suspects were there—the men and women who took ineffable pleasure in going along, as often as possible, to religious festivals, especially those celebrated at country chapels."[iv][8]

The worshipping community of Skiathos is characterized by its fundamentally traditional character. Its composition is not based on ideological, social, or professional criteria but embraces all the people on the island. It includes men and women of all ages—young and old, middle-aged and children. When people of all ages participate in the Divine Liturgy and other services of the Church, the two parishes of Skiathos resemble a many-colored mosaic, and their exodus toward the country chapels takes the form of a sacred pilgrimage. Recollecting memories of his own childhood, Papadiamandis writes: "When we were children with time on our hands…if a conscientious priest went off to celebrate the liturgy in some country chapel…we would evade our parents' supervision and tag along behind these good Christians."[9] None of the children, the unlettered pilgrims gathered in the country chapels of Skiathos, or even the nearly illiterate parishioners worshipping in the chapel of St. Elisha in Athens had difficulty understanding the services, as is often suggested today. Everyone understood and actively participated in what was taking place because they knew that they were members of the same body. Their participation in Church was not intellectual or ideological, even less legal or juridical, but existential and loving. Their participation was the natural result of a personal relationship: loving, giving, and serving.

In "Easter Chanter," Papadiamandis describes how some of the women who gathered in the chapel of St. John the Forerunner "cut bundles of twigs from the scented shrubs, terebinth and ilex and sage, tied them up with twine to make rough brooms, and proceeded to sweep the church floor and the porch with

---

[iii]*Phrónima*: Mindset or character. It also suggests one's upbringing and how this affects one's mindset and development of character.

[iv]In Greece and other traditionally Orthodox countries, it is common for the faithful to travel to different churches when the feast (of the patron Saint) of the church is celebrated.

The chapel of St. John the Forerunner, just outside the Castle walls

quick, even strokes."[10] Meanwhile, Granny Mathino and Aunt Seraino, the color-bearer of the feasts, "started to trim the wicks, pour oil into the icon lamps, and cross themselves fervently. An inexpressible joy and sweetness welled up within them,"[11] when they found themselves in the tabernacle of the Lord of Hosts. In the story "Sweet Kiss," Aunt Areto knows how to say "thanks be to God" even in life's most difficult situations and goes daily to all the nearby country chapels to light the vigil lamps, as "the selfless church warden and willing decorator of all the country chapels."[12]

The simple faithful collaborate with the priests and consider the Church to be their home. The liturgical ethos and the offering of ecclesiastical service are not limited to the clergy but are also distinguishing marks of the people. The network of relations between clergy and laity in Skiathan society and the genuine love of all for the Church ensure collaboration, and, above all else, they maintain the essential place of the laity in basic ecclesiastical ministrations and spiritual service, asserting their presence in the life of the Church as a vital necessity.

The Laity as Liturgical Concelebrants

Papadiamandis's Skiathans do not appear in worship as simple spectators of what is taking place but as co-ministers and participants. Today, there is a mistaken impression common among

Orthodox Christians, and found in Orthodox liturgical booklets, which makes a distinction between ministers/celebrants and followers/laity in worship. The conception of the church as a theatrical space largely dominates the contemporary life of worship. This conception has led to additions and changes to liturgical texts such as, "For all those *following* the service of this bloodless celebration."[13] The experience that Papadiamandis expresses, however, is completely different. In his conception of the Church, expressed eloquently through his stories, laymen view themselves as concelebrants.

In the story "The Halasohorides," Uncle Anagnostis concelebrates with Papa-Soteris and "offers his part so that the mystagogy could take place" at the church of the Three Hierarchs.[14] In another story, "Easter Chanter," the term "concelebrant" is used when referring to the chanters and,

Church of the Three
Hierarchs, Skiathos

more generally, to other laymen. In this story, a certain Konstantos promises to go to "do the chanting and concelebrate the Resurrection," and, when the priest saw that he was late in coming, "he wanted to send one of the herdsmen to the town, to look for someone and bring him back to help celebrate the Liturgy."[15] Papa-Dianelos was concerned lest he be unable to celebrate the Divine Liturgy of the Resurrection, "[f]or, obviously he could not celebrate without an assistant."[16] The simple priest realizes that which the whole Orthodox tradition knows and lives, that "a Liturgy cannot be celebrated without at least one chanter or reader."[17] For this reason, when the priest is concerned about the delay of the chanter, Aunt Mathino suggests that she could serve as canonarch,[†] and recite as much as she knew by heart. She continues, "[i]f I could read what it says on the page, I don't think

---

[†] The canonarch reads the text to be chanted just before the chanter actually chants it.

it would be sinful to do the chanting myself."[18] Today, among the educated and among theologians, one seldom encounters the ecclesiastical consciousness of this simple woman.

Of course, these ordinary lay people and even the chanters sometimes incorrectly render the words of the hymns. However, it should be noted that Papadiamandis's priests do not harshly correct or discourage them, but encourage their participation nonetheless. Aunt Mathino presents her own offering, chanting slightly altered versions of the hymn, "Let us purify our senses and let us see," and the hymn, "Come let us drink a new drink," while other simple folk chant their own rendition of "My every hope."[vi] In the years during which our author lived in Athens, he would spend Easter in one of the villages outside the city with his friend, the nobleman, John Penteliotis—a chanter with a special love for the style of chanting used in Constantinople. Papadiamandis would chant with him, and there, during Holy Friday, "a whole squad of impromptu chanters, each of them holding a leaflet with the text of the Good Friday burial service, and who feel duty-bound to chant the Praises in ear-splitting discord, manage in the process to demolish, with their comical blunders, even the few words in the leaflets which are printed correctly."[19]

Papadiamandis also refers with admiration to unlettered laymen who have been educated and cultivated through the Church's life of worship. For example, he presents "Uncle Anagnostis, an old villager who knew the Easter service by heart" and though he could not read anything "from the book," he still wanted to chant the hymn, "Receive the Body of Christ."[20] Neither the corruption of the words during the chanting and recitation of passages, nor the ignorance of the exact meaning of what is being chanted keep the simple people from participating in worship. These things do not impede Uncle Pipi (in the story "Roman Easter") when, rather than chanting "Hosanna in the highest,"

[vi]In Greek, "Katharthómen tás isthíseis ki oupsómetha," "Deúte póma píoumen kinón," and "Tín pásan olpída mou." These are all cases where the text is slightly changed due to the mishearing of the text. To a Greek ear, these mistakes are still basically comprehensible and charming in their guileless inaccuracy.

he chants, "as an adversary in the highest."[21] His mistakes do not bother Papadiamandis, who lovingly tries to correct him and to explain to him the meaning of the passage. Likewise, Uncle Kitsos participates in the joy of the Resurrection by chanting the hymn "Christ is Risen," in his own unique fashion.[vii][22] It is, in fact, pointed out that "despite its singularity, no one ever sang a sacred song with more Christian feeling and enthusiasm."[23] Despite all their mistakes, Papadiamandis regards these as the "true Orthodox Greeks."[24] When Papa-Phrangoulis is going to the castle for the Divine Liturgy of the Nativity, he asks Alexandros the chanter about the meaning of the passage, "He who raised our horn."[25] Alexandros thinks that "your raising up" actually means "your nephew," and that "the spoils of Babylon of the kingdom of Zion,"[26] refers to some dogs.[viii][27] Papa-Phrangoulis does not make an issue of it. He knows how to make use of the least of talents in the building up of the Church and realizes that, despite the unintentional mistakes made, the service may still be celebrated in a joyful and reverent spirit.

When the clergy make use of the gifts and abilities they find in the body of the Church, they do not compromise or lessen their own offering or ministry. Instead, this sharing of the work of the Church among its members affirms the authentic liturgy and functioning of the ecclesiastical body. In addition to the work of the chanter, there is also the ministry of the churchwarden. The contribution of the warden in the Church is mentioned many times and in a variety of ways in Papadiamandis's texts. There are people who perform this ministry with great sensitivity and selflessness. Antonitsas's son Panagiotis, for example, does not tire of caring for the country chapels; his dedication is so great that the municipality decides to recognize him as a permanent warden of all the churches in the countryside.[28]

Except for a few examples, however, Papadiamandis does not praise the wardens. This is usually because they do not exhibit an

[vii]"Crisis lads, Crisis risen, from the dead by death, chomping down death, and to those, those in the tombs life most blessed!"

[viii]The confusion comes about because the Ancient Greek word for "spoils" and the Modern Greek word for "dogs" sound identical [skýla].

The country chapel of St. Elissaios (previously the chapel of
the Prophet Elijah), which was renovated in the 1980's

ecclesiastical ethos, nor are they distinguished for their selfless
service. They limit the Church by limiting themselves to the
economic care of the church and by not showing the proper
sensitivity and reverence for the place itself. Papadiamandis
tells of a certain John, who was the warden at St. George of
Kastodoulitsas and of all the country chapels where feasts would
take place, and who would take the half-burnt vigil candles (that
had gotten stuck together in a large mass) from the candle-
stands, step on them with his shoes to extinguish them on the
church's tile floor, allegedly out of fear that if he left them to burn
down they would flare up. He would also hold out a beautiful
tray, going about the ranks of feast-goers, raising funds "for
the churches to be fixed up." Papadiamandis rhetorically asks,
"God forgive us for thinking such a thing, but isn't it possible
that his hands were not entirely clean?"[29] Papadiamandis's
descriptions of the wardens in Athens were generally negative.
His experience was that the living eucharistic community, with
its charismatic character of ministries and service among the
lay members of the community, did not exist in the capital. The
Athenian churchwardens were usually characterized by vainglory
and vanity, and had often obtained their positions by pleading
with those in power. Some of them had zeal for the Church,
but the work of most of them was limited to putting out the
half-burnt candles of the pilgrims. This is why they were called

"light-snuffers." Generally, their presence in the churches of Athens was tyrannical and anti-ecclesiastical, as they "lorded it over the priests, the cantors and the sacristan."[30] They imposed their opinion, not only on questions of the typicon and times of the services but also on purely spiritual questions.[31] They also became domineering with the simple faithful. Because of their vanity, their desire to flaunt the prestige of their office, and their lack of liturgical ethos, many wardens caused more disturbance and disorder during the Divine Liturgy and other church services than those who they were supposedly trying to keep in line. With a critical and disparaging pen, Papadiamandis records the unseemly behavior of certain churchwardens of his day in Athens. He describes a certain Giambis, a churchwarden who, during the services of Holy Week, would stroll around the aisles meant for women parishioners and reprimand "poor, young mother[s] for the whimpering" of their infants.[32] Among the wardens in Papadiamandis's Athenian stories are some described as "vulgar" and "ignorant" people who "insidiously, audaciously, and without permission introduce...sham and fake gold objects" into the churches, trying to make them more lavish.[33] At the same time, there are those who strive to properly beautify and adorn the churches.[34] In all of this, the office of the churchwarden is not to blame, but the mentality and the ethos of certain people. While some wardens have liturgical sensitivity and true love for the Church, others are bereft of these qualities.

The roles filled by laymen are not restricted to chanting and the care of the church building, but extend to broader pastoral work. Laymen stand behind the priests, working and serving together with them in the mystery of salvation; they are their co-workers.[35] Many times, seemingly insignificant and invisible people prove to be valuable co-workers, because of their living relationship to the Church and their disposition to help others. Aunt Sophoula, the *Sarandanoú* (or *Sarandanonoú*),[ix] had served as the godmother for forty people. The most admirable aspect of her work as godmother was not the expense she undertook for the Baptisms, but the love, interest, and affection that she

[ix]Both variations mean "one who has been a godparent to forty people."

showed her godchildren afterwards. She felt responsible for their catechism and education. In addition, because she had baptized both boys and girls, "she took care to give precise notes to priests and spiritual fathers, so that in the future there would be no match, by any chance, between one of the boys and girls she had baptized...."[x][36]

In his story "The Unchurched," Papadiamandis depicts with remarkable vividness the synergy between priests and the faithful in the work of the salvation of souls. The figure and behavior of the monstrous Uncle Kolia, "the unchurched" one, represents all those people who, due to various circumstances, find themselves living far from the liturgical life of the Church for many years. Like Uncle Kolia, these people usually hide a kind disposition, but the proper loving approach of other Christians is needed to bring them back into the Church. In the story, the kindly priest Papa-Gariphalos, moved by true paternal and pastoral concern, makes the initial overture to Uncle Kolia. However, the ministry of the priest's co-workers, the ecclesiastical community, also proves decisive. In particular, the shepherd named John plays an important role in the return of "the unchurched" one. "He held him firmly by his arm and said, Where are you going, Uncle Kolia? Now I won't leave you.... That's all behind us now! This year we're going to celebrate the Resurrection together!"[37] This approach proves to be salvific for Uncle Kolia, who, as the text confirms, "wanted to come, but was ashamed. He was very unusual and wanted them to push him to join them."[38] John acts out of genuine love "as though he had penetrated into the soul of Kolia"[39] and displays a true liturgical and ecclesiastical ethos— an ethos that desires all creation, and especially all people, to be gathered together in the body of the Church. This simple layman exhibits great fraternal care, desiring the happiness and salvation of his brother, and this is because he does not consider

[x]According to the canonical tradition of the Orthodox Church, men and women who have been baptized by the same person are not permitted to marry one another. This is based on the principle of the spiritual family, part of the purpose of which is the extension of the love of the family to the wider Church.

the Liturgy as a religious display for certain chosen people, but as a possibility of communion with all people.

Religious Brotherhoods

The belief that worship is the liturgy of the whole body and not of a chosen group of people also informs Papadiamandis's stance regarding the religious brotherhoods[xi] that had begun appearing in his day. In a particularly derisive tone, he refers "to the great growth of variously named associations—the various Resurrections, Reformations, Renaissances, Stirrings, and Regenerations—promising renewal. Among all the doctrines and convictions, throughout the nation, it is firstly the call of religion and patriotism that rallies the people."[40] His criteria for judgment are always clearly ecclesiological, and his unwavering opposition of the brotherhoods is thus the reaction of a genuine ecclesiastical *phrónima*.

The theological education of the people and other matters of pastoral care are ecclesiastical duties that must be undertaken in a responsible manner. The lay theologians of the ecclesiastical brotherhoods, who "wander about the churches and in Church circles spouting off words and sermonizing,"[41] are not the

[xi]The word "brotherhood" is used in place of the word "organization" (as it appears in the original Greek) as this is the English word that makes the concept most accessible to the reader unfamiliar with modern Greek ecclesiastical life and history. These brotherhoods appeared at the turn of the twentieth century as an attempt to meet the spiritual needs of Orthodox Greece. Monastic life was in decline at the time and many regarded the brotherhoods as the successor to monasticism. That this view was gravely mistaken is revealed through Papadiamandis's critique of the brotherhoods, as well as through his account of Apostolos Makrakis and his Protestant-influenced "School of the Word," which was officially censured by the Church in Greece as being unorthodox. Monasticism, as with all true aspects of the Church's tradition, never fully disappeared and was powerfully re-kindled in the life of the Church in Greece in the twentieth century, giving further witness to the fact that irregularities in Church life are not solved by external measures, foreign to the ethos of the Church, but are healed from within, through the living breath of the Holy Spirit moving within the ancient tradition that He established.

responsible pastors given the authority to do this work, as they have not been anointed by the Church through the Mystery of ordination. The tradition of the Church indicates the proper place of Her grace-filled ministers. Although the clergy are necessarily to be found at the head of the people, to show the way and to guide the flock responsibly, they are neither outside, nor above the Church. While Papadiamandis emphasizes the importance of the gifts and service of the laity in the Church, in the story "The Teacher" he questions the "extemporaneous stupidities"[42] of certain self-ordained and self-titled lay "pastors" who make a "living from piety."[43] He recognizes and questions the Protestant character of these laymen's meetings, sermons, and prayers: "What innovations, what foreign elements, what vain chatter is this? Are we Protestants here?"[44] Despite his clear preference that sermons be given by well-trained and virtuous clerics, Papadiamandis did not have an objection to laymen, with a special blessing and the analogous gift, "wearing the holy garment"[45] to serve from the pulpits of the churches. This should only be done, however, with the exhortation and blessing of the Church's shepherds.

In the story "The Eternally Deluded One," Papadiamandis records his views concerning Apostolos Makrakis and his followers. In his critique he does not simply ask whether Makrakis and those who followed him were truly "good" or "ethically beneficial." Papadiamandis discusses the crucial issue of man's relationship to the ecclesiastical body. His views witness to the nature of the only genuine Orthodox ecclesiastical ethos. Only within the framework of the Church can responsible ecclesiastical service be understood and can a genuine ecclesiastical ethos be cultivated. The parish constitutes the cell, the basic building block of the Church organism. Whatever takes place outside of the parish under various pretexts and names exists outside the accountability of the Church and Her tradition. A contemporary bishop has noted that spiritual endeavors pursued in the world, outside the life of the parish, "definitely achieve one goal, to overrun and to split the unity of the Church."[46] By not working through the parishes, Makrakis worked outside of the Church; as a consequence, the Church in Greece formally declared him and his organization heretical and unorthodox. Papadiamandis gives a balanced and fair assessment of the situation when he writes the following:

> There is no doubt...that many of the Makrakians are good people and that Makrakis could have been very good and beneficial.... But, what can I tell you, "the good law is good, the bad law is bad." If, for example, it is officially declared by doctors that such and such a house is infected with cholera or smallpox, would you ever dare to disregard the quarantine and enter it?... Even more so, this holds true with Makrakis. Those qualified—that is to say—the Holy Synod, have declared him unorthodox and heretical. Until it is proved to the contrary and until the judgment of a higher court, such as the Great Church and the other Patriarchates, reverses the action of the Holy Synod of Greece and declares Makrakis healthy as regards the faith and Orthodox, every Christian is bound to be obedient to the visible representatives of the Church, whether they be sinners or Saints, and should not approach Makrakis. Otherwise, it would be anarchy.[47]

In other stories and articles, Papadiamandis further reveals reservations regarding Makrakis, the leader of the "School of the Word," and regarding the practices of the religious brotherhoods in general. Papadiamandis takes issue with Makrakis and the brotherhoods on three main points. In the first place, the brotherhoods transfer the center of the Church's life and worship from the parish and the church to the auditorium.[48] Secondly, the lay theologians in the brotherhoods of his day present an easy, fashionable Christianity. In their sermons, they hesitate or are ashamed to speak of the Saints and miracles, of fasting and asceticism, of the battle against the passions and evil spirits.[49] Thirdly, Papadiamandis takes issue with the type of religious man that the piety of the brotherhoods fashions and the pride and hypocrisy that the moralistic one-sidedness of the religious unions cultivate.

In contrast to the simple, unaffected customs and piety of the inhabitants of Skiathos, the "pious Christians" of Athens involved in the various religious brotherhoods are distinguished for their duplicity and hypocrisy. Papadiamandis regards these vices as epidemic sicknesses and unavoidable side effects of these groups. In his story, "The Lady Supporter of Makrakis," Mrs. Giorgoula, who is a reader and chanter and "would regularly go to the School of the Word," pretends to be the peacemaker for the family of Mr. Kaisaras Ordinarios and "the willing redeemer and consoler" of the husband of Mrs. Dionysoula.[50] However she accuses them to Mrs. Rinis behind their backs and publicizes their economic and domestic situation to prevent them from renting her home.[51] Supposedly good and honest, she manages to be regarded by all as a good Christian. "'A good Christian!' Mrs. Rinis said to herself. 'Good for her! She tells the truth!...' 'A good Christian!' said Dionysoula to herself. 'She is untiring in doing good. You see, those who go to the Teacher... learn Christian conduct.'"[52]

Papadiamandis's position regarding the religious brotherhoods is further revealed in two articles he wrote in 1891.[53] The first was a response to the report in Makrakis's religious periodical *The Word* [*Lógos*] regarding a charge Makrakis had brought against two priests of Skiathos, Sakellarios John Maniotis and Papadiamandis's father, Oikonomos Adamantios Emmanuel. Living in Athens at the time, Papadiamandis sought further details regarding Makrakis's "missionary journey" to Skiathos. Instead of a few details, he received an extensive letter from Skiathos explaining the situation. Agreeing with the information he received, he thought the wider public should hear the priests of Skiathos's side of the story and sent it for publication on July 22, 1891. Despite its sharpness of tone and harsh characterizations,[54] the article is an eloquent discussion of the consequences that heresy and schism have for the Church. Although Papadiamandis's position was criticized as "religious intransigence" and the prejudice of a half-educated person "against a person who ha[d] studied abroad,"[55] this is not what emerges from the text. Characteristically viewing all things through an ecclesiastical prism, Papadiamandis recognized Apostolos Makrakis as a "dangerous and much more unremitting opponent" than even "the cosmopolitan modernists and the atheist Kleona Ragavis." While "the Church [has] never [been] overly concerned with the attempts of the 'resuscitators' (Ragavis)...it [has] always vigilantly stood against heresy (Makrakis)."[56] Heresy constitutes a denial of the Church and not just a new interpretation of ecclesiastical faith; it is an innovation and not a spiritual regeneration, a new invention and not a renewal. It does not just change one part of the ecclesiastical tradition that it does not want to accept as a tradition of the Church but inevitably adulterates all of Her life.

The second article appeared when the Makrakians defamed Papadiamandis in *The Word* by raising some ecclesiastical scandals and accusing him of being an atheist because he refused to take a position regarding the scandals. With his profound ecclesiastical consciousness, he responded:

> I am a genuine child of the Orthodox Church, which is represented by Her bishops. If it happens that many of them are sinners, only the Church is qualified to judge, and we need only to appeal to the endless mercy of God. We do not confuse the authority and unity of the Church with the sins of persons, as you para-ecclesiastics do. It is not possible for us, personally, to have proof regarding the guilt of anyone, nor in suspicion and from stray rumors should we judge. "He that is without sin among you, let him first cast a stone." Otherwise, the word stands, that "God does not direct the paths of all men, but works in all men."[57]

As usual, Papadiamandis does not fail to analyze the pathology, interpret the symptoms, and present the deeper cause of these phenomena. He points out that the faithful long to hear "the Christian doctrine, albeit adulterated, wherever this is preached, because when the springs and fountains grow cloudy, with those in authority concealing the clear spring waters, men and beasts, dying of thirst, will prefer to drink from the cloudy stream, finding some slight hope of deliverance in this, rather than die of thirst...."[58] In his story "The Grumblers," Papadiamandis further discusses the symptoms of lay para-ecclesiastical expressions of worship and provides another example in which the piety of the people is exploited due to the lack of true pastoral care. He believes that the cause of the sickness manifested by these symptoms, both the lack of pastoral care and the para-ecclesiastical forms of spirituality that result, tragically lies in the inadequacy and decline of the bishops—individually and as a Synod—from the time that the Church in Greece received its autocephaly. Papadiamandis speaks of the tragic deterioration of the Church itself into an *organization* and *union*, when it cannot act as the Body of Christ. He says that "except for this body [the Body of Christ]...we can hope for absolutely no other good."[59] Still, there is always hope where there are clergy and lay Christians who, out of selfless love for the Church, work from within to bring about a resurgence of Her reputation and rekindle interest in Her life.[60]

Church and State,
Church and World

Ecclesiastical criteria also govern Papadiamandis's views regarding Church and State relations. He argues that any interference of the Church in politics is a deviation and only guarantees division. He argues that "the [essence] of the Church is not one of division, but of unity and of agreement."[61] For this reason, he does not approve of any interference by priests in politics or their support of various parties. In his story "The Two Monsters," he describes a pre-election period on his island in which "all the impure election demons have been let loose on the street, the elite have allied with the mob, and the yellow monster has called for the help of another monster—the red one."[62] (Yellow and red are the party colors of the two candidates for mayor.) Unfortunately, certain priests and other ecclesiastical entities had gotten embroiled in the political campaign fervor. In an obviously derisive tone, Papadiamandis describes the situation:

> The house of one priest had been covered with a red flag, indicating that he wouldn't accept offerings from both parties, but only from that party. Another priest, not wanting

Katholikon of the Monastery of the Annunciation

to appear obvious in his support, told his wife to put all the beautiful red carpets out the windows and over the balcony, supposedly to air them out. Beside the same house, a great pole or column had been erected, which was at the edge of a precipice...On this pole a bunch of red banners, ribbons, and pennants had been hung certainly with the tolerance if not the recommendation of the priest. Uncle Ioannis, who in his later years took refuge in repentance at the Monastery of the Annunciation, had postponed his tonsure from election to election, remaining a novice. Each time he promised that he would be tonsured a monk once the election had passed. This was because the candidates would treat the voters to smokes, raki,[xii] and roast meat with pasta, as well as rolls of dimes. Now, once again, he earnestly promised to receive the tonsure after the election of Uncle Mari to mayor and to thereafter look after his soul.[63]

[xii]Raki: A strong Greek aperitif.

Papadiamandis believes that "the Church should be far from every governmental dependence and imposition."[64] He argues that "the Church is victorious in the world without the slightest cooperation of the State; in fact, on the contrary, the Church has been much persecuted and exhausted by the State. Today, the Church can be victorious over every persecution when its leaders, having the consciousness of their high calling, seek the good of the Church in every way."[65] Papadiamandis insists that the Church must not only distance itself from politics but also from the State in general. The Church must be particularly strict when a corrupt State asks Her, not only for small compromises but to commit sins on its behalf. He believes that the Church must be managed by the faithful themselves and not from the outside. In particular, the election and ordination of clergy must take place according to purely ecclesiastical criteria and procedures, and the Church should not be forced to accept the "swarm of priests, boors and philistines that corrupt politics have many times imposed upon the eminent hierarchs to ordain."[66]

While Papadiamandis insists that the Church must remain far from politics, he does not believe that it should remain far from the world. The members of the Church militant, the clergy and the people, are not a community of people cut off from the world, living and acting in an ideal, sinless, and blameless way. Christians are, of course, "called to be Saints,"[67] and the battles and struggles of life are intended to set them on the path to this sanctification. Christian life is a life of sinlessness,[68] but this does not mean that the faithful are perfected Saints. This especially does not mean that they make up a caste of "pure ones." The Church is comprised of the repentant. This is why a repeated petition of Orthodox worship asks that the faithful be able to pass the rest of their lives "in repentance"[69] and, when the time comes for their departure from the present world, that Christ might receive them in "repentance and confession."[70] Christ Himself guarantees that the kingdom of heaven, the militant Church on earth, is like "a net that was cast into the sea, and gathered of every kind."[71]

Papadiamandis's faithful are presented as the people of God who live and move in the world, as did the first Christians. Like the early Christians described in the *Letter to Diognetos*,[72]

Papadiamandis's heroes do not separate themselves from other people in the world—not as regards to where they live, their language, or their daily habits. While they follow the local customs regarding dress, food, and the everyday aspects of life, they evoke admiration for their unique otherworldly conduct. They constitute the soul and the center of the society in which they live, and live and move within the world as if they belong there quite naturally.

Papadiamandis's depiction of the people of God as the Church agrees with the position of St. Maximos the Confessor. According to St. Maximos, the Church and world should not be sharply separated into two distinct entities; rather, they cooperate with each other in the process of the world becoming the Church.[73] Papadiamandis's texts present precisely this theology. It is characteristic that he is not interested in interpreting, defining, and judging the religious level and "spirituality" of the people he describes. He loves them all, and he empathizes with them. As he once remarked, "the heart tends to prevail over the head."[74] Although he may not have regularly started up conversations with the frequenters of the shoreline coffee shops of Skiathos or the denizens of the Athenian taverns, he knew how to converse with them and to immortalize their passions and aspirations on paper. The trials and misfortunes of the people he met and wrote about do not just skim the surface of his life but enter into him. They shake him to the core, become his own sufferings, as he experiences and lives the reality of the Church as one body. The coupling of his proclivity to live the ecclesiology of the Church with his extraordinary talent for expression enables Papadiamandis to raise the individual troubles of the people of God to the level of the universal suffering of the world.

In the mystery of the Church, the faithful are joined as members of one body and fill what is lacking in one another. Men and women of all ages and classes work in an inseparable unity. Papadiamandis's writings confirm and remind us that the Holy Spirit was given to the Church, in the words of St. John Chrysostom, "so as to unite those who are of different generations and manners. The old and the young, the poor and the rich, the child and the teenager, the woman and the man, and

Photo taken from the chapel of the Prophet Elijah,
overlooking Skiathos and the harbor. In the distance on the
far right is the island of the Great Tsougria, mentioned in
Papadiamandis's story, "Watchman at the Quarantine Colony."

every soul become one"[75] in the body of the Church. In the texts
of our writer, one becomes acquainted with a remarkable variety
of people, each one living and cultivating his relationship with
God and the Church in his own way.

Papadiamandis likes to portray humble and scorned people
who may seem strange or scandalous, but, through the author's
lovingly perceptive eyes, the reader comes to value them for the
unique truth expressed through their lives. One such character
is Aunt Skevo who dresses like a man in order to travel to the
small island of Tsougria, set aside as a sanitarium, where only
certain men are permitted.[76] Her son has been quarantined here,
along with other cholera patients, and Aunt Skevo wants to take
care of him. In this adversity, she is able to comfort those around
her, encouraging them to repentance, while she takes refuge in
prayer and finds support there in her trial. In another story, a
teacher named Christina lives outside marriage with Pangagis, a
politician who takes advantage of her while promising marriage

and a teaching position.[77] She yearns for the liturgical life and the ecclesiastical community, but in order to avoid the critical looks of the "respectable" ladies of Athens, she only goes to church with the servants and nannies on weekdays and other times when there are no major feasts. In another story we meet the barren Seraino who patiently endures the maltreatment and humiliation of her husband and even takes care of the eight children born to him by his second wife, Lelouda. When the villagers go to her tomb three years after her repose,[xiii] to dig up her remains, "a gentle, divine fragrance like basil, musk, and rose wafted up to the nostrils of the priest, the gravedigger, Lelouda, and the other two women there. Her bones had become fragrant."[xiv 78]

In other stories, simple people pray with such belief, boldness, and selflessness as if to compel God and the Saints. They undertake self-sacrificial actions for the good of their fellow men, without expecting human reward. One of these is the simple shepherd who, learning of the approach of imminent danger to the village and finding himself opposite the chapel of St. Sozonos,

> made the sign of the cross three times and pleaded with the Saint to appear now, not to prove his name false... [H]e didn't daydream about a reward or some payment, for by his actions, he had offered a great service to his compatriots, by warning of the terrible impending danger and saving all the village from fear and plunder. These are (how could one say?) "sacred things," and if there is some reward, he had a certain feeling, it will be somewhere else.[79]

In a similar way, the simple women of Skiathos would often cry, "My Panagia! My Panagia!" in times of peril and danger—a spontaneous cry of faith that saved the world from many misfortunes.[80] These simple, devout women went by foot to the country chapel of the Honorable Forerunner[xv] for the feast on

---

[xiii]In Greece it was common for the bones of the reposed to be exhumed three years after their repose.

[xiv]It is not uncommon for the bones of those whom God has sought fit to honor to be found fragrant and yellow from the presence of divine myrrh.

[xv]This is a title given to St. John the Baptist.

The country chapel of St. Anastasia, "the deliverer from poisons."
To the left of the chapel can be seen the ruins of a 4th century tower.

the twenty-ninth of August. When they would see some boat in danger on the sea, "they would chant the *Supplicatory Canon* before the large, old icon of the Saint."[81]

Papadiamandis believes that no one should be turned away from the Church, even though his or her expressions of devotions may seem unconventional or strange. Papadiamandis accepts and indulges his cousin Mahouli, who

> circled the church [of St. Anastasia] seven times [earnestly serving, on her own, a special liturgical service out of motherly affection] with a hundred-headed candle that she had fashioned by hand...and she called upon the Saint to destroy the magic, to enter into the mind of her son, lovesick and drunk from bad witchcraft.[82]

Nor does Papadiamandis reject Konstantios, who, when he found himself in danger with waves buffeting his small boat, "unlearned, for the moment, the blasphemies he knew and busied himself with saying his prayers."[83] Nor is the son of Aunt Kyrastos, the one called "the American," rejected. Absent for years in America, immediately on his return to Skiathos, he showed his special devotion to the church of the Three Hierarchs: "even though he did not cross himself when he saw the church, he took off his hat in the darkness and put it on again, as if he had met an old friend and was greeting him."[84] Faith in God exists as a deep experience in people who at first glance do not seem pious, while the Church remains a point of reference even for those who do not attend.

In the final analysis, if one admires something particular in Papadiamandis, it is his ability to reveal how all people are children of God, the people of God—the priests who roam about the island and struggle to serve Liturgy in distant and isolated chapels, and the laity who accompany and concelebrate with them; the immigrants who return and those who are fatigued by their travels; the fishermen on the Skiathan waterfront; the drunkards of the bars of Skiathos and the frequenters of the coffee shops along the Athenian docks; the somewhat shady characters, the lovesick and the nostalgic, as well as the old ladies who work to raise their children and to help their widowed daughters with their orphaned children. In the pages of Papadiamandis, all have their place and all are valued because they are children of God, who become the Church and exist as the Church. People and human society are transformed into a divine-human society, a eucharistic gathering, and an ecclesiological reality. The literary talent and ecclesiastical experience of Papadiamandis gracefully depicts the great potential whereby people of the world can be changed, in the Church, into sons of blessing and transformed into partakers of the Eucharist. He reveals how a finite world can become infinite and how a society of pain and tears can be transformed into a doxological and eucharistic community.

4

THE TRADITION OF THE CHURCH

Biblical Tradition as Liturgical Tradition

In the *corpus* of Papadiamandis's works, the number and nature of passages from ecclesiastical literature—Biblical, patristic, hymnological, and synaxarian—are much more than a simple annotation of sources.[1] This is why it is not easy "to locate the sources (literally and metaphorically) of the waters that flow into the 'all-consuming sea' of Papadiamandis's text."[2] Often, these passages are perfectly assimilated with the text and become difficult to distinguish from his own words. In his writing, Papadiamandis does not just use certain disembodied fragments of ecclesiastical phrases remembered from his childhood years. He was the son of a priest and, from his earliest years, regularly followed his father to the Divine Liturgies and other services. He continued to live the liturgical tradition of the Church in his subsequent years, mostly at the chanter's stand.[3]

Events from Holy Scripture, especially from the Old Testament, appear frequently in Papadiamandis's works. A characteristic example is the inclusion of the story of the idol of Baal,[4] in his story, "The Witches."[5] Also, in his articles published in newspapers on the occasion of Church feasts, he interprets events and stories from the four Gospels and from the Apocryphal Gospels.[6] Most of Papadiamandis's biblical references are to passages from the Psalms, Prophets, Gospels, and Epistles—especially from those passages that are read in worship.[7] These biblical references appear in many other stories—sometimes as unedited biblical passages underlined or in quotation marks and sometimes inserted with a free rendering. In his story "The Watchman at the Quarantine Colony,"[8] Papadiamandis writes, "But Christ speaks, concerning some future day, when the Lord of the vineyard will come" suggesting the passage from the Gospel which says, "He will come and destroy the vinedressers, and give the vineyard to others."[9] Later in the same story, it is written that "the demon of fear had found seven other demons more evil than himself and had taken captive the spirit of men."[10] This excerpt echoes

Christ the True Vine

another Gospel passage: "Then he goes and takes with him seven other spirits more wicked than himself, and they enter and dwell there; and the last state of that man is worse than the first."[11] When a Jewish docker who had been given a ride from Thessalonica refuses to help Captain Iraklis because it is Saturday, Papadiamandis comments on his position.

> Tsiphoutis didn't know that "It is lawful to do good on the Sabbath," nor did he know that "the son of Man is Lord also of the Sabbath."[12] He only knew how to be saved, by the sweat of Greek sailors, who were sailing on the day of the Sabbath....He was, it seems, a genuine descendant of those of old, who would split hairs and pretend not to see the camel.[13]

As is evidenced by the texts, Papadiamandis knew and used the Holy Scriptures as naturally and readily as one uses his native tongue.

For our author, Holy Scripture is not read or interpreted alone, nor is it the only foundation of faith. Holy Scripture is studied and used within the Church, for it is the Church that preserves its content and meaning. It is part of the Church's recorded tradition, the witness and experience of the Prophets, Apostles, and Evangelists within the life of the Church. Whenever and wherever the Church acts synodally, it is the communion of the

Saints and incarnates the ecclesiastical tradition. The Lutheran dogma of *Sola Scriptura* reveals man's rationalistic attempt to insure a safe and immovable foundation of "tradition." In the final analysis, however, Luther replaces the Pope (who places himself above the Church) with a "paper pope," as Western theologians themselves have rightly called it. Because reformers in the West had only experienced the idea of the Church as understood in Catholicism—as a confession governed by the Pope—and not of the fullness, communal nature, and tradition of Orthodoxy, these reformers could not understand that the Church is something more than Holy Scripture. All the texts of the Church (including scriptural, patristic, hymnological, canonical, and other writings), which over time have taken on dogmatic-symbolic meaning[1] in Orthodoxy, are witnesses to the ecclesiastical tradition. These texts have never, however, been understood as the absolute bearers of the Church and Her tradition. They indicate Her limits without exhausting Her fullness. The whole tradition exists within the life of the Church. Papadiamandis knows that an intellectual acceptance of the tradition does not suffice. For this reason, he chose a different path for himself: to live humbly within this tradition. Thus, his own life also became a part of this tradition, along with his work. Having been enveloped and grafted into the ecclesiastical tradition, Papadiamandis could still approach and appreciate other traditions, such as that of the dervish in his story, "The Fallen Dervish."[14] The biblical foundation of Papadiamandis's texts and the liturgical stance in them are essential parts of the basic source of our writer's work: the Orthodox tradition.

All of Papadiamandis's short stories, novels, poems, and articles have deep roots in the Orthodox tradition. These roots support and raise before us the trunk of his person and the many-branched tree of his work, justifying his insistence on preserving these roots and safeguarding this tradition. He does

[1] The terms "dogmatic" and "symbolic" were used by the Fathers to designate the truths of the faith as preserved in the dogmas of the faith, which were contained in the symbols of faith (such as the Nicene Creed).

not consider changing it for any reason. He may be likened, in a certain way, to David Pargolas, who Papadiamandis describes in this way: "Concerning this man, a tradition is preserved that he had rejected the dignity of being Ecumenical Patriarch, which had been offered to him by one of the Iconoclastic Emperors on the condition that he would join the other camp, because he preferred to be a simple monk and to remain Orthodox."[15]

The Orthodox tradition is the starting point and axis of Papadiamandis's work. References to it are made even in his philological texts. For example, in describing the *Anaphiótika,*[ii] he turns the readers' attention to "lit vigil lamps in small alcoves, in old enclosed altars, incense, candles, worship...the *Unknown God.*"[16] He does not hesitate to speak of the passing, in Athens, of the

two visions [who] occasionally appear there. The one wears a ratty tunic, and a cloth thrown upon his shoulders. He holds a staff. A Galilean, with a beak-like nose, bald in front, is snatched up to the third heaven. The other one wears a phelonion from cloth textured with red crosses, a stole [*epitrachílion*] embroidered with angels, and an omophorion from sheep's wool. With a straight nose, a great beard, venerable, he once went up as far as the upper hierarchies and described the orders of Angels. Both visions are lofty, commanding respect, sublime. The first is named Paul, the second Dionysios.[17]

Papadiamandis's rich knowledge of and daily experience of Holy Scripture, within the context of the Church, enable him to successfully make universal theological connections and

[ii]This is a district of Athens near the Plaka (at the foot of the Acropolis), whose name comes from the island Anaphi, in the Cyclades island chain. His reference to the "unknown God" is undoubtedly a reference to the Areo Pagos, right by the Acropolis, where St. Paul gave his famous speech to the philosophers.

descriptions in his texts, leaving future generations with exquisite works of literature that present the Orthodox tradition.

Patristic and Synaxarian Tradition

In addition to Papadiamandis's use of the biblical tradition in his works, his texts also reveal his masterful assimilation of the patristic tradition. Many of his stories make reference to patristic texts, while his whole work is an attempt to reconnect and re-introduce Greeks to the Fathers and to the genuine patristic *phrónima*. In "The Monk," Papadiamandis refers to a passage in St. John Chrysostom's *Address to Evtropios*[18] that states that the scrutiny of friends is better than the kisses of enemies.[19] When he speaks about usury, he refers to St. Basil and uses his imagery: "Whether or not the earth brings forth, whether or not the trees bear fruit, the interest doesn't stop. Assets give birth. The fertile have ceased bearing (as St. Basil says), but the unfertile have started to and continue to bring forth."[20]

Bearing within himself the synaxarian tradition and the lives of the Saints, Papadiamandis often refers to them in his texts. For Papadiamandis, a Church without Saints is unthinkable, so he frequently refers to their lives in his texts. In an article written to honor the memory of St. George, he presents the folk traditions concerning St. George together with the synaxarian elements and, through them, expresses the great love and reverence that the Great Martyr evokes, not only in the Greeks but also in other Eastern peoples.[21] The narrations in this text are reminiscent of the *Evergetinos*.[iii] [22] In another text, he describes the chapel of the Archangel Michael, which has a spring with an abundance of cool water in the recess of the holy altar. Using the synaxarian account of the Archangel Michael's miracle in Chonais (Kolossais) of Phrygia, which our Church celebrates on the sixth of September, he explains why nearly

---

[iii]Evergetinos: A collection of ascetic texts centered on the ancient ascetic fathers, compiled in the eleventh century by Paul of the Monastery of the *Evergetinos*.

every church dedicated to the Archangel has one such spring.[iv] With his extensive knowledge of the *Synaxarion* and of history, he interprets another event of modern Greek history recorded by a non-Orthodox writer, "a reliable foreign witness," where a similar miracle of the Archangel Michael is authenticated.

> Whoever reads through the history of the Greek Struggle of the philhellenic General Gordonos, will learn from a reliable foreign witness what happened in the Anatolikon, not far from Mesologgio, when the besieged Greeks began to lose heart due to an absence of water. A bomb fell and exploded in the wall of the [church of the] Holy Bodiless Ones, which caused an abundant spring of cold water to gush forth from the foundations of the church of the Archangel. The valiant men took courage and didn't capitulate.[23]

In "The Watchman at the Quarantine Colony," Fr. Nicodemos the monk mentions the reading of the *Synaxarion* and the *Lausiac History*;[24] in another story, the synaxarian relationship of St. Theodore of Tyron and of *Osios*[v] Joseph the Hymnographer, poet of the canon of the Akathist "living book of Christ,"[25] is discussed. Elsewhere, he shows that when babes and young people have untimely deaths, Christians can find consolation in synaxarian accounts and traditions.[26] In addition to these, many other stories include allusions to the lives of the Saints or references to texts of the Fathers, revealing the great influence of the synaxarian and neptic traditions of the Church on Papadiamandis.[27]

[iv]St. John the Evangelist, while preaching in Phrygia, prophesied that God would send the Archangel Michael to a certain spot in that area. This happened and at that place a miraculous spring appeared with great healing powers. A beautiful chapel was built there by one of the faithful whose daughter had been healed. Later, a young man named Archippus settled there, so as to live the ascetic life. He was greatly aided in his spiritual struggles by miraculous interventions of the Archangel.

[v]This is an appellation given to monastic Saints.

The Hymnological Tradition: "The Songs of God"

Being steeped in the hymnology of the Church, Papadiamandis introduces and incorporates the hymns of the Church into his work. In his story, "The Furnace," he writes, "But from breasts that have run dry, as from a barren rock, you ask to suck milk, *a new drink*, as from a source of incorruption,"[28] which is reminiscent of the hirmos of the third canticle of the canon of the Resurrection—"Come let us drink a new drink, not one wonderfully brought forth from a barren rock, but the source of incorruption, springing forth from the grave of Christ, in Whom we are established."[29] When he refers to the sea-furnace, the sea-cave, he cites the verses of the *Parakletike*:

> The furnace, O Savior, hast Thou cooled,
> The dancing children chant;
> O God of our fathers, blessed art Thou.[30]

Describing the beauty of nature in the springtime, he borrows verses from a troparion that is chanted in churches on Great Friday: "For Thou didst wear the crown of insult, Who didst paint the earth with flowers; and the red mantle of revilement didst Thou wear...."[31] In another text, he recounts a resurrectional Divine Liturgy in which the participation of Christians in the Mystery of Holy Communion is characterized as "communion from the new fruit of the vine."[32] In "The Monk," the reader glimpses the depth of Papadiamandis's knowledge of the Psalter, ecclesiastical hymnology, and the Orthodox tradition in general by witnessing this same wealth expressed in his character, the monk Samuel.[33]

As a chanter, Papadiamandis was thoroughly familiar with the hymns of the Church.[34] He reveals the spirit of Orthodox hymnography through his stories, especially through several passages in his short story "Songs of God." The first example describes the reaction of the little Toto to the hymn, "This is the day of Resurrection."

[Upon hearing the] allegro, the first hirmos, that is to say, of the canon of the day...[she] leapt for joy, and her little face lit up. Her eyes, her mouth, her cheeks, all became more beautiful and smiled an ineffable smile of joy. It moved me. It seems that those inspired songs of our holy Church truly have an ineffable fragrance and beauty, witnessed to from the mouths of babes and sucklings.[35]

A second example comes from Maria, a child of seven years, who also speaks out with joy, "Those aren't troparia that you are chanting, sir.... Those are like sweet, sweet little songs."[36] In a third instance, little Angeliki, the daughter of Papadiamandis's friend Nicholas, approached him during a vigil at St. Elisha, greeted him, and told him, "You, Uncle Alexandros, you sing the songs of God."[37] The continuation of the story shows how pleased Papadiamandis is with this characterization. He is happy with it not only because it comes "from the mouths of babes," but also because it completely resonates with what his childlike soul believes—that the hymns of the Church he chanted are the songs of God.

Canonical Tradition

Papadiamandis's extensive knowledge of the canons of the Church (another important aspect of ecclesiastical tradition) also becomes apparent through his stories and articles. For example, when referring to the very strict fast of Great Saturday, which has always been observed by the Church, he refers to the sixty-sixth apostolic canon and to the fifty-fifth canon of the Penthektis Synod, which state that there "is no fasting on Saturday and Sunday, except on only one Saturday."[38] He does not, however, stop there. Because the canonical tradition began in the gatherings of ecclesiastical worship and was completed in the gatherings of the Fathers—the synods—he connects the canons with the liturgical tradition of the Church. Consequently, in the continuation of the text, he cites the canon's rationale based on the liturgical practice and on the theology of worship. "Some

Christ blesses the children

ancient Christians didn't eat anything at all on Great Saturday; formerly, on this day, the catechumens would be baptized. All night long a vigil would be served."[39] He also shows that the instruction provided by the God-inspired canons permeates all of life, such that worship continues beyond the bounds of the worship gathering, as a liturgy after the Liturgy, transforming all of life into the worship of God. For him, the canons are not historical texts or dry forms, unable to influence the life of the Church. Rather, he discerned that their neglect and the arranging of the life of the Church according to the laws of the State was the beginning of the disaster that obstructed and continues to obstruct the path toward the proper functioning of the Church in Greece.

While Papadiamandis is against the systematic violation and infringement of the Church's canons, he does not, however, approve of their observance just for the sake of appearance or the folk superstitions that have grown up around them. He also disagrees with the mentality that only clerics are qualified to know the canons and *The Rudder*[vi] and that laymen should not have an immediate and personal knowledge of them, a mentality according to which "the people never [take] *The Rudder* into their hands, to see how many and which canons it contains."[40] According to this mentality, *The Rudder* and the *Nomocanonas*[vii] are considered to be sacred, and the use of them by laymen is forbidden, lest they desecrate them by holding them in their hands.[41] Papadiamandis addresses this mentality with pointed irony in the following dialogue between the wife of a priest and a simple townsman who dares to ask her for *The Rudder*:

"And what do you want with this book?" Papamanolaina asked him.
"Don't you worry," Minas answered. "I want to read something and I'll give it right back to you."
"Isn't this the book that has the *Nomocanonas*?" the suspicious presbytera[viii] asked once more.
"Yes," cousin Minas said, wincing.
"My priest says that it isn't right for anyone that's not ordained to take hold of it." "Don't take it with your naked hand," cousin Minas answered. "Use a clean towel."[42]

Papadiamandis argues that the conscience of the people and their needs should be placed above the letter and theory of the canons. "This [pious] impulse [of the people] prevailed over the stricter and more canonical view."[43] If, however, he rejects both the devotion to the letter and the distancing from the spirit of the canons, even more so does he condemn the elasticity and Economy[ix†] dictated by sinful expediencies.

[vi]*The Rudder* is a collection of the Church's canons compiled by St. Nicodemos of the Holy Mountain (one of the leaders of the *Kollyvádes* movement) in the eighteenth century.

[vii]The *Nomocanonas* is a compilation of the ordinances and decisions of the Holy Synods.

[viii]Presbytera is the Greek title for the wife of a priest.

[ix]The Church's use of this word derives from the "Economy" of Jesus Christ, which was His condescension, as God, to become man in the Incarnation. Though man deserved death, God reached out to man in love, to save him. Economy involves the altering of a given rule, requirement, or practice in a specific concrete case so that the therapeutic aim of the rule can be fulfilled.

Papadiamandis's works deal with Greek traditions and lifestyles that are in harmony with and are watered by the tradition of the Church.[44] He does, however, distinguish the true ecclesiastical customs that were born in the Orthodox liturgical tradition and that express Her ethos from various local traditions, which are crude and contain worldly elements.[45] For Papadiamandis, the tradition of the Orthodox Church provides the criteria by which every kind of folk belief and tradition is evaluated. Many of the truths of the Orthodox faith were preserved by the faithful who passed them down orally from generation to generation, and many of the folk traditions have been profoundly influenced by the patristic and ecclesiastical tradition. Regarding folk songs (the characteristic songs of the people), Papadiamandis notes that "some [of these songs] have the feast of the day as the subject of their lyrics but without following the sacred texts; they go over the subject with poetic colors and with the help of the popular legend."[46] He views these songs as "wonderful in their simplicity," because they express the Greek and Orthodox patristic tradition. Commenting on a verse from a popular song for New Year's, "St. Basil is coming from Caesarea, bearing paper and glue, paper and quill pens,"[47] he points out that "Hellenism's innate love of learning, which survived through so many hardships and sufferings, used the fame of the Greek Saint [Basil] (who was an educator) as encouragement for the young people to study and learn, so that after many centuries the great light of Caesarea appeared as if writing a second *Admonition to Young People*."[48] His conception of Hellenism is noteworthy as he does not limit the Greek Orthodox tradition to the bounds of the Greek State, but views it extending much further than the geographical bounds of the borders of Greece.[49] When, however, he speaks of national traditions it is clear that he does not agree with nationalism, just as, when speaking of the Orthodox tradition, he does not agree with intolerance and fanaticism.[50]

Papadiamandis knows that the Church's tradition is ensured by its catholicity, and the catholicity of the Church is realized in Her tradition. Tradition is only possible within the framework of genuine ecclesiastical communion, in the one Body of Christ.

Outside of the Body of Christ, in every heretical manifestation, it is impossible for the ecclesiastical tradition to survive. Papadiamandis locates the roots of and the spread of heresies in improper thinking and, above all, the improper living of the Orthodox tradition.[51]

In his articles, Papadiamandis uses historical and theological points to explain the differences and the mutual influences between the Eastern tradition that he lives and the Western tradition, which he seems to know well. Writing about the feast of Nativity, he points out that "in Western Europe they developed and formulated the feast such that it took on a unique form—a special ethos, customs, and traditions that combined with and, in turn, influenced the feast."[52] Taking into consideration the temperament of Western people, he explains the development of a whole philosophy derived from the *Contes de Noel*—also known as the *Christmas Tales*, many of which are incredibly beautiful works, which were written by distinguished writers. He observes that the annual *Christmas Numbers* (the special leaflets in colorful magazines that were published every Christmas) could fill a whole library. "It is not at all strange," he notes, "that this tradition developed in the West, for that is where this feast has its origins and creation. When St. John Chrysostom was ordained Patriarch of Constantinople at the end of the fourth century, some came from the West, making known the customs pertaining to the feast, and he instituted the celebration of the birth of Christ throughout the East on the twenty-fifth of December so that the confusion that prevailed regarding the date of its celebration would come to an end in the East as well."[53]

Papadiamandis also notes that well-educated Westerners—Jesuits and others who published and commented on the Eastern Fathers—spoke with heartfelt admiration for the ecclesiastical poetry, the typicon, and the ceremony of Orthodoxy. Some of these people, in fact, had the patience to translate word for word—even preserving the rhythm—a myriad of troparia and hymns chanted in the Eastern Church, as the Orthodox Slavs had once done. However, Papadiamandis sadly notes that it is not always Westerners who are affected by Orthodoxy, it sometimes works the other way around: "Occasionally, some of us are so confused as to admire the Papist Church!"[54] An example of this may be found in a book by Roidis[x] who, among other things, writes: "Personally, if some foreigner studying to become a Christian asked my opinion as to which of the Christian churches he should choose, I would counsel him to enter into the Western [Catholic] Church, as it has instrumental music and songs."[55]

Papadiamandis derisively describes the assault of foreign customs and traditions, which imposed a different ethos and a foreign way of life on Greek families. He derides people who express pride in dancing European dances and who argue that Greek dances are an unbearable monotony.[56] In the stories "The Dance at Kyr Periandros" and "The Provisions of Grandeur,"[xi 57] he describes the capture of Greece by foreign traditions. When he came to Athens in 1873, a city of fifty thousand inhabitants, most people had lost the way of the Orthodox tradition. The small Greek State of 1830, aided by Europe and the immigrant army of "enlightened" Greeks, had begun to throw away, one by one, whatever had been preserved of the spiritual inheritance of its ancestors and set the direction—without understanding what it was doing—to become, even in its "spiritual" orientations, a modernized European State. Papadiamandis saw this new anti-tradition spreading quickly, which is why he wrote the following introduction to his Easter story "Easter Chanter," to awaken his countrymen.

[T]he nation of today, unfortunately, has not progressed as much as they say it has. The Greek nation, at any rate the enslaved portion of it, is still lagging behind, and the free portion cannot run far enough ahead without the whole rupturing, as it

---

[x]Emmanuel Roidis (1836-1904): A well-educated writer of prose and a literary critic from the island of Syros.

[xi]The title is, very likely, a sarcastic play on words, for the Greek word we translate as "provisions" (opsónia) has the metaphorical meaning of "wages," as in the expression, "the wages of sin."

has already, alas, ruptured.... An Englishman or a German or a Frenchman is able to be cosmopolitan or anarchic or atheist or anything he likes. He has done his patriotic duty; he has built up a great country. Now, thanks to the luxury of his freedom, he can give rein to unbelief and pessimism. But for the Greek of today, sorry figure that he is, to want to act the cosmopolitan or the atheist, is like a dwarf standing on tiptoe and striving to emulate a giant. The enslaved portion of the Greek nation, and the liberated also, has and will always have need of its religion.[58]

Living the tradition of despised *Romyosíni*,[xii] he sees that the "enlightenment" that the Greeks brought from all over created an increasingly impenetrable darkness of ignorance. In his story "Supplicatory Canon," which he wrote at the Monastery of Venerable Dionysios of Olympus, he beseeches the Saint to "give mystical illumination to those entering the darkness of despair."[59] Papadiamandis writes his stories on the borderline between these two worlds—he uses a foreign literary type, the novel, to present the Orthodox tradition through particular persons and things, rather than as a device to analyze ideas. He limits himself "to the description of persons and things, which is, narrowly and precisely, our work."[60]

The "enlightened" translators of pagan wisdom who came from abroad in Papadiamandis's day and afterwards, were an epidemic that paralyzed every traditional inclination and creation. Those people thought that Europe was a prototype to be copied, so that the *Romyoí* might become Europeans. Few were those who, studying in or about Europe, took only that which would be truly beneficial to Greece. Instead, the great mass of them wholeheartedly adopted European ways as a ready solution and imported them, unskillfully and dangerously transferring European traditions, beliefs, and customs to their homeland. Papadiamandis discerned that many small-minded persons were hiding behind the European veneer. He knew that

[xii]*Romyosíni*: "Romanism," that is, the culture of authentic Orthodoxy.

people of substance can discern what is valuable and critically and productively make it their own.[61]

Papadiamandis was not afraid of the world outside Greece or of communication with other peoples. In fact, he learned two European languages, English and French—which was unusual in his day—so he would be better able to communicate, read the texts, and learn the culture of those peoples. He did, however, fear the Greeks' immaturity and lack of spiritual foundation that allowed them to easily accept the unassimilated influences of foreign traditions. With sadness, he records how "public personalities, people from all over...[have returned bringing] with them...*napoleana*[xiii] but, even more, new habits, blasphemies, controversies, impudence, insobriety, and provocation."[62] This characteristically anti-traditional disposition appeared in Papadiamandis's day mainly as a result of various Roman Catholic and Protestant theological books, full of intellectualism and metaphysics, being read as ecclesiastical theology, both by those who went abroad and by some within Greece. These texts, translated by admirers of rhetoric, were offered as the height of theological science. This anti-tradition rose up ceaselessly and severely against our author—more after his death than during his life—through the writings of the literary critic Constantinos Dimaras and the academic and professor of Patrology Demetrios Balanos.[63]

Diachronicity[xiv] *in Tradition*

Papadiamandis has a gift for connecting persons and events in the Christian tradition with corresponding persons and events in the wider span of Hellenism. Knowing that Christianity superseded idolatry, he has no trouble in viewing the tradition diachronically. Those who complain about the presence of pagan elements or hidden pagan tendencies in his work forget that

---

[xiii]These were the coins made during Napoleon's reign.

[xiv]Diachronicity: A theological term referring to the perseverance of truth throughout time.

Papadiamandis does not express the fragmentary and particular, but the unified and the whole. The center of his life, the Church, incorporates and transforms everything, which is why, in his thought and writing, these two seemingly contradictory traditions find continuity and unity within each other. This unity of traditions appears, for example, through his description of a church: "Its name was St. Anastasia's. Once upon a time it had perhaps been a temple of Kore from Hades or Hecate the Venomous (Pharmakis); and the Christians, natural heirs of dying paganism, had baptized it and made it, out of a spirit of contrariness, into a church of the *Pharmakolýtria* ("Deliverer from poison"), or else of the *Romaía* ("the Roman Woman"), deriving the name straightforwardly from the building."[64]

In another story, "Reverie of the Fifteenth of August," he describes the condition of his hero's soul by using the poetry of Homer, while referring to verses from the Psalms of David and troparia from the hymnology of the Church. He presents Old Phrangoula, who lives all alone, sitting in the courtyard of the church of the Panagia of Prekla on the eve of the feast of the Dormition of the Theotokos. Old Phrangoula thinks both

Ἡ ΚΟΙΜΗCΙC ΤΗΟ ΘΕΟΤΟΚΥ

about Koumbo, the daughter he lost at fourteen years of age, and about his troublesome creditors. He now lives alone, on the road to old age,[65] and recalls the verse of the Psalter, "Do not cast me off in the time of old age.... Now also when I am old and gray headed, O God, do not forsake me."[66] He pours out his lamentations in mournful tones to the Panagia with troparia from the *Great Supplicatory Canon*: "The distractions of life have encircled me, even as bees in the honeycomb, O Virgin...."[67] He calls upon the Panagia, "the Sweetness of Angels, the joy of those who sorrow," to come in sympathy and help in his difficulties—"Take hold of me and deliver me, from eternal torments...."[68] In his short story "A Drop of Water...," while describing the offerings made by the people, Papadiamandis interlaces hymnological troparia and Homeric verse in an excellent synthesis: "The older people inscribed the whole final troparion of the Service of the Saint [the troparion that begins 'Shocked at the wounds wrought by man'][69] onto an artist's canvas, and this offering was made to last a lifetime for the healing of fevers that had been brought by the Dog of Orion[xv] to the downtrodden people."[70]

In the same story, Papadiamandis footnotes verses of Pindar in a graceful way,[71] showing the diachronicity of the Greek tradition while interpreting events from the age before Christ using events that took place after Christ. With obvious admiration for ancient poetry, he points out how the ethereal Pindar invokes certain hymns, wonderfully personifies them, and asks them to chant together to one God, hero, and man. According to Papadiamandis this greatest lyricist of antiquity "somehow *prophecies*," and this prophecy is fulfilled in the hymns of the Orthodox Church that hymn Christ who is true God (as one of the Holy Trinity), the greatest hero (who threw out the devil and through the Cross defeated death), and the most true human (as the son of man): "Pindar's perplexity is also assuaged, as that of every chanter or poet, finding in one and the same person, the union of the three attributes: of God, of the hero, and of man."[72] Thus, according to our author, both Pindar's *Anaxiphórminges*[xvi] and the Church's hymns manifestly hymn "the true God, hero, and man—our Lord Jesus Christ."[73]

Papadiamandis's insistence on the diachronic nature of tradition provides him with a clear position—an unusual thing for his and later periods—regarding the Greek language question. In the only interview he gave, he reveals the bitter truth that none of his contemporaries were bold enough to tell. He refuses to allow Psiharis[xvii] to pretend to represent the demotic [popular] language, because Papadiamandis does not see in him any resemblance

---

[xv]According to an ancient mythological understanding, fevers were caused by the evil dog of Orion.

[xvi]*Anaxiphórminges*: A Homeric word referring to the musical notes that are more glorious and melodic than those made by any other musical instrument.

[xvii]John Psiharis (1854—1929): A linguist, philologist, writer, and university professor who championed the demoticization of the Greek language.

to the tradition that gave birth to this language. "The demotic language that Psiharis saw, which he learned, which he studied? He is from Chios, nearly a foreigner, an aristocrat Phanariot, attempting, with a warped dialect, to assert himself as the creator and teacher of the whole nation. No! Languages are not imposed in this way (all of a sudden)...on people!"[74]

Similarly clear is his stance regarding the likewise warped dialect of the advocates of Purist Greek—of the Soutsons[xviii] and Mistriotis[xix]—who limit the Greek language in the opposite way, unaware of how the language could have developed naturally. "The Greek language should have radiated far, as a radiant lighthouse, the bright glory of antiquity, a lighthouse shining without end. The lighthouse guides to the port; it is not itself the port."[75] The statement made by Papadiamandis's earlier publisher, G. Baleta, that he was apparently "blinded by prejudice"[76] when he spoke against Psiharis, is unfair in light of Papadiamandis's disapproval of the other extreme—Purist Greek. Rather than champion either extreme (each trying to change the Greek language in its own way) Papadiamandis remains ever faithful to the tradition.

The language Papadiamandis uses in his texts expresses and provides witness for the diachronicity of the tradition. His critics, however, often misjudged his masterful synthesis of the various stages of the Greek linguistic tradition, considering it to be inconsistent, and demanded more linguistic caution and consistency from him.[77] Papadiamandis does not simply appear to be a Byzantine; he truly is one. Living and writing within the seeming inconsistency of the diachronic Byzantine tradition is liberating and natural for him, so he cannot help but express himself in a way that reflects this tradition.[78]

This "inconsistency," in fact, characterizes the entire ecclesiastical tradition. We hear the language of Homer in the iambic canons, and Attic and Hellenistic *Koíne* in hymnology

[xviii]The name of a famous family of the Phanar, three members of which are particularly famous for intellectual and political reasons: Alexandros, Michael (Vodas), and Panagiotis.

[xix]George Mistriotis (1839-1916): A classical philologist from Tripoli, university professor, and champion of Purist Greek.

Iconostasis in the country chapel of the Prophet Elijah

and patristic theology. We read Byzantine Greek in later writers and new Greek in St. Nicodemos the Athonite's *Synaxarion*. The latter, in fact, speaks so freely that he does not hesitate to call the Prophet Elijah's chariot a "cart," [*karótza*] and translates the "platter" on which the Honorable Forerunner's head was transferred as a "plate" [*tzanáki*] while, at the same time, using datives and infinitives.[xx][79] For the same reason, Papadiamandis's use of Homeric, Byzantine, Purist, and Skiathan Greek should not seem surprising or inconsistent, as they all speak of the same tradition.[80] It has been rightly observed that Papadiamandis works traditionally,

> without trying to, for he lives his place, his time, his life, and his work truly, authentically, with ancient endeavors. He has assimilated within himself thousands of years of the life of this land, beginning from his Indo-European inheritance, passing through the ancient world, and ending, through the brilliance of Byzantium, at this which he truly is: a simple and unpretentious *Romyiós* Orthodox.[81]

All three of Papadiamandis's novels—*The Immigrant, Merchants of the Nations*, and The *Gypsy Girl*[82] —provide insights into his

---

[xx]That is to say, he freely used both new words to replace ancient ones, as well as ancient constructions (such as with the dative and infinitive) that had fallen out of use.

upbringing in a world characterized by the spiritual continuation of the tradition. The stance he takes regarding history and the former (pagan) spiritual tradition of his people is particularly apparent in *The Gypsy Girl*. He describes how the people of the Renaissance regarded history, a position that was strange to the Byzantine mind. He sees the Renaissance and its spiritual successors cutting and dividing the Greek Orthodox tradition into two parts, the Greek and the Christian. He knows, however, that this divides humanity and destroys the natural continuity of life.

Papadiamandis is a complete man—a true Greek and a true Orthodox Christian—who discovers Byzantium through his Hellenism and finds ancient Greece through Byzantium. In his thought and life, both remain inextricably linked. Ancient Greece resembles a flower that, wilting from its desire for the truth, then bears great fruit in the warmth of the Sun of Righteousness. Papadiamandis himself was never in danger of being severed from this warmth because he realized that it is not legitimate to assess Byzantium by means of ancient Greece but to do precisely the reverse. *The Gypsy Girl* was his answer to those advocating a return to some vague, true-blue ancient Hellenism. In an attempt to confute Fallmerayer's[xxi] claim that contemporary Greeks are descended from the Slavs, the advocates of Ancient Hellenism fell into the same mistake Fallmerayer had made—they were ignorant of and disparaged the Byzantine and post-Byzantine links that organically bind ancient history to the modern, links that ensure the organic continuity and path of their tradition.

Contact with Papadiamandis is contact with the living spiritual tradition of his land. Living tradition is at odds with fossilized traditions preserved in books or museums.[xxii] Living tradition is a people's way of life and organically links all the elements that constitute its presence in the world. It includes the upbringing

[xxi]Jacob-Philip Fallmerayer (1790-1861): a German historian who argued that contemporary Greeks are descendents of the Slavs.

[xxii]Dr. Keselopoulos here uses museum and book as adjectives to differentiate between two approaches—the living, organic, "subjective" approach and the dead, "objective" approach, which he identifies with museums and, more generally, the fossilization of tradition in some dead form.

and education of children, the illumination of the elements of its culture, and the meaning found in all aspects of its life and path through history. Living tradition always develops naturally from its archetypes and roots. These roots determine, even irreversibly, the life, character, gifts, and, more generally, the path of a people. Tradition is not bronze and copper vessels, textiles and embroidery, nor the various types of folk art. It is living, and there is no authentic life outside of this developing and living tradition.

In his stories, Papadiamandis does speak of shepherds' crooks, gourds, and traditional ways of life, but it is clear that he does not limit the tradition to these things. He regards tradition as the existential truth of a people and not its folkloric appearance. The most essential element of this tradition is that it is inexorably bound to the life of the Church. The Church liturgizes and is liturgized, because it is living. There is nothing dead in the Church's liturgy, not even the dead, for they also serve "in the hope of Resurrection and eternal life." Papadiamandis's stance as regards the tradition is wholly Orthodox—he retains its continuity, not by some conservative connection to the past, but by giving it life in the continuous present. This is how he manages to present the tradition in an authentic way, as life and not as a dead form.

Papadiamandis is fully aware, on a personal level, of his dependence on the spiritual tradition of Greece.[xxiii] Rather than appear to be a conservative, a progressive, or a leader, he prefers to just be Orthodox, consciously learning from life and simultaneously enriching—perhaps unconsciously—the saving tradition of the Orthodox Church and its "wealth-bearing Orthodox theology."[83] His testament to the Greeks of his age— as well as to those who followed—does not come as the voice of a gentle whisper but as a word sharper than any two-edged sword. He expresses his concern for the survival of the tradition that he has lived existentially and not merely intellectually. His

[xxiii]Greek last names beginning with "Papa" refer to the presence in one's lineage of a priest, as the word "Papa" is a diminutive for priest. Papadiamandis's name reflects the priestly lineage of his family.

A midnight vigil on the eve of Nativity:
Church of the Nativity of Christ in the Castle, Skiathos

struggle for the tradition was the most substantial attempt to restore the true Greek tradition since the foundation of the independent Greek State:

> They (the so-called upper class) must not disdain whatever is obviously old, whatever is native, whatever is Greek. The imitation of foreign customs, the aping of foreign ways, the emulation of European manners must all be fought. The religious and familial traditions must not be falsified. The dignified Byzantine tradition must be cultivated, as regards worship, the decoration of the churches, music, and painting. We must never imitate the Papists or the Protestants. We mustn't marvel at foreign things. Let us feel affection for and honor the things of our fatherland. It is gross national shamelessness for us to have heirlooms and not to take care to preserve them. Let them who have the greatest responsibility judge well their responsibility.[84]

5

PAPADIAMANDIS'S LITURGICAL THEOLOGY

Influences from the Monastic Typicon

The Church's liturgical life and tradition transform Her members and guide them to salvation in Christ Jesus.[1] The Christian's life in the Church does not consist of joining some group or embracing some ideology, but of accepting and becoming familiar with the revelation of Christ, which is taught through the services and worship of the Church. The liturgical tradition is received and passed down, not as a dead form but as essence and life that are constantly renewed and developed. The Church on earth, however, does not live the fullness of the Kingdom of God but sees as "in a mirror, dimly."[2] She shares Her life with humans whose nature is fallen and whose weakness is hereditary. This is why, in sharing their life, She is forced to use forms and symbols through which She presents the essence of Her message. The Church uses definitions, symbols, and dogmas to express and preserve the faith. In the same way, in order to express and maintain worship, She uses liturgical forms that are preserved in the Church's typicons. History gives clear witness to the vital role played by the typicons in the preservation of both the liturgical order and the essence of the Orthodox Church; it also reveals the extent to which monasticism honors and respects them. The typicons make it possible for worship to be offered "decently and in order,"[3] leading the faithful to understand the reality of the

The iconostasis in the *katholikon* of the Monastery of the Annunciation

words of the hymn, "being found in the church of Thy glory, we think we are in heaven."[4]

It becomes clear from Papadiamandis's descriptions that the liturgical life of the two parishes and the country chapels of Skiathos were greatly influenced by the monastic liturgical typicon, particularly that of the monasteries of the Holy Mountain. The presence of the *Kollyvádes*, with their Athonite liturgical tradition, left a lasting impression on the Church in Skiathos.[5] In particular, the Monastery of the Annunciation was a visible and living presence that preserved the *Kollyvádes'* Athonite liturgical tradition. In the stories "Hatzopoulos"[6] and "The Black Stumps,"[7] Papadiamandis describes the establishment and liturgical life of the monastery. Papadiamandis is always quick to point out the great respect and authority accorded to the liturgical typicon by the monks. It is this holy fidelity that ensures the cautious and unhindered celebration of the divine services in the monastery and the preservation of this living liturgical tradition throughout the passage of time. This dedication to the liturgical typicon ensures the ecumenicity and catholicity of the liturgical tradition. The ecumenicity and catholicity of the liturgical tradition, in turn, give the necessary assurance of the tradition's authenticity and its place in the life of the Church.

Monastic Typicon in the Monastery

Papadiamandis's profound knowledge of the Athonite typicon is revealed in many of his short stories. In "The Monk," he suggests that monasteries in the world (those not on the Holy Mountain) bring back "the old *typika*, with the vigils and pre-dawn Matins, with all the appointed verses and readings from the Psalter."[8] In that short story and in others, he mentions the *ktitoriká*—a special service in commemoration of the founders of a monastery—that is served on the day after the festal celebration of the *katholikón*[i] of the monastery. In "Easter Chanter," Papa-Azarias "abbot of this isolated monastic community" of St. Charalambos asks the chanter Konstantos to help in the church on the eve of Great Saturday "since I go along with the old order of the Church and read from the *Acts* on Good Saturday evening."[9] Papadiamandis, explaining the priest's words, writes in a note, "According to the old typicon, the *Acts of the Apostles* are read in the Holy Monasteries on the evening of Holy Saturday before the vigil and the Paschal Matins."[10]

Elsewhere, Papadiamandis records all the details of the typicon for the vigil of the Nativity, which is celebrated in the little Monastery of the Panagia of Kechrea. He notes that the six monks who have recently come from another monastery (on an island in the Cyclades island chain) begin the evening with Vespers of the feast—without the usual Service of Entreaty[ii]—and, on the day of the feast, they serve the Liturgy of St. Basil. "It was daybreak on Monday and Vespers hadn't been sung that morning nor had the Liturgy of St. Basil the Great been celebrated on the previous

[i]The main church in a monastery.
[ii]In Greek, *litíya*.

evening."[11] The Liturgy of St. Basil is celebrated in the Church ten times a year, including the day before Nativity, after the Vespers service of the feast has been sung. However, when the day before Nativity is a Sunday, the Liturgy of St. John Chrysostom is celebrated along with the Matins of Sunday (with hymns for the eve of the feast), while Vespers of the feast is sung along with the Service of Entreaty on Sunday evening. The Liturgy of St. Basil, which otherwise would have been celebrated on the day before the feast, is moved to the day of the feast, Monday. Being an expert on the finer points of the typicon, Papadiamandis preserves even this detail, simultaneously noting another habit of the monastic typicon—the reading of the panegyric of the day, a homily of one of the Fathers of the Church that sheds light on the content and meaning of the feast.[12]

Papadiamandis describes the unique monastic typicon, still used today in many hermitages and communities on the Holy Mountain, where the repetition of the prayer "Lord Jesus Christ have mercy on me" takes the place of the service of Vespers or Matins. In the story "The Watchman at the Quarantine Colony,"[13] this typicon is used at the dependency of the Monastery of the Annunciation by Fr. Nicodemos, who serves the early morning service "in his unique way, using the prayer rope and the infinite repetition of 'Lord Jesus Christ.'"[14]

In the monasteries, the typicon is not described or taught theoretically but is learned through continuous use. Its order regulates the liturgical life of the monastic brotherhood, which lives within it and is experientially taught by it. Its directives establish the liturgical order and the proper path—both for monastics and for Christians living in the world—that leads toward the immediate and final goal of the Christian life: experientially living the salvific life of the Church.[15]

Monastic Influence on Parish Life

Influences from the Athonite typicon also appear in stories that are not set in the monastery but in the churches and country chapels of Skiathos. In "A Pilgrimage to the Kastro," Alexandros the chanter sings all the troparia during the Service of Entreaty

To ΠΕΡΙΒΌλι τῆς Πλναπίας.   ἍΓΙΟΝ Ὄρος.

Mount Athos, The Holy Mountain

and reads the Psalm "I will bless the Lord" at the end of the Divine Liturgy, providing examples of the influence that the Athonite typicon had on the church services on Skiathos. Other examples appear when Papadiamandis describes the extended Matins, Liturgy, and memorial service during the exhumation of the reposed: "We chanted Psalm 118 (119), 'Blessed are the Blameless,' as is the custom on the Holy Mountain, and that venerable canon of Theophan, 'In the Heavenly Chambers.'"[16] Emphasizing that this was the custom on the Holy Mountain shows the difference between the monastic—and particularly the Athonite—typicon and the parish typicon while also showing the influence and the attraction that the former had for Christians living in the world. The liturgical tradition of the Holy Mountain fed the zeal of the Christians on Skiathos and inspired them to emulate this tradition.

In addition to the influence of the monastic liturgical typicon, other monastic practices influenced the parishes of Skiathos. In the story "A Village Easter," not only the length and the typicon of the services but also the way in which the faithful are called to worship is monastic. Uncle Anagnostis prepares a makeshift *símantron* from a solid piece of walnut wood and—as with the monastic *tálanton*—goes about the houses hitting the wood rhythmically with a hammer so as to awaken the townspeople.[17] Along with abundant allusions to the typicon and the hymnology of the Nativity services, in the story "Delisiphero," Papadiamandis also refers to the tradition of the canonarch—one who goes back and forth between the chanter on the left and the chanter on the right with the open *Menaion*, reading the words of the hymns verse by verse before the chanters chant them.[18] Today the tradition of the canonarch continues to be used in the liturgical life of the monasteries of the Holy Mountain.

In three of Papadiamandis's stories,[19] the reader finds descriptions of vigils for Nativity, while another four stories[20] include references to Easter vigils. From these stories we can draw out valuable information regarding the typicon and the hymnology of these days. The simple Skiathans love all-night vigils, from which they receive an indescribable spiritual sweetness. In the story "Fey Folk," a certain Aggalos finds himself at an all-night vigil in the church of the Panagia of Kechrea. Once he satisfies his curiosity as to which monks are chanting, he decides to leave, even though the vigil is still only at Vespers. He wants to go home and return in the morning with his family for the Liturgy. However, just as he is about to leave, he hears a voice within him saying, "I'll stay a bit longer."[21] He decides to remain in the church because of the sweetness he feels during the vigil. "[I]t was already approaching midnight without him having felt at all tired. For he found the sweetness and decorum of the chanting most pleasing."[22]

In the story "John's 'Christ is Risen'," Papadiamandis notes which all-night vigils are celebrated during the feasts of the country chapels of Skiathos,[23] while in the story "Reverie of the Fifteenth of August," we have an analytical description of the order and typicon of a normal all-night vigil. According to Papadiamandis's descriptions in this story, the eve of the feast begins with Small Vespers followed by a frugal fasting meal. Phrangoulis Phrangoulas, the one celebrating his name's day, "prepares a makeshift wooden *símantron*, impromptu, in imitation of those that tend to be used in the monasteries, and circles the church three times, striking it on his own, initially in trochean meter—'*ton Ad-am, Ad-am, Ad-am*' and then in iambic meter—'*to Ta-lanton, to Ta-lanton*.'"[24] Small Compline follows, and the vigil begins immediately afterwards, lasting eight hours without a break. The description of the typicon of the vigil is quite detailed, mentioning the doxastikon of the *Octoechos* of Vespers, the three and the forty "Lord have mercies" of the Service of Entreaty, the reading from the *Synaxarion* at the end of Vespers, the readings from the Psalter, the Polyeleoses,[iii] the Prokeimenons[iv] and the two canons of Matins, the Hours, the Service of Preparation for Holy Communion, the Typika, Macarismoi, and the "All generations,"[v] in place of "It is truly meet" during the Divine Liturgy. The vigil concludes with a festal meal at which "all sit together and eat and are glad."[vi 25]

It was not, of course, only in the churches of Skiathos that all-night vigils were celebrated. Papadiamandis's Athenian stories show that, despite the evident secularism of its ecclesiastical life, the Greek capital preserved some pockets of Christians who struggled to live the liturgical tradition of the all-night vigil. In "A Different Type," a sea captain living in Piraeus, Uncle Mark, would come to Athens and "often went to a chapel where, on feast days, all-night vigil services would take place."[26] In his autobiographical story entitled "The Adopted Daughter," Papadiamandis makes reference to his frequent participation in the vigils at the chapel of St. Elisha when he was in Athens. He reminisces, "I would return home in the morning, when a feast

---

[iii]It means, literally, "great mercy" and comes from Psalms 133, 134, and 135, which are sung at Matins line by line, each one ending in the refrain "for his mercy endureth forever, alleluia."

[iv]These are verses of the Psalms read before a reading from Holy Scripture.

[v]These are the first words of one of a series of hymns of mourning chanted around the funeral bier of Christ on the eve of Holy Saturday. In this case, the hymn is addressed to the Theotokos on the eve of the feast of her dormition.

[vi]It is worth noting that many of the festal celebrations of Skiathos's country chapels are still celebrated according to the manner and ecclesiastical order described in Papadiamandis's stories. The liturgical tradition has a regenerative power that helps its preservation for future generations. [Au.]

day dawned, having passed the night in the vigil service at [the church of] St. Elisha."[27]

Papadiamandis and the Monastic Typicon

Three of Papadiamandis's contemporaries confirm in writing his experiential contact with the Church's liturgical life. In "All-Night Vigil at St. Elisha,"[28] Gerasimos Vokos, "'a man most likely neutral,' clearly sketches the world where Papadiamandis, even while drifting about as an exile from Skiathos, found consolation."[29] Vokos describes the vigil and its participants:

> Alexandros Papadiamandis and Alexandros Moraitidis—the twin[vii] short-story writers from Skiathos, those sensitive writers—these true and pious Christians [were chanters at the church of St. Elisha]. The first one, the colleague at the *Akrópoli* [newspaper], became enraptured in the fulfillment of these holy tasks. A shine of absolute joy would enlighten his shaggy countenance, with his frizzy black beard and thick hair of the same color. He was unrecognizable; that countenance, so sad during the hours of work here in the office, became animated at the chanter's stand. The author of "Homesick" chanted earnestly and with true passion....[30]

The second testimony, by Constantine Psachos, is entitled "Alexandros Papadiamandis."[31]

> For many years now this wonderful person [Papadiamandis] regularly chants in the humble, privately owned chapel in honor of the Prophet Elisha in the courtyard of a home beside the old barracks. This little chapel does not let a major feastday pass without serving a vigil until morning, as prescribed by the typicon of the Holy Mountain. A certain group of people comes to these vigils, passing the night and praying in unfeigned compunction with the sound of perhaps the greatest music, truly necessary for these vigils,

---

[vii]They were called twins because they were both named Alexandros, they both came from Skiathos, and they were both writers.

[dedicated] to the glory of the Highest. Papadiamandis is always found in his place.[32]

Finally, the third testimony, "The Authentic Chanter, Alexandros Papadiamandis," by I. Th. Tsoklis,[33] asserts Papadiamandis's competency as a chanter and the depth of his knowledge of the typicon, as revealed during the vigils at St. Elisha's:

Papadiamandis knew all aspects of the celebration of such an all-night vigil, particularly what the typicon prescribes and the ecclesiastical hymns. He knew, by heart and in all its details, the typicon of St. Savvas, which among other things contains the extensive orchestration of the typicon of these all-night vigils. The particularities and variety of Polyeleoses and *Eklogón*[viii] hymns, as well as the similarly unusual

The symantron is used in monasteries to call the monastics to services

and completely unfamiliar (to the musical world of the cities) Prosomoia executed in the Athonite style—all these things were so wonderfully and faithfully engrained in Papadiamandis's ear that everyone listening to him chant these things would develop a firm conviction that this man *had received an extensive instruction on the Holy Mountain, though he [Papadiamandis] had never come into contact with such things* [emphasis is Tsoklis's].[34]

Although there are serious reservations today regarding the phrase "*though he had never come into contact with such things* [i.e. Byzantine music theory],"[35] the other part of Tsoklis's testimony, that Papadiamandis was a lover of services and master of the typicon,[ix] remains unshakeable.

[viii]This word means "option" and is the name given to the third set of polyeleos hymns, which change according to the feast being celebrated that day (for a Saint, a feast of Christ or the Theotokos, and so on).

[ix]This refers to the person who is in charge of following the orchestration of the typicon.

The Divine Liturgy—the chief gathering of the body of the Church, whose heart is the Mystery of Holy Communion—enjoys a central place in the thought of Papadiamandis. His theology does not deviate from the liturgical experience of the patristic tradition, and includes all the daily services, Mysteries, and sanctifying actions. All these appear in his works as preparation for, or as an extension of, the one Mystery, the one Liturgy—the Divine Liturgy—which is the fullness and crowning of all the joy and blessedness that worship offers. St. Nicholas Kavasilas eloquently expresses this sentiment when he writes that "[the Liturgy] is the goal of life, and, if we reach it, we do not need anything else to attain the sought for joy."[36] Papadiamandis lived this blessedness from his childhood years—on Sundays and also during the daily services and minor feasts—concelebrating with his father in the church of the Three Hierarchs in the village and in the country chapels of Skiathos. In his texts, the Divine Liturgy is presented as the space in which the communion in Christ is realized and where true interpersonal relationships among the faithful are formed. The Divine Liturgy is the womb of the spiritual life that brings renewal to Christians; it is the continuous movement toward the perfection that the faithful anticipate in their eschatological existence. At the same time, it is bound directly to the daily needs and problems of the faithful, concerning which many of the prayers and supplications are offered.

Papadiamandis points out that the Church, through the Divine Liturgy and Her broader liturgical life, prays not only for spiritual but also for material needs. When the women of Skiathos pray at the chapel of St. Nicholas of the Castle, interceding for the safe travel of their relations who are sailors, and at the church of St. Anastasia for the healing of some sick person, they are in complete harmony with the prayers of the Divine Liturgy that ask that "the Gifts [here] offered work as is necessary for each one."[37] They act in harmony with the patristic sense of Eucharist, whereby Christ grants a variety of gifts and answers all human needs, material and spiritual.[38] Their actions are also consistent with the spirit of the Church's hymnographer who petitions St. Nicholas for that which each person needs in his personal life, without distinguishing between material and spiritual: "The sick [seek] a doctor; those in danger, their savior; the sinful, their defender; the poor, their fortune; those in mourning, their consolation; those that travel, their companion; those at sea, their navigator; wherever one has need, He comes [swiftly] to help us."[39] For the Christians of Skiathos, the Liturgy is not an abstract spiritual offering, nor do they regard it simply as an expression of religious faith. It is not even an opportunity to be strengthened for the [fulfillment of their] work, as many religious circles regard it today. The Divine Liturgy is not the means to an end, but the goal itself; it is their very life.

Throughout his works, Papadiamandis does more than simply attempt to preserve forgotten traditions. His emphasis is on essentials—he presents the fundamental Christ-centered ecclesiological reality lived by the Church through Her worship. The Church lives the essence of the Liturgy, beginning with the *proskomidí*[x] and reaching a climax near the end of the Liturgy with the gathering [*systolí*] of the Precious Gifts in the Holy Chalice after communion. The priest gathers into the Holy Chalice everything left on the *diskário*[xi] except for the Lamb. In this way, those represented in the portion—the Theotokos, the orders of angels, all the orders of Saints, and all living and reposed members of the Body of Christ—are commemorated by name during the *proskomidí*, all of whom mystically serve the Divine

[x]This is the preparation of the bread and wine before their consecration into the Body and Blood of Christ. This process is at the heart of the Liturgy, which is in turn the heart of the liturgical life and the broader spiritual life of the Church. The theology contained in these prayers and actions of the priest summarize Orthodox faith and practice.

[xi]The *diskário* is where the priest prepares the sanctified bread before it is combined with the sanctified wine. Each section of the special bread used for Holy Communion is carefully cut, each section representing a certain person or group of people who are remembered in prayer before God. The Lamb is the central section of the bread and during the *proskomidí* represents Christ Himself.

Liturgy along with the serving priest. Through commemoration, the names of the faithful remain in the memory of the Church and are preserved in Her unity and communion. The vertical communion of each believer with Christ is accomplished, as is the horizontal union of all the members of the Body between them. St. Maximos's definition of the Church may thus be understood: "The holy Church...is an icon...of God...because the same union that works with God works also among the faithful."[40]

Papadiamandis also strives to show the dependence of the faithful on God's grace; the love of the faithful, weak and burdened with sin, is not sufficient to realize their union with Christ in the theanthropic body of the Church. This presents another patristic teaching—it is the love of God that freely offers the Body and Blood of Christ to the faithful in the Mystery of the Holy Eucharist, where the faithful are really united with the Body of Christ and do not merely form an image of this union. Only in the Holy Eucharist where, in the language of Papadiamandis, "we are liturgized,"[41] do the faithful become members of Christ, since the Church, with the Holy Eucharist, is the Body of Christ. Here it is particularly worthy of note that the Fathers did not separate the Body of Christ, the Church, from the Body of Christ offered during the Holy Eucharist.[42] Papadiamandis's emphasis on the Church's unity offered by Christ in the Eucharist leads him to reject the institution and mentality of the private Divine Liturgy.[xii]

[xii]The liturgies in the country chapels of Skiathos are not private liturgies as they are announced ahead of time to everyone and anyone who wants can participate in them. The faithful gather at daybreak at the "Good Spring" outside of the village and walk in groups to the chapel where they are serving Liturgy. After the Divine Liturgy, they eat and converse together, thus liturgizing communally in the other aspects of their lives. In Papadiamandis's stories, only in the case of a certain John, do we see the privatization of the Liturgy, in this case because of human pretension. This John gathers other shepherds and goes with Papa-Angelis far away to a country chapel so as to celebrate Easter. He does this "in order to free himself from the burdensome spectacle of his second cousin Yannis Ladikas at St. George's of K'stodoulitsa, or that of Yorgis, Panayotis's son, at St. Charalambos's, where respectively they presided and discharged the duties of churchwarden...and in general [were] boss of everything both inside and outside the church." ["At Saint Anastasa's," *Complete Works*, vol. 2:355.] [*The Boundless Garden*, 191.] Through the dialogues that precede and with the events that follow, Papadiamandis clearly reveals his opposition to the privatization of worship. [Au.]

Although Papadiamandis's descriptions of the ecclesiastical life are centered on the Divine Liturgy, they are not restricted to it. His stories are full of abundant references to the whole mysteriological and liturgical life of the faithful.[43] Papadiamandis makes special reference to Confession and records his views concerning the practice and theology of this Mystery. One of the most characteristic examples is in *Merchants of the Nations*, where he describes the confession of Sister Agapi to Elder Ammoun.[44] The Elder speaks boldly about the essence of confession and commends Sister Agapi's unfeigned and forthright way of confessing. Papadiamandis contrasts it with the established way of confession at that time, whereby a spiritual father would mention acts for which people usually feel the need to be forgiven. The Elder, who is described as a holy figure, "during every Great Lent of his service" had heard many women confessing "slander, lying, arguing with their spouses…and would very often recount, with delight, their virtues or would speak poorly of neighbor and friend, pretending that they were supposedly confessing."[45] They do not, however, confess their deeper sins. Concerned lest the essence get sacrificed for the sake of the form, or lest the performance of the Mysteries of the Church be compromised, Papadiamandis asks an important question through his character Elder Ammoun, who has begun to worry about the superficial and insincere nature of some confessions: "To what purpose is Confession and why this institution?"[46] It is not by chance that, after pondering this question and then hearing an insincere confession, the Elder sensed "that the deserts of the Thebaid… opened their melancholy caverns and that from them myriads of demons came out," so he deemed it necessary to read, not the prayer of forgiveness to the woman confessing, but the exorcisms of St. Basil.[47]

In Papadiamandis's texts and in the Church today, the Mystery of Confession is not practiced by all priests but only by specially ordained spiritual fathers. In his stories, it is priest-monks, in particular, who descend from their monasteries to the villages, usually on the eves of great feasts, who hear the confessions of the faithful. Papadiamandis believes that the relationship between spiritual father and spiritual child should not be a casual one. It is not sufficient if this relationship is limited to a rushed forgiveness of sins (especially if only done on the eve of Nativity or during Great Week), without extending to a continuous relationship ensuring serious spiritual guidance.[48] In the story "Oh! The Little Heartbreakers," Fr. Isaac, "the venerable spiritual father, venerated by all,"[49] descends from his monastery to hear people's confessions in the small dependency of the run-down Monastery of St. Nicholas. Although very old, Papa-Vangelis, in "A Village Easter," performs similar labors:

> The parish priest, Father Vangelis, who was also the abbot (and only monk) of the small monastic establishment of St. Athanasios, had been appointed by the bishop to take charge of the villages on the opposite shore. Though already an old man, he would take the boat across four times a year, during each of the main fasts, to hear the confessions of his unfortunate parishioners —the "hill-people" or "mountain-scarecrows" as they were called...[50]

There are also those who fulfill this service in their monastery or hermitage. In the story "The Death Agony," Fr. Jeremiah "who lived monastically (in the *hesychastírion* of the Prophet Elijah), solitary and independent for decades, without ever going down to the town,"[51] hears the confession of Captain Georgakis, a prosperous forty-five year old businessman. George had lived "so many years without absolution. He still had all the sins of his youth loaded on his conscience, passions of the flesh and all the rest. However, he confessed and didn't leave anything unsaid, unless he forgot a few things,"[52] for he felt his sins weighing him down and depriving him of true communion with God and the Church. The Elder does not restrict himself to a simple hearing of confession but extends his love beyond the performance of Mysteries; as he says "why doesn't our brother [Peter, a monk living with the Elder] accompany you...to give you a spiritual word."[53]

Fr. Ezekiel, abbot of the brotherhood that had settled at the church of Panagia Kechrea, hears confessions in the same spirit. Aunt Synodia and her daughter Aphentra take refuge in him in the story "Fey Folk." Aunt Synodia has a heavy conscience both for having spoken poorly of people, out of a lack of love and unity with others,[54] and for having the passion of malice.[55] She feels the need to confess and to get truly reconnected to the Church. Similarly, her daughter Aphentra, who had fallen into the sin of witchcraft, finally finds the courage to confess it. Both readily receive the counsels and penance of Fr. Ezekiel, which are not vindictive but pedagogical in that they aim at reuniting the penitents with God and, in turn, with their brethren against whom they sinned. In the faith and theology of the Orthodox Church, confession is not a private matter but an action with the deepest social and ecclesiological meaning.[56]

Papadiamandis's Liturgical Realism and Freedom

Although the divine aspect of Orthodox worship always precedes its human aspect, this does not devalue its human character. Papadiamandis does not attempt to make the Church's ceremonies and liturgical services either "mystical" or "respectable." The priests in his stories do not cultivate the atmosphere and spirit of "angelism," which first appeared in Western confessions and was followed by attempts to transplant it into Orthodox lands. This vague mysticism is foreign to the realism of the worship of the Orthodox Church. While Orthodox worship is directed toward God, the faithful offer the hymns of worship as one body, conscious of the presence of their brethren. They live and move with ease and freedom, as though they are in the house of their Father. They do not feel that they need to act in a certain way or that they should display an ethos different than the one they have in their life outside the church.

The faithful of the Church in Skiathos live in this spirit of freedom and love in Christ. They are not disturbed by Aunt

Marios, a troublemaker who makes a fuss if another woman takes her seat in church. They accept both the eccentricity of old Daradimos, who has the bad habit of saying out loud whatever the priest, the reader, and the chanter are about to say, and the annoyance of Captain George Konomos, who casts scornful expressions at Daradimos for doing this.[57] The authenticity and unaffectedness of the Orthodox liturgical ethos are observed in the description of a vigil in the story "John's 'Christ is Risen'":

> The chanting continued throughout the night. Fifty to a hundred men and children—they had usually eaten and drunken too much—were sleeping outside, among the bushes, and eight to twelve women and three of the elderly were sleeping upright in the stalls or on the floor of the church. Occasionally, the snoring of the priest could be heard from inside the altar. The chanter was very tired and made prostrations standing in his stall, and old Demetrios, the former church sexton and warden of the country chapels, without his mind becoming disconnected from the moneybox and the candles, took "two troparia" (that is to say, he slept a little bit) standing in his stall. John (the son of Lekas, who was mentally disabled and constantly laughed but was never absent from a vigil) was vigilant and did not stop laughing.... During the vigil (usually after midnight), either old Demetrios from Epiros, the sleepwalker, or Fr. Ioakeim, the homeless monk (usually without shoes and bareheaded), would come to the chapel. When John saw this monk, he would feel a great joy and delighted in looking at him. Ioakeim would stand at the far corner of the iconostasis, to the right, and usually the chanters would give him the Psalter to read. John never had his fill of looking at him and laughing, laughing with unspoken delight.[58]

Whatever hour the faithful go to the service, they are well received, for all feel that each person is a member of the Body and of their community. They all live the communion offered by the ecclesiastical gathering in a human but substantial manner, not insincerely, as a matter of habit, or pietistically.

The relationship between precision and Economy in the implementation of the liturgical typicon and the canons of the Church has always concerned Christian communities. This important issue appears in a number of Papadiamandis's stories. One example is found in his story, "A Different Type," through the dialogue of Papa-Gregory and his wife. All year long Papa-Gregory serves vigils at the many country chapels around Athens without leaving out even one troparion from the service. He rises three hours before the sun appears and, in front of the iconostasis in his home, he reads the whole service from the Midnight Office and Matins through the Hours "awaiting the first twilight of the dawn to appear so as to go to liturgize at a country chapel."[59] While he is a fervent advocate of the precision of the typicon, Papadiamandis does not believe that the ethos of worship should be different than the ethos of the other aspects of one's life. For this reason, he advises Papa-Gregory through the mouth of the priest's wife: "What good does much reading do you, my father?... Have brotherly love!...it doesn't matter if you say one less glory of the Psalter, or if you leave out a few little troparia from the *Parakletike* or from the *Menaion*."[60] It is, nevertheless, difficult to argue that Papadiamandis completely shares these opinions of the priest's wife. Clearly, the point of this passage is not to disdain or extinguish zeal for the precise keeping of the typicon, but for the priest to unite his love for the services with brotherly love and selflessness.

Papadiamandis confronts another problem concerning the Church today—the chasm between worship and daily life. He advocates the connection between liturgical practice and daily life, arguing that the words and actions of worship must have an effect on the rest of life. In his story "The Hushing Up," he refers to Cosmas, a generally unruly man "with the nature of an Epicurean," who has "three or four mistresses with whom he had lived at various times" and has "sown illegitimate children in all the neighborhoods." He finally promises "to be crowned"[xiii] with Rini, who has managed to "pull him together" and to rear "the last illegitimate child, whom he had had by an unknown mother and who was completely unruly."[61] In the text, "to be crowned" is in quotes, to indicate the colloquial expression—to get married—and to show the disparity that often exists between the liturgical act of "crowning them with glory and honor"[xiv] and the reality of the life, behavior, and attitude of those being crowned. Nevertheless, "our Holy Church makes a practice of crowning everyone without distinction, as 'lawfully struggling.'"[62] Attempting to preserve the truth and authenticity of the liturgical life, he suggests "that it would be good, in many situations, for the crowns to be replaced with hoods, as much for symbolic reasons, explaining the verb *'koukoulóno'* which people are accustomed to using in such circumstances."[xv] [63] His desire to preserve the truth and authenticity of the liturgical life leads him, in another story, to recommend a political marriage in such situations.[64]

Although Papadiamandis is concerned with the implementation of precision, as much as possible, in the Church's liturgical life, he knows that the Church's genuine liturgical ethos lies beyond the letter of the law and is above all characterized by humility. In "The Visit of the Holy Bishop," the liturgical ethos of the simple priests of the countryside is contrasted with the self-promotion, theatrics, and exhibitionism that characterize certain bishops. Papadiamandis refers to a certain bishop who, in his "pastoral" visit to Skiathos, speaks disparagingly of a priest of the island. This priest, being a provincial person unacquainted with hierarchical services, had said "Through the prayers of our holy Fathers" at the end of the doxology instead of "Through the prayers of our holy Bishop," which is the proper way to end a service when a bishop is present. Papadiamandis comments on this characteristic pastoral practice of the bishop and wonders how "the poor priest...could have known, as he had not seen it

---

[xiii]That is, to get married. In the Orthodox Church the Mystery of marriage includes the crowning of the bride and groom.

[xiv]From the Orthodox Marriage Service.

[xv]In addition to the meanings "to cover," "to hush up," "to suppress," this word has the metaphorical meaning of "to force into marriage."

written anywhere?"[65] Forgetting that the Divine Liturgy is noble in and of itself and does not need superfluous movements to highlight its majesty, the bishop, "when he served on Sunday, showed another example of his pastoral care. At the 'Always, now and forever,' he suddenly grabbed the eldest, most experienced, and best educated priest by his arm that was holding the Holy Chalice and forced him to stand at the door of the altar for a full minute, so as to say the 'Always'" more slowly and with more drama, "as though...they were going to give a second Communion."[xvi][66] Papadiamandis points out that the *Evhológion* [Book of Prayers] only indicates that "the priest looks toward the people" and not that he stands at the Beautiful Gate at this point in the service. With this scene and the rest of the story, Papadiamandis describes the sickness of episcopal despotism (common for his age, and ours), the unseemly and empty pastoral care of many bishops, and the accompanying lack of liturgical ethos and the most basic piety.

The limits of liturgical precision on the one hand and the discerning application of Economy as regards the typicon on the other engage not only liturgicists but also many pastors of the Church. The Christian cultivation of the liturgical ethos is directly connected to the form and length of the services. The liturgical canons regulating the typicon of the services are not theoretical forms. Rather, they are the fruit of liturgical experience cultivated through the ages in the atmosphere of worship that is imbued with the Holy Spirit, which is why they need to be preserved with respect and precision.

Although it is crucial for the preservation of the liturgical tradition and for the unity of the Church that these liturgical canons be preserved with respect and precision, they are the creation of other eras distant from our own, both chronologically and qualitatively. They are often characterized by a universality that has not been adapted to local problems or particularities.

[xvi]This refers to the action of the priest who, soon after giving Holy Communion and returning to the altar with the chalice, brings the chalice before the congregation for a moment, before returning once again to the altar.

This is why the Church, in all aspects of Her life, "without violating or overturning Her canons, 'uses Economy,' adjusting and regulating things in a spirit of indulgence and condescension, always looking to Her stable goal—the salvation of people."[67] Perhaps this justifies the existence of different typicons in various parts of the Church. Every discerning application of Economy undertaken in the Church "is the extension and specialized application of divine Economy, of the revealing of God to the world for its salvation and renewal."[68]

Through his stories, Papadiamandis manifests knowledge of liturgical precision and discernment in questions of liturgical Economy that surpasses that of many specialists. He knows that the Sabbath was made for man and not man for the Sabbath.[69] The precise following of the typicon has value when it facilitates worship and not when it makes it more difficult. In "Easter Chanter," the priest's preparation for the Divine Liturgy is described extensively—the way he says the entrance prayers, his robing in the holy vestments, and the *proskomidí*.[70] Papa-Dianelos knows that this whole process should take place during Matins, when the chanters are chanting the passages from the Psalms (kathismata) and the canon. However, in dealing with the tardiness or the potential absence of Konstantos, the chanter who is late, he thinks of leaving the altar to go to the chanter's stand to chant Matins on his own. The simple priest "realized that he would either have to postpone the offertory [*proskomidí*], or break off the service" as "these things required Economy."[71] Nevertheless, he struggles within himself as to "how they were going to manage the Liturgy."[72] This is because he knows that the presence of at least one layman, to respond and answer the petitions of the priest, is not a question of form but is an essential aspect of the Mystery, which does not allow for any Economy.

We find another example of Papadiamandis's understanding of Economy in "The Godmother." Among the families of shepherds on Skiathos, when it was winter and difficult for the priest from the village to travel to read the prescribed prayer for a woman who had given birth, there was the following custom of liturgical Economy: a relative or neighbor would fill a bottle of water, either from the holy water of the Holy Archangels or from the pure water of the Prophet Elijah,[xvii] and bring it down to the priest in the village. Wearing his priestly stole, he would open the *Evhológion* and read the prayers "for a woman after giving birth" over the bottle of water. The blessed water would then be taken back to the hut on the mountain and sprinkled on the new mother, the babe, the bed, the crib, the midwife, and whoever else happened to be at the birth.[73] Through this application of liturgical Economy, those regionally isolated Christians could experience the presence and blessing of the Church.

Papadiamandis did not generally have a very good impression of the churches in Athens and their lack of faithfulness to the typicon.[74] Naturally, he understands the particular difficulties of city life and is not ignorant of the justifications for this situation, for "in Athens multitudes of people throng into the churches on these [festal] days. The groups are noisy, and it is impossible to keep good order and precision."[75] This, however, does not imply that we need to violate or get rid of the typicon. For the preservation of liturgical unity in the churches of Athens, Papadiamandis suggests that the typicon of the Great Church of Christ[xviii] be used as a common base. He points out that the Great Church of Christ, the Ecumenical Patriarchate, in the framework of its administrative and pastoral responsibility, with discernment and vision "foresaw all, and cut from the typicon whatever was possible to cut, leaving out the *stichiología*[xix] and the readings, and decreasing from twelve to six the troparia of each canticle of the canon (for Great Week). It couldn't do more than this...."[76] Beyond this, anyone within the jurisdiction of the Ecumenical Patriarchate who applies the typicon differently acts high-handedly, placing himself above and usurping the authority of the Ecumenical Patriarchate, which has been given the authority over the canonical and the liturgical order and unity of those areas of the Church under its jurisdiction.

[xvii]These were areas around which the families of Skiathan shepherds would live. [Au.]

[xviii]This is a nickname given to the Church in Constantinople.

[xix]These are verses (often from a Psalm) read before a hymn is chanted.

The keeping of a common liturgical typicon—including a common ecclesiastical music, chanting, and reading—acts as a safeguard, which is an essential presupposition for the unity of our liturgical tradition.[77] Despite not having a formal theological education, he senses that it is only with a common liturgical typicon—with the same words, movements, and actions—that the unity of the Church is expressed on the liturgical plane and enables the Church to offer its doxology to God "in one mouth and one heart."[xx] A common typicon provides a common spiritual education that, along with common worship, establishes and guides the liturgical community to the same faith, the same *phrónima*, and the same life. As a practical remedy for the liturgical irregularities of the churches in Athens, Papadiamandis suggests that, in the absence of an ecclesiarch[xxi] or a master of the typicon, the chanter on the right-hand side of the church[xxii] regulate the typicon for the services, only taking directions and listening to observations from the most senior and head priest of the church. Though this suggestion is still relevant today, it was particularly applicable in Papadiamandis's time because, although the priests and chanters were certainly competent students of the typicon, they lived under the harsh and coercive administration of the wardens.[78]

For Papadiamandis, exiled from the Skiathos of the *Kollyvádes*, the churches in Athens that preserved liturgical order and the typicon were true oases. If there was haste and disorder in the central churches of Athens, ignorance of the typicon (with its accompanying negative effect on the performance of the services) usually prevailed in the churches of the countryside. However, when he visited a village of Attica (just outside of Athens) during Great Week, he was happily surprised and wrote, "I discovered a priest who read humbly, but also perfectly, the

[xx]This is from the Liturgy of St. John Chrysostom.

[xxi]This is the person who cares for the church building, lights the candles, and so on.

[xxii]When parishes in Greece have two choirs (at the front right and front left of the church) the head chanter of the right choir is called "first-chanter" and has priority among the chanters.

twelve Gospels of the service of the Holy Passion.... I found a priest who knew the order of the Service well, who wouldn't allow even one disturbance or pause. I also found a rational flock, piously listening to the service."[79] This passage reveals another  precondition for ecclesiastical and liturgical order—in addition to a basic knowledge of the typicon, an education in worship and a liturgical ethos are necessary for both the priests and the faithful. The same priest, faithful to the precision of the typicon, arranged to have Psalm 118 (119), "Blessed are the Blameless" read on the evening of Great Friday after the canon "Waves of the Sea,"[xxiii] and before the Eulogies (*Engkómia*). As Papadiamandis observes, these typicons "do not prosper in worldly churches, but, according to the typicon of the Great Church, the 'Blameless' should not be cut and needs to be read."[80] Naturally, he was glad when he heard it read there "in an appropriately quiet place, where the people were not impatient."[81] This enthusiasm for the keeping of the typicon of the Church is not conservatism but, literally, a liturgical approach to life, which is reminiscent of some of the verses from the "Blameless" itself.[82]

Form and Essence in Worship

In Orthodox worship, as with many things, the form exists to protect the essence, and without the essence the form is empty. Papadiamandis has a clear understanding as to when and to what extent the form serves the essence. For this reason, as much as he cares about the keeping of the typicon, he is far from every form of legalism. He argues that the forms are useful "as long as they have the essence as their soul and meet a human need, but as soon as the created need departs and the life-giving spirit goes out of them, they fall dead and are transformed into ugly skeletons, create stumbling blocks, and hinder progress."[83]

[xxiii]It is a hymn derived from Psalm 118 (119).

A classic example that exemplifies Papadiamandis's words is that of Papa-Kyriakos in "A Village Easter." Initially, his behavior seems to be liturgically out of place, as he attempts to empty the Holy Chalice into the mouths of the faithful because he feels the need to go to Confession before partaking of Holy Communion himself.

> "Oh Lord," he exclaimed with all his heart, "I have sinned, I have sinned! You gave yourself up for our sins, and in return we crucify you daily!" He turned around and hurried back up towards the church to continue the service. "And I was actually going to drink water![xxiv] I am not fit to celebrate! But what can I do? I can't take communion! I shall say the office without taking communion—I am not worthy! 'Behold the first fruits of the vine!' I am not worthy!"
> He re-entered the church, and the villagers greeted his return with joy.
> He celebrated the divine mystery and administered the Holy Communion to the faithful, taking care that every last drop from the chalice passed through their lips.[xxv] He himself abstained, vowing to tell all to his confessor—and ready to accept whatever penance he might impose.[84]

This action of the simple priest is an authentic spiritual reaction against legalism. He understands that, as beautiful and important as adherence to the liturgical order and typicon is, the loss of the essence of the Liturgy may be similarly dangerous if there is not true communion and relation with that which is taking place. The scene that Papadiamandis presents to us resembles that of the priest from Mardaros of Kilikias, in the *Spiritual Meadow* of John Moschos, who refused to begin the Divine Liturgy if he did not feel the overshadowing of the altar by the Holy Spirit.[85]

[xxiv]Orthodox Christians traditionally abstain from eating or drinking before partaking of Holy Communion.

[xxv]This would be a solution to his dilemma, for otherwise he would have to consume what was left in the chalice.

One cannot have a substantial relationship with worship without truly participating in it. This is not simply an ethical position but a deeply ecclesiological one. In the absence of a personal experience of worship, liturgical actions and services cease being understood as saving energies of God and instead are viewed as actions of a magical rite and a sick religiosity. Granny Ourania, the widow, watches her son drinking and sleeping in the streets and on the beach and attributes his situation to sorcery. She is ready to do forty days of Liturgies to break the spell, but she considers it necessary that he participate in the struggle, so as to "beat the temptation."[86] This reveals the Orthodox teaching, where salvation is the fruit of the synergy between the grace of God and the freedom of man, where liturgical life is not separate from the rest of life but intimately connected with it. When truth and essence are absent, the typicon degenerates into sterile legalism and ritualism, which are not salvific and only complicate faith.[87] According to the Orthodox understanding, the whole world is created to become Eucharist. In facilitating this transformation of the world, the meaning and substance of the typicon become manifest.

The Orthodox liturgical ethos does not seek intellectual and emotional satisfaction in worship. In the Orthodox Liturgy, we are called to meet and be united both with Christ, by eating His Body and drinking His Blood, and with our brethren—not superficially but truly.[88] Man's balance is lost when he does not have a bodily sense of, and relation to, his Creator. This is why the Mysteries of the Eastern Church touch the flesh—from Baptism to Holy Communion. We participate in these things with the body, and we commune with all the members of the body of the Church. In order to acquire the Orthodox liturgical ethos, it is not sufficient to simply perform the Liturgy with a proper liturgical typicon. Similarly, seeking after God with only the intellect does not testify to an Orthodox conscience.

An example of Papadiamandis's concern for preserving the substance of liturgical forms was manifested when the Duchess

Alexandra[xxvi] reposed in 1891. The Jews of Athens wanted to pay their respects to the Palace and decided to publicize in the daily news that they served memorial services in their synagogues "for the rest of the soul of the Orthodox princess."[89] Papadiamandis, who knew Orthodox ecclesiology and believed that worship flows from the faith and dogma of the Church, objected. He argued that "these are deceptions, ostentations, and flatteries, and we are unjustly lost in them. Supplications for her healing, while she was struggling, could, of course, be chanted by all religious communities, and they did well; memorial services for the rest of the reposed one, however, only Orthodox Christians have the right and obligation to serve."[90]

Papadiamandis's Liturgical Catechism

Papadiamandis's short stories constitute an Orthodox liturgical catechism and a sure initiation into the world of worship.[91] Papadiamandis's liturgical catechism appears throughout his works—both in the subjects he chooses to write about and in the details he provides—thus enabling the reader to enter more fully into the spirit and essence of worship. In his short story "Kosmolaitis," speaking of the small Polyeleos, he feels the need to clarify that it is "a Psalm of which all the verses end in the phrase 'for His mercy endureth forever,' which is why the hanging, many-candled [chandelier] in the middle of the church, which is swung when this Psalm is sung, is also called 'polyeleos.'"[92] In his novel *Merchants of the Nations*, set in the women's Monastery of St. Cosmas, he records the beginning of the service of Matins at the hour during which the Six Psalms are being read: "There was darkness in the church. The wicks of the vigil lamps were trimmed, and barely glimmered with their weak light.... In the stalls appeared, here and there, some human forms—nuns—unmoving as statues, with hoods let down over their eyes, without breathing, without looking, without apparent life."[93] The time during the reading of the Six Psalms symbolizes

[xxvi]A Russian princess who was married to King George of Greece in the late nineteenth century.

the anticipation of the Second Coming. The nuns live this anticipation, with the extinguished candles, the soft light of the vigil lamps, the evocative atmosphere, as well as their intense prayer. However, just when the Six Psalms end, the light returns to the church. The dark and somber period of the anticipation of the coming of Christ, Who is the True Light, ends, as suggested by the verses immediately following—"God is the Lord and hath appeared unto us."[xxvii] Behind every liturgical form is the essence, the theological reason for which it was established.

Liturgical references also abound in Papadiamandis's newspaper articles. They may, in fact, contain even more exhaustive and practical commentary than his short stories, as they were intended for the reading public of the newspapers who were not necessarily familiar with the liturgical practices of the Church. He interprets liturgical forms and symbols, offering a substantial theology of worship and a liturgical catechism that provides real instruction for all—a body of work that amazed the specialists. In other places he makes typological and symbolic references to subjects relating to the Church calendar and liturgical life, and in this way he continues the Alexandrine tradition of biblical interpretation, in this case regarding worship.[xxviii] In these articles, published on the occasion of great feasts of the liturgical year, Papadiamandis follows the liturgical practice of the Church, insisting that worship should be approached through personal experience and that its participants should, as the Psalmist once wrote, "taste and see."[94]

In one of his articles entitled "Holy Theophany," Papadiamandis observes that "on this day[xxix] in the ancient Church, catechumens would be baptized, and truly this is the most appropriate of days; therefore, in place of the Trisagion during the Liturgy, the Church directs the hymns toward those baptized: 'As many as are baptized into Christ have put on Christ. Alleluia.'"[95] Elsewhere, he offers a theology of worship that leads

[xxvii]This is a hymn sung after the Six Psalms during Matins.

[xxviii]The Alexandrine tradition of biblical interpretation tended to view Scripture as metaphorically expressing deeper meanings.

[xxix]That is, January 6, the feast of the Baptism of Christ by St. John the Baptist.

from the symbol to that which is symbolized and from the form to the essence, thus providing historical grounds for, and a theological interpretation of, various practices and traditions related to Easter. He explains why the week after Easter is named "*Diakainísimos*" or "*New*": "It is thus called since in antiquity the catechumens were baptized at Easter...and thus began a new period and era for them and for the Church. The Latins called it week "*in albis*" (in white), as those baptized would traditionally dress in white clothing, in profession of their soul's purity."[96] He discusses the characterization of Sunday as the "first of Sabbaths" or the "one of Sabbaths" and describes the historical reasons behind the reading of the Gospel in different languages during the Agape Vespers: "This is an ancient practice; it was the first Gospel that the baptized Christians would have heard. Because they were of different nationalities it was read as they would have understood it in their various tongues."[97]

Papadiamandis's liturgical catechism appears in other places as well—through his interpretation of the biblical readings read during different services,[98] his analysis of the canon of Great Thursday, "the magnificent piece of art [composed] by St. Cosmas, the bishop of Maimos, who had similar zeal and who was on a par with his adopted brother, St. John of Damascus,"[99] and the explanation he gives for the linkage of the Divine Liturgy of St. Basil to Vespers.[100] With wonderful clarity, he describes the influence of the monastic typicon on the world,[101] including the origin of the three canticles in the canons of Great Week and the typicon of the all-night vigil for the service of the Resurrection.[102] He also gives an explanation for the fasting of Great Saturday[103] and the absence of the Divine Liturgy on Great Friday: "Today the Liturgy is not served. The Liturgy is the remembrance of the Crucifixion of Jesus Christ, but today we celebrate this Crucifixion...it would be unfitting to serve it as a remembrance."[104]

Papadiamandis's liturgical catechism is offered in a language that is understandable to common people, and is more than an explanation of how worship is orchestrated according to the regulations of the canons. What he presents, especially in his newspaper articles, is more than a simple *ritus* or that which is taught in the West—and even in Orthodox theological and ecclesiastical schools—as Liturgics (the study of "rubrics").[105] While Liturgics was considered, even in Orthodox theological schools, as simply "a more or less detailed practical study of ecclesiastical rites, combined with certain symbolical explanations of ceremonies and ornaments,"[106] Papadiamandis's approach reaches beyond the "how," extending to the "what" and "why" of worship. In explaining the meaning of the actions and experience of worship, and by clarifying the role of liturgical tradition in the life of the Church, he develops a theology of worship.

6

ART IN WORSHIP

The Meaning of Liturgical Art

The Divine Liturgy unifies scattered people; the Church is not only spiritual but also has a material dimension. Through the Church's art, material things do not remain foreign, soulless, and dead, but become familiar and living. Christian faith, love, and worship of God are expressed through a variety of art forms including architecture, painting, hymnography, and ecclesiastical music. These arts are called ecclesiastical, since they were born and developed in the Church, and Byzantine because of their cultural and chronological framework.

The arts help purify man's senses through mystagogical and compunctionate communion with God. They are not paths or objects in and of themselves, but they act as a means for raising man up to God. This is why man's relationship with God defines the Church's position regarding liturgical art. In remaining faithful to this principle, the Church has always required that the arts, cultivated in Her worship, not disturb the unity and harmony of man's communion with God. Liturgical art not only helps man become sanctified during worship, but itself becomes sanctified. When art illustrates the unity, sanctification, and salvation of the members of the Church, it is itself sanctified. Liturgical art has deep roots in the rich earth of the ecclesiastical tradition. While it sweetens the senses of the pious, it is also used in the Church's Liturgy, which is why it is characterized primarily as a liturgical art.

Papadiamandis's works have a generally ecclesiastical character and liturgical orientation, and he makes reference to the art of the Church, which is tightly linked to Her liturgical practice and life. Churches and icons appear in Papadiamandis's works, and are presented in such a reverent and elegant manner that these descriptions themselves become representations, poems, and melodies that lead to the rational worship of the Church. Rather than expounding his own theories regarding art, he presents the life and tradition of the Church as they have been expressed for centuries through various art forms. The story "Sweet Kiss," for example, contains his longest description of the structure and architecture of a church:

The four walls stood, still unbroken, on a stone foundation, preserving a small coating from olden days around the southwest corner, mossy and black-green around the northeast corner. A rafter held up the roof, still bearing a few tiles and slabs, with many beams of hard chestnut wood. On the walls all around, high above the lintel of a door and on the eaves of the roof, small, beautiful painted canvasses from years past were hung, in the shape of a large cross, in the concave of the holy altar toward the East.... Another two crosses hung to the right and to the left, above the two windows of the chanters' stands, and a fourth cross hung above the doorstep of the entrance—toward the West. The old beautiful plates were all colored—azure, viridescent, yellow, and white—with branches and with flowers and with little people and with birds, done with a skillful love of beauty [*philokália*] and elegantly placed, polished like the sun, easy on the eye, heirlooms sitting up high, soundly placed in their recesses, otherworldly offerings, relics of ages past....[1]

Other noteworthy descriptions are found in his poetic work, especially in the four poems dedicated to the icons of the Panagia of his island.[2] Even more enthralling are the descriptions of the icons and wall paintings of the churches:

> The small, beautiful icon, with the pale face of the Panagia joined cheek to cheek with the pale, God-inspired face of her worshipped Babe, had an ineffable sweetness and was a perfect expression of motherly affection, a sweet fruit budding as from a bitter root, with the pains of birth combining immediately with the cares and struggles of child-raising.[3]

Papadiamandis's vivid description effectively portrays the sweetness and affection of the icon without excessive discussion of technique or aesthetics. The depiction of the icon is philokalic[i]— it exemplifies the love and pursuit of the heavenly beauty [*kállos*] that sanctifies man and all of creation. The icons' translation into a narrative in the story, its descriptive presentation by Papadiamandis, is on the same level. In describing an icon of the "Sweet-Kissing Mother of God," another writer—even more, another iconographer could easily end up with a misleading or accidentally heretical description; to theologize is always a difficult and dangerous endeavor. Papadiamandis is not sidetracked into sweet emotionalisms, which would present the relationship of the Panagia to Christ as Nestorianism[ii] would; nor does he err toward Monophysitism, which would depreciate the human nature and attempt to present it as immaterial and disincarnate. The above

---

[i]In Modern Greek the word may be rendered as sensibility, good taste, and love of beauty. Here, however, Dr. Keselopoulos uses the word theologically, with its patristic meaning. In this case the word, while including the above definitions, has a deeper meaning as its understanding of the "good" and "beauty" is theological. It was used by the Church Fathers to describe the love of the good and beauty as the fruit of one's spiritual and ascetic struggle for God. Similarly, the Greek word *kállos*, which is the second part of the word *philokália*, refers to this unique heavenly beauty. *Kállos* has the sense of a beauty that is solid, essential, eternal, which springs forth from within, while the other word for beauty that is found often in ecclesiastical texts— oraíos—suggests a passing external beauty that is often deceptive.

[ii]That is to say, with an over-emphasis on Christ's humanity, separating it from His divinity.

passage is a good example of a balanced description that avoids the scholasticism of art historians and the absolutisms common in such descriptions.

The continuation of the story, which refers to the wall paintings of this church, is also revelatory, both for its synaxarian connections and for its presentation of the cycle of iconography in an Orthodox church. "To the right on the iconostasis was the icon of Christ and the icon of the Forerunner. To the Left, the Panagia 'Sweet-kissing Mother of God,' the protector of mothers, and St. Stylianos, the friend and guard of infants." On the walls there were a few more Saints "painted from ancient times"—St. Elevtherios, "the liberator of the pregnant," and St. Marina, "the protector of those in anguish." Saints George and Demetrios

St. Moses the Ethiopian

appear along with Saints Barbara and Kyriaki "with their Crosses and palm branches in their hands." The monastic Saints, "Venerable Antony and Euthymios and Savvas" also appear, "with their heads wrapped,[iii] with their white beards, their prayer-ropes, and red crosses."[4] Further along the wall is a wall painting of St. Moses of Ethiopia, whom Papadiamandis characterizes with iambic verses from his entry in the *Synaxarion*—"A man in appearance and a god in his heart."[5] Moses was a robber who was sanctified, "and went to find his old fellow-workman [the Good Thief],[iv] that one, who, as the tradition says, the Panagia had once nursed in the desert during the flight to Egypt, during the time of the slaying of the Innocents."[6] The reference to "his old fellow-workman" is not by chance. The feast of the side-chapel of the church of the "Sweet-kissing Mother of God" on Skiathos is celebrated on

---

[iii]The wrapping of their heads indicates that they were desert-dwellers.

[iv]According to the tradition of the Church, that "fellow workman" was the Good Thief on the cross next to Christ (Luke 23:40-43).

the twenty-sixth of December, the feast of the Synaxis of the All-Holy Theotokos. In the Sporades and Cyclades island chains, December 26th and the days following are called the *Epilóchia*' and on the island of Pelio, during which the faithful call upon the Panagia as the protector of bed-ridden new mothers and their babes and as a helper in nursing. As a conclusion to his description of the chapel's wall paintings, Papadiamandis recites the iambic verses from that day's entry in the *Synaxarion*: "New virgin mother, mother who never knew a man."[7]

Papadiamandis asserts the freedom of the iconographer, a freedom that enables him to present themes that, while not specifically based on the *Synaxarion* of the Church, expresses the iconographer's eschatological expectation. An example of this may be seen in the presentation of the military Saint, St. Mercurios, who appears in his deep helmet, armor, gaiters, and shield and "pierces the cadaverous transgressor, sitting upon his throne, with his spear." The anonymous iconographer, living during the Turkish occupation and anticipating the final victory of the Orthodox against every persecutor and conqueror, has the martyr Mercurios (who lived during the years of Decius and Valentos, in the third century) killing Julian the Apostate (who lived at the end of the fourth century). This gives the impression that the iconographer is unlettered and ignorant of basic chronologies and events of history. It is more likely, however, that he is not ignorant of them but intentionally goes beyond them, proving that he knows the language and canons of iconography. Just as "the *Synaxarion* does not simply recite events of the lives of the Saints, but expresses and interprets them,"[8] Byzantine iconography "does not depict, but...reflects on its subjects."[9] The goal in both cases is not the presentation of historical fact on the surface but the truth hiding behind it. This basic principle allows iconographers to express the faces and bodies of the Saints "otherworldly, immaterially, supernaturally, and schematically—that is to say, included in the framework of a general type, which exhales piety and expresses not the natural face of the Saint but the eschatological form of his divinized existence."[10]

'This word signifies days of celebration after a birth.

The meaning of the Church's architecture and painting is deeply theological; they prove to be divine art that transfigures the Church into an earthly heaven where the heavenly God dwells and moves. At the same time, the represented Saints, all the faithful, and the material things of the church unite together, participate, and concelebrate in worship. In "A Pilgrimage to the Kastro," Papa-Phrangoulis travels to the chapel of the Nativity of Christ in the Castle with his convoy to serve the Liturgy, and Papadiamandis takes the opportunity to describe the divine beauty of the church:

Christ the Pantokrator

The entire church was aglow, and in the dome the Pantokrator shone down with majesty and grandeur. The gilded and finely-carved icon screen glimmered, with its beautiful icons in the finest Byzantine style and the great icon of the Nativity, "Where the Virgin sits imitating the cherubim," in which the figures of the divine infant and immaculate Mother sparkle exquisitely and the angels, magi and shepherds appear life like; one thinks that the gold actually shines, the frankincense wafts fragrantly and the myrrh sends forth its comfort—to the extent that if pictures could speak one would expect at any moment to hear "Glory to God in the highest!" At the centre of the church hung a great, many-armed brass candelabrum encircled by another in the shape of a crown, which was adorned with icons of the prophets and apostles. It was beneath this glimmering assemblage that in the old days the rite of holy matrimony for Christian couples was celebrated. And all round, the figures of the martyrs, saints and confessors covered the walls, still, dispassionate in their bearing, the blessed inhabitants of Paradise, who focused their gaze straight ahead, as if they were clearly beholding the Holy Trinity...

Art in

153

Worship

In the apse of the sanctuary, high up, hovered the Virgin "Wider than the Heavens," crowned by angels. Lower down, around the altar, stood in silent solemnity the sweet-smelling figures of the great Fathers of the Church, the Brother of the Lord, Basil, Chrysostom, and John the Theologian, and they seemed on the brink of great gladness, as if about to hear once again the prayers and hymns of the Eucharist that they themselves had composed, inspired by the Holy Spirit. All around them, both in the sanctuary and in the nave of the church, were depicted with admirable skill the cycle of the twelve great feasts, the ranks of angels, the slaughter of the Innocents, the Righteous residing in the bosom of Abraham, and the thief who confessed Christ on the cross...

But when the priest emerged to chant "Come, Faithful, behold where Christ is born," the figures of the saints on the walls seemed to delight; "Let us follow whither the star leads" the priest continued and Kyr-Alexandris, filled with enthusiasm, took up the long rod and set the candelabrum swinging with all its candles alight. "The angels hymned there without ceasing," and the whole church trembled from the thunderous voice of Papa-Frangoulis when he chanted with passion: "Saying, 'Glory to God in the highest,' to the one who was born today in a cave...," and the painted angels that encircled the Pantokrator high up in the dome bent their ears to hear the familiar strains.[11]

The description begins with the most tangible things and concludes with the significance and meaning that they take on in their particular liturgical space and time. The judgments regarding the artistic/aesthetic value are only as many as are necessary to present the divine beauty of the holy figures. In this, as in other similar descriptions, the references to the historical and chronological problems are infrequent. Papadiamandis, who had an inborn sensitivity to divine beauty, systematically avoided the aesthetic or purely scientific treatment of the icons—as is clearly witnessed by his work—though he was quite capable of also approaching his subject historically, as his studies and historical novels show. This reveals his general stance regarding liturgical art, which was for him, finally, a stance towards life.[12]

The Theology of the Icon

In the passages of the short story "A Pilgrimage to the Kastro" quoted above, the whole church—with its architecture, wall paintings, Saints, and faithful—becomes an icon of the Incarnation of the Son and Word of God. At the same time, all that is officiated there—the whole service, hymns, typicon, lighting of the vigil lamps and incense, the movements of Papa-Phrangoulis, and the chanting of Alexandros the chanter— reveal the same incarnational reality in a different way. Art serves worship, and worship internally enlightens art from different angles, bringing out its meaning. "The whole mystagogy is like an icon of a body that lives as Christ taught us, in all of its parts from the beginning to the end; between them there is an order and harmony that guide our thought and vision...."[13] In this concelebration of all things, even the "many-armed brass candelabrum," the "gilded and finely-carved icon screen," and all the other material things of the church concelebrate, and the contribution of every particular element, person, and object is understood properly in the liturgy of the Eucharist of God.

Through Papadiamandis's descriptions, it becomes clear, not only how the church is built or how icons are painted but also in what atmosphere they thrive and grow. The architecture, wall-paintings, and icons of the church of the Nativity of Christ in the Castle speak in a soundless voice while the voice of Papa-Phrangoulis and the sound of the chanted melodies illustrate another, invisibly seen, icon. In Papadiamandis's description, both individuals and things, people and art, take on their true dimensions and achieve their full potential in the Church. The colors can speak and the faithful at prayer can paint and chant, with their every movement "representing the Cherubim"[vi]—

[vi] A verse taken from the hymn sung immediately prior to the Great Entrance in the Divine Liturgy of St. John Chrysostom.

all these things taking place "without some bodily organ speaking, but as if using the absence of movement as a source of a beautiful sound."[14]

An additional three descriptions of portable icons reveal our author's way of approaching the Orthodox icon. The first refers to *Trímorphi*, the well-known composition of the Deisis where Christ is painted and under Him the Panagia and the Forerunner are in a stance of supplication:

> [H]er gaze remained intentionally fixed on the lamp burning before the icon of the Three Holy Figures that she had received as her dowry, depicting Christ in the middle, standing erect, blessing with his right hand and holding a book in his left, with his gentle expression, his beauteous form, his slightly parted fair beard, his blue raiment and red seamless robe. To Christ's right was the Holy Mother of God, to his left St. John the Baptist, both bowing with arms crossed at either side of the Lord.[15]

The second description refers to the icon of the Panagia with Large Eyes, found in the beautifully preserved chapel of the same name, which celebrates its feast on the Saturday of the Akathist:[vii] "Firstly, he lit the vigil lamps of the Panagia with Large Eyes. It was a large, ancient icon of the Theotokos, with sharp features and a face twice the size of a regular one, with large, very large eyes, and with Christ, a babe with a very large head, wearing a gilded robe, radiant, 'who coverest [Himself] with light as with a garment.'"[16]

The third description, of the *Pepoikilméni*,[viii] the icon of the Dormition of the Panagia of Kechria, proceeds along similar lines. In describing it, Papadiamandis simultaneously gives information regarding the hymnographers of the two canons of the feast.

[vii]This is the fifth Saturday of Lent.

[viii]It is the first word of the katavasias (the first troparion sung in a given ode of a canon) for the Dormition of the Theotokos. The same name was given to an icon of the Dormition in the country chapel of Kechria on Skiathos. The word first appears in ecclesiastical literature in Psalms 49:10 and 144:14; these psalms are used in priestly prayers during the *proskomidí*.

Icon of the Dormition

It had been ten years since I had kissed the old venerable icon of the Dormition, where are painted on either side, on two upper sections, holy Cosmas (that superb poet of the *Pepoikilméni*)[17] [and] the divine Damascene, opening two wide volumes, toward the bottom of the icon, in which two troparia are written—"the Mortal Lady, but supernaturally also Mother of God" and "As a living being rightly receiving heaven within...."[18]

Papadiamandis's descriptions of icons do not focus on their history and technique but affirm the essential and personal relationship that the faithful may have with them. They express the canonical formulation of Orthodox theology regarding icons that was fixed during the period of Iconoclasm and that came into conflict with the scholastic-ethical-didactic understanding of the icon that prevailed in the West.[19] The icon is regarded as a means of ascent and not as an autonomous object. According to Orthodox teaching, the proper understanding of the icon comes through its connection with the Church's Christological dogma.

While Papadiamandis does not disdain historical knowledge or aesthetic evaluation (his own work witnesses to his rich sensitivity),[20] he does disagree with making art into an autonomous value in itself. In the three descriptions discussed above, there is a relationship established with the icon through prayer and worship. The same may be seen in "Easter Chanter," where Papa-Dianelos and the women who travel with him appear before the icons with the same prayerful and worshipful stance. Their relationship to the icons is not aesthetic but liturgical. When they enter into the church, "to trim the wicks, pour oil into the icon lamps, and cross themselves fervently. An inexpressible joy and sweetness welled up within them."[21] For this reason, they feel a living relationship with the persons represented in the icons:

The face of Christ the Lord, to the right of the Royal Doors, shone with divine light. To the left, the face of the Lady Mother of God, holding her Holy Infant, was bright with unspeakable bliss. The countenance of the Holy Baptist, with one curl of hair quivering upwards as if it had remained on end at the touch of the brutish executioner who severed the venerated head of the greatest man ever born of woman, radiated a mystical joy at the side of Him upon whose hallowed head he had been permitted to lay his hands in consecration.[22]

With their liturgical ethos and prayerful relation to the icons, Papa-Dianelos and the simple women "preach Christ our true God and honor His Saints in words...in churches, in images."[23] The focal point of Papadiamandis's work is always the person and personal relationship.

Many icons are considered by Christians to be miracle-working and living. They bear witness to the life and resurrection that the grace of God bestows, not only on the souls of the Saints but also on the clothing or objects that they used and in the icons in which they are represented. For this reason they can speak through signs and miracles, not only to the faithful but also to the distrustful and unbelievers. Papadiamandis, without taking shelter in positions, arguments, and apologetic theories, presents his personal faith and certainty in his description of the icon of St. George of the Monastery of Zographou on the Holy Mountain:

> The icon of St. George, made "without hands" from the bloody gore of the slaughter of the Martyr, is preserved there, where, because a bishop didn't believe the story, he checked it with his hands to test it and was rightly punished for his boldness. When he placed his finger on the icon, his finger stuck to it, and he was forced to cut off his finger so that he might be saved through repentance, weeping in the church of the Saint. This icon is there and the finger remains visible on the icon, after so many years.[24]

Papadiamandis believes that intellectual training is not necessary to understand the icon; rather, one needs to have a personal relationship with it. This belief is revealed in other stories as well, through his presentation of simple people who truly converse and communicate with the icons. The represented persons—the Saints—become familiar persons, like relatives of the faithful. In "The Watchman at the Quarantine Colony," it is recounted that Skevo "knelt before her *Panagítsa*,[ix] the small silver *Panagítsa* about the same size as the tender forehead of an innocent three year old girl. She knelt before her St. Nicholas, the one that had traveled along with her husband on his trips, a companion swimmer and savior of those at sea."[25] Skevos's husband, Captain Gialis, had brought from Russia a small icon of St. Nicholas "wearing a crown and the silver *epigonátion*,[x] and holding the Gospel; it was an image about the same size and shape as a pocket Gospel book."[26] His relationship with it is completely personal. The captain had sunk three times at sea, and, each time, this icon (though it was kept back in the dressing room with a vigil lamp burning before it) was found at his breast, as if it were saying to him, "As a Saint, I'm saving you. Save me as an heirloom."[27] Feeling an unusual lightness while swimming, he seemingly sailed on the waves and rose above the fear of his crew and thus survived.

St. Nicholas

In Papadiamandis's descriptions, icons do not simply help the memory to recreate persons or events from the past, but they also create and impose a sense of presence. They bring the faithful into a personal relationship with the represented Saints. "Eyes and lips and heart...need...to venerate and embrace the icons."[28] In his short stories, Papadiamandis uses tangible examples to illustrate the Church's teaching on icons. This teaching includes that of St. John of Damascus, who points out that icons are "unquenchable

[ix]This is the diminutive form of the word Panagia.
[x]It is a square made of cloth that a bishop wears while serving in Church.

preachers teaching, in a soundless voice, those who see them"[29] and how the Christian, simply by seeing one icon, can find his salvation. He reminds us of the mindset of the Fathers who first confirmed the value of icons: "Because not all people know the same amount of letters and because not many spend time in reading, the Fathers agreed that, as at the common table [it is easy for all to eat], these things should be written on icons, for quick remembrance."[30] This is affirmed by St. Nilos the Ascetic, who points out that it is possible for "those who do not know letters, observing the painting, [to] remember the true servants of the True God, who served Him by doing good works."[31]

Through Papadiamandis's stories, the relationship between theology and iconography is expressed. The interpenetration[xi] and inherence between the truth that an icon expresses and the divine beauty that it offers becomes tangible. The patristic tradition points out that just as the "word of history comes to the mind through listening, to the same extent, iconography, like silent writing, shows the same thing through imitation."[32] In this way, iconographers, the painters of the Church who "consent to unite with the divine beauty,"[33] now portray through icons the Truth that was hypostatically incarnated through the Theotokos and was dogmatically formulated by the Fathers of the Church in the Ecumenical Councils. In the Church, all these things take place with the power and enlightenment of the Holy Spirit and are different revelations of the Incarnate Word of God. Just as one must be endowed with spiritual senses to become a partaker of the mystery of the Incarnation, to know Christ, and to be initiated into the "mystery of theology,"[34] the same is necessary for one to be able to discern and understand the divine beauty of the icon. As theology is not a science—not even a holy science, as it is often called—but the mystery that mystagogically guides man to what is above nature and above the senses, in the same

[xi]A theological term used to describe the way in which the three Persons of the Holy Trinity co-exist in the one Godhead. The word is also used to describe the way in which the two natures of Christ co-exist within His one Person.

St. Theodore the Studite,
11th-century mosaic from Nea Moni monastery in Chios

way, the icon is not a simple work of art or a religious painting
but an inalienable and holy liturgical vessel that sanctifies man
and brings him into immediate contact with the grace and
hypostasis of the represented Saint. As St. Theodore the Studite
notes, "the icon exists and is seen and is venerated because of its
relationship to the prototype."[35]

Turning Liturgical Art into Museum Pieces

In his discussion of the icon and, more generally, the
vessels used in worship, Papadiamandis expresses his views on
another important issue affecting this type of liturgical art—its
exploitation and conversion into museum pieces. In short, he
considers whether, and to what extent, it is permissible for the
icon to be deprived of its liturgical function by becoming part
of a museum exhibit. The extent to which he disagrees with
Greece's exploitation of its Byzantine wealth and its transfer
from the churches to the museums is shown in "Easter Chanter,"
where he clearly articulates the dangers of such a conception of
liturgical art and warns against it.

The beloved disciple,[xii] too, was there still, rejoicing in the Resurrection, although lines of care furrowed his high forehead, caused by the foreknowledge that a shameless church robber would shortly seize him from his setting and carry him off to Athens to place him not in a church and a place of sacrifice and a sanctuary, not in a place for oblations, but in a Museum. Almighty God! a Museum, as if Christian worship had ceased to be practiced in this country, as if its vessels belonged to a buried past, objects of curiosity!... Have pity on them, Lord![36]

About seventy years after "Easter Chanter" was written, Zisimos Lorentzatos—bearing an exceptional theological perception, though not considered an "official" theologian—speaks in the same way about art and displays the same intuition of the dangers that threaten it. It is not by chance that he shares the same point of view as our author as regards art, for he also lives, moves, and breathes the same tradition:

Another question, which is worthy of amazement (and that no one has noticed), is the purely aesthetic or historical stance that we hold as regards the living tradition of Orthodox iconography, Byzantine and Modern. It comes from our lack of participation in the tradition. As we do not participate in the spiritual content of the icon, which painting serves, we are left with the painting (art for art's sake or the history of art). The art-lover and *Kunthistoriker* take over from the faithful lover of icons. We boast, for instance, how [Greece] is the first country in the world to have a Byzantine museum. This makes us, somehow, pioneers—we imagine—in the scientific branch of Byzantine studies. Truthfully, we should be saddened.[37]

Scholars assert that these words refer to the new understanding of Christian art introduced during that period by George Lampakis (1854-1914), founder of the Christian Archeological Society (1885) and the Byzantine Museum and lecturer of Christian and

---

[xii]That is, St. John the Evangelist.

Byzantine Archeology at the Theological School of Athens.[38] Using the authority his titles and positions[xiii] gave him he organized (at Zappeio)[xiv] in 1891 a large exhibition of religious paintings of the Bavarian court and of the Roman Catholic Loudovikos Theirsios (Triersch) and supplied propaganda for their propagation, believing their Nazarene/pre-Raphaelite style to be an "improved Byzantine school" appropriate for Orthodox churches.[39] Lampakis's affiliation with this painting is easy to explain. On the one hand, he had a position in the courtly environment where the conventional emotional painting of the past century found wide approval, those paintings that had already infested Russia and were being brought en masse from there to Greece. On the other hand, he was immediately connected with the Greek Nazarenes— who had studied mainly in Munich—among whom was his brother Emmanuel. The same year that "Easter Chanter" was published (1893), the collection of the Christian Archeological Society was transferred to the National Archeological Museum, so it would be available to the wider public.[40]

It was natural that Papadiamandis would object to this situation. It was completely foreign to his sense of the tradition and of art. He objected both to the distortion of Orthodox ecclesiastical art by the addition of foreign elements and to its conversion into museum pieces. There was no response to either part of his objection, at least not in his day. It was probably deemed unnecessary. For many years, this protest would echo as the voice of one crying in the wilderness, or else be considered as naive provincialism. The whole of Orthodox Greece—including the Holy Mountain—seemed to accept and cultivate the modern renaissance religious art, architecture, and painting. Athens and other cities even incorporated modern European music into worship. Today the bibliography dedicated to Byzantine and ecclesiastical art has enjoyed an unprecedented development, which is attested to by the splendid published volumes that

[xiii]He was special secretary to the Russian-born Queen Olga. [Au.]
[xiv]An exhibition area in Athens.

display the great artistic achievements of Byzantium. Similarly, renaissance-style icons, which most iconographers painted until recently and were often passed out as gifts to the children of the catechetical schools, have begun to disappear. Though a century has passed, today one can finally speak of the vindication of Papadiamandis, who fought for faithfulness to Orthodox ecclesiastical art and tradition.

Regarding the conversion of ecclesiastical art and objects into museum pieces, the situation in Greece is not very optimistic. The State, along with the Office of Archeology of the Cultural Ministry, insists on keeping splendid Byzantine churches as archeological areas, forbidding the continuation of worship there, so as to reap the benefits of the income from their use as museums. For the same reason, it takes these churches' icons to enrich the Byzantine Museum. At the same time, however, the position of the official Church is not clear. In Papadiamandis's day, many ecclesiastical leaders hurried to congratulate and help the founder of the Byzantine Museum by giving gifts of icons and holy objects. A brief look at the news in the Bulletin of the Christian Archeological Society during this period is enough to show the truth of this statement. At that time, no one spoke out to share the grief of Papadiamandis, which flowed from his deep ecclesiastical consciousness.[41]

Many years later, now that Byzantine art has become fashionable, objections are raised to the predatory tactics of the State. Sadly, however, these objections do not spring from theological insight, but from a desire for publicity or to exploit this art for material gain. Thus, we have reached today's contradictory situation, which shows the extent of our theological stupor. The official Church often refuses to relinquish icons and liturgical vessels for their safekeeping in museums on the grounds that they make up— rightly, of course—objects of its divine worship. At the same time it rushes to place those very objects in ecclesiastical museums of the Metropolises.[xv] The phenomenon also appears when monasteries

[xv]The Metropolis is where the Metropolitan (bishop) of an area is located. The Metropolis in Greece is a spiritual and cultural center that often also has an ecclesiastical museum.

King Otto of Greece,
by Joseph Karl Stieler (1781–1858)

that find themselves in a period of reconstruction and growth come up against the refusal of the ecclesiastical museum (of the metropolis to which they belong) to return old icons or other holy vessels to them, which they had taken from the monastery during periods of depopulation or decline. They would prefer that these be found "not in a church and a place of sacrifice and a sanctuary, not in a place for oblations, but in a Museum."[42]

The liquidation of most of Greece's monasteries and the confiscation of their possessions was undertaken during the years when Otto was king. It was then considered necessary to gather the icons and liturgical vessels into museums to save them from smugglers of antiquities and antique dealers. Papadiamandis was not ignorant of this problem. In "Sweet Kiss," he discusses the "relics of ages past, those things saved from theft and from various plundering. Alas! Little safer than from the mania of new archeology and of the illicit antiquities trade."[43] In "Disenchantress," he writes with the same anguish:

The chapel of the Saint had fallen into decline and pitiful neglect, for religious piety had greatly declined since that time. Only two oily and deteriorating icons were on the decaying iconostasis.... The icons of the Panagia and of the Honorable Forerunner had disappeared. Perhaps they had been taken by the hands of those that love antiquities or by the lovers of Byzantine art.... There were only two vigil lamps half-broken or cracked.... The altar and the table of oblation, naked and without cover, were completely dusty.... The sanctified chapel...was no longer used.[44]

His pain is manifold. He refers to the devastation of the church, the removal of the icons, the coat of lime over the wall paintings, the decay and neglect of the icons that remained, the rotting of the iconostasis, but, more than anything else, he refers to the fact that the chapel has been left without worship. This is the cause of all the rest of its devastation, plundering, and ruin, for it "arouses the mania of today's archeologists and of the illicit antiquities trade."[45] Papadiamandis is not ignorant of, nor does he want to ignore, the problem of endangered icons and liturgical objects in abandoned churches. However, his position regarding the problem is different. He believes that "the mania of archeologists and of the illicit antiquities trade are two sides of the same coin, that is, of the de-sanctification of the object of worship and of its change into an alien element—to an exhibit item that obeys the rules of aesthetics and art history or a trade commodity."[46]

For Papadiamandis, ecclesiastical treasures and liturgical art are not only witnesses of the past but also bearers of a living tradition. The old churches are not archeological areas, nor are old icons archeological objects with only memorial value. Papadiamandis deftly portrays how unified the Orthodox tradition is in all its expressions of art and of life. The natural place for the icon continues to be the church, where it acts as an organic element and not as an autonomous aesthetic value. Even on purely scientific grounds, the icon that is moved to the museum is wronged, as it loses the presuppositions necessary for its interpretation. For example, an icon of the Lord taken from an iconostasis and placed in a museum could not be properly interpreted, as its position in the church and on the iconostasis

Icon of Christ the Pantocrator,
from the church of Christ in the Castle

would be unknown, as would its relation to worship. Its description would be necessarily limited to its artistic-historical elements or to trite touching words, while one's relationship with it could not become a relationship of participation, unable, in that setting, to surpass the relationship of the simple visitor or spectator.

Papadiamandis argues that the icon functions properly when it is used liturgically. Conversely, when it is cut off from its environment, it is reduced to an object, a sum of lines, colors, and forms—possibly perfect from an historical or technical perspective, but empty of that which differentiates it from the exhibits of secular art surrounding it. The goal of the icon is to guide the pilgrim to transcend it, to guide him beyond the phenomena and what is meant, the symbols and representations. If the icon limited the faithful to the icon itself or to its particular elements—to its form, color, aesthetic, history, and technique, that is, to the created world—it would be an idol and would not have been worth the struggles made and the blood shed for its restoration. The liturgical icon is a contact with and a fruit of the Incarnation of the Word, witness and guide to the theosis of man.

In 1889, Papadiamandis's article, "The Nine-Hundredth Anniversary of the Great Lavra" was published.[47] In this text, he notes that "the inherited distortion of the religious life, from the viewpoint of art" is not simply a change of style and technique in ecclesiastical painting.[48] He asserts that this change is the result of a deeper decay, which deforms the Orthodox *phrónima* and the liturgical ethos of a people. The building of a church or the painting of an icon reveals not only the ethos of the architect and iconographer but also of the particular liturgical gathering—or of the whole Church—that accepts it. There is an essential relation and correspondence between the ecclesiastical-liturgical ethos and the representational (*eikastikó*) style of art. In Papadiamandis's day and earlier, the liturgical community built the church according to its needs and abilities, while its wall paintings were usually painted, not by an iconographer-businessman, but by someone who had fasted and had asked for the enlightenment of God for this work. There was even a living tradition of people who built the churches, painted the wall-paintings, created mosaics, composed hymns and melodies, shaping soulless matter with spirit, with the sense of the Liturgy and of co-liturgy. These people would not individually improvise or idolize their inspirations but expressed the life of the Church as a Body, as a liturgical community that was guided by the Holy Spirit. Just as priests served the sacrifice of Christ on behalf of the people, the architects, builders, painters, poets, and hymnographers of the Church served in the same way, practicing their sacred art as a spiritual ministration.

In the ecclesiastical community of Skiathos, there was a living liturgical tradition and a genuine eucharistic ethos. There were people such as "the blessed Athanasios Kephalas, from Epiros, a spiritual struggler, well-educated, fluent in many languages, eloquent, and a painter" who painted the beautiful icon of the Panagia "Sweet-kissing Mother of God."[49] Such strugglers knew how to live and paint as Orthodox Christians. The contemporary practice of

"The lumps of cement..."

entrusting the construction of a church to a contractor and its adornment to industrially made icons, iconostases, and stalls, was completely foreign—and unacceptable—to the tradition that Papadiamandis represents. The lumps of cement, which people today imagine to be "Byzantine style churches" and copies of the church of the Holy Wisdom,[xvi] were not common then. One reason for this was that the people who were "hard-working, ground down, poverty-stricken, burdened with peasant chores and scattered in hamlets and villages, lacking as they did the funds to build large and resplendent churches, instead built numerous less pretentious ones."[50] Another reason was that those people had a sense of the originality and uniqueness of every building and did not neglect the unbroken development and inexhaustible diversity of Byzantine architecture, which never built two churches exactly the same. Similarly, they did not have a slavish attachment to one particular school of painting, nor did they disdain the painting of the united, unbroken, and continuous Orthodox tradition that in every era was able to express dogma in its own style. They would never have been able to interpret the senseless and mechanistic transfer of icons and wall paintings from other places and periods as traditionalism in liturgical art. They would not have considered unchecked improvisation to be the mark of their freedom, nor would they have affirmed the audacity of the inspiration of the moment. Ecclesiastical art occupies a place in tradition where faithfulness and freedom interpenetrate one another, are in harmony with one another, and include one another. The dynamic relationship between this faithfulness and freedom requires creative members of

[xvi]This is the most famous church of the Byzantine era, built by the Emperor Justinian in fifth century Constantinople.

a living ecclesiastical community, which makes possible the continuity and creation of the tradition.[xvii]

In Athens, however, there was a different situation. Orthodox sensibilities as regards ecclesiastical art and decoration had begun to lapse, especially in the large churches. Simplicity and authenticity in art were usually exchanged for luxury clothed in bad taste. In one of his articles, Papadiamandis vehemently points out the danger of the distortion of liturgical art. He notes that many Christians of that era preferred going to church in small chapels rather than in the large and luxurious churches. However, he does not regard this demanding piety of the faithful as unwarranted, especially when one considers that extravagance is completely forbidden and unacceptable in churches.

> The unique characteristic of Christian churches is their modesty and sublimity. Poverty does not preclude this characteristic.... Forgeries and things made of fake-gold, which you see in some Athenian churches, are insidiously and audaciously imported, completely unauthorized, by uneducated and tasteless people, so-called wardens of these churches; they should have been stopped.[51]

Papadiamandis senses that the genuine divine beauty, the Church's *philokália*, has no relation to the interference of these wardens or of many today who rush to supply churches with the most luxurious holy vessels and furniture they can find. These theologically indefensible and aesthetically unacceptable interventions into the physical space of the church come into opposition, as much with the principle of the ancient Greek tradition ("We create things with divine beauty [though] with little money"[52]) as with the practice of the Fathers of the Church.[53]

[xvii]Creation and tradition are often regarded as diametrically opposed, though in the Orthodox understanding they are not only complementary but also completely necessary for the life and survival of one another. As Dr. Keselopoulos explains, through Papadiamandis's faithfulness to and living within the Church's tradition, his own work was permeated with the tradition and became an authentic expression of it—his work is simultaneously traditional and creative.

When, however, the tradition is not lived properly and when an authentic liturgical life is absent, it follows that there will not be genuine art. The absence of this life witnesses to an ecclesiological crisis that, in turn, deteriorates into formalism and the demise of all living forms and expressions of art.

Church Hymnography and Music

Papadiamandis argues that ecclesiastical poetry (hymnography) and the music of the Church were created together. Living during a period when the first calls were made for translations of the hymns of the Church and the first symptoms of the Europeanization of ecclesiastical music appeared, he was tireless in his struggle for the preservation of hymnography and music within the framework of the Orthodox tradition. With sobriety and a critical disposition, he confronts the intellectuals who had studied in Europe and been influenced by the Enlightenment. With the same stance, he confronts the spirit of secularism that had begun to assault the worship of many churches in Athens. The advocates of the popular language (Demotic Greek) maintained that the ecclesiastical hymns had to be translated into the popular idiom, supposedly so they would be comprehensible to the people. These advocates ignored the fact that the language of ecclesiastical poetry makes up only one of the symbolic aspects of Orthodox worship, while all ecclesiastical arts and liturgical actions together make up, as symbols, the language of worship in the broadest meaning of the word. All attempts that are limited to the translation of hymns or other liturgical texts (out of a desire for intellectual understanding) without a simultaneous attempt to live the other symbolic means with which the Liturgy is connected remain irresolute and ineffective. Papadiamandis asserts that, were one to attempt to translate a troparion into the common language, he would realize that that language—so able to express the heroism and love songs of the people—is cold, "unto apparent death, for the troparia."[54] Still, he does not reject the composition of new hymns, as long as they have the necessary presuppositions. "Without the existence and bestowing of inspiration," it is impossible "for life to be breathed into a place where the soul is missing."[55]

Papadiamandis maintains that the hymns of the Church become dear and familiar to the ears of the faithful when combined with the traditional music of the Church, which helps to make the language of the hymns comprehensible even to the illiterate. The words of the holy Gospels, accentuated with this music and melodic reading, become more accessible to the ear and thus penetrate deeper into the hearts of those listening. For this reason, the language in which the Gospel and hymns of the Church are written has the unique honor throughout all the world of remaining, at least in hearing, still living after two thousand years.[56]

Papadiamandis argues, furthermore, that the melodic way of reading in Church is the most ancient practice and authentically Greek, being descended from the ancient tragedies. Westerners then borrowed this form to create their Gregorian church music. This way of enunciation, which extends the sentence and all the syllables, imitates the sermon and the voice of the preacher.[57] While it is common for the Epistle to be recited in a variety of keys and pitches, the Gospel is recited simply and plainly. In Papadiamandis's ecclesiastical consciousness, the melody used in melodic reading is consonant with the tradition of the Church. Some modernists of his era rashly criticized it as nasal and distasteful, so they found some priests who were convinced by their suggestions, abolished the melodic way of reading, and read the Gospel passages loosely. Since this style of liturgical reading is not the tradition of the Church, Papadiamandis suggests that those in authority, the bishops in each area, prohibit this novelty.[58]

Grounded in the Greek ecclesiastical and musical tradition, our author argues that, in every ancient and modest music "the melody reigns, while the rhythm serves."[59] The ancient melodists of the Church arranged the rhythm as subservient to the melody, which appears very clearly in the prosomoia,[xviii] creating the

[xviii] These are set melodic pieces used for liturgical hymns. The same melodic piece may be used a number of times each week, though the words of the hymn change according to the Saint or feast celebrated on any given day.

melody before adapting the words to the rhythm. A modern musician could not accentuate an ancient hymn better than the poet who wrote both its words and melody.[60]

During the time of the Peloponnesian War, everyone in Athens was modernizing their music, seeking what they considered to be richer and more perfect melodies and criticizing the older ones as simple and inferior. Plato, however, deplored this tendency in his contemporaries and vigorously preached that this innovation was a debasement and corruption of music.[61] Papadiamandis appeals to this example to point out the pathology of his era concerning this question. The tendency of many of his contemporary Orthodox Greeks to imitate the Europeans and to betray their own tradition made them ridiculous, even in the eyes of those whom they wanted to emulate. Papadiamandis perceptively refers to one such circumstance:

> I don't recall which one of our own [people], two years ago, it seems to me, sent to the son of one of the leaders of Europe, and an admirer of Greece, some European piece he had written—a waltz, I think, or a polka, or I don't know what. The good prince received the gift and replied to him in a way that more or less meant, "Good, thank you, blessed one; but don't you know how to write something of your own to send me, something Greek, native? I'm saturated with European music." From the publication of the prince's letter...it is not clear if he [the composer] understood the subtle lesson.[62]

Another example of this pathology may be seen in the argument that the Byzantines did not use four-part harmony in their ecclesiastical hymns because they were unaware of it. Four-part harmony, they argued, is a newer discovery. They believed that if the Byzantines had known it they would have ushered it into worship. The adherents of these arguments also implied that there might, in fact, have been four-part harmony in Byzantium of which historians were not aware. Papadiamandis maintains that newer does not mean better. He even cites a more modern type of music that echoes the form of Byzantine music—the operetta, where the main characters principally sing arias, while the orchestra only keeps the drone note. Any polyphonies of the choir, he says, are on the periphery, while the arias make up the center and axis.

The tendency of some Orthodox to imitate Western confessions by introducing musical instruments into the churches, led Papadiamandis to write an article giving the Orthodox interpretation of the often-misinterpreted psalm verse, "Praise Him with stringed instruments and flutes."[63] He points out that many passages from the Old and the New Testament are interpreted allegorically. The hymnographers of the Church interpret the praising of God "with stringed instruments and flutes" as praising Him, "to the sound of the cymbals of our pure lips, of the harmonious harps of our hearts, of the sweet-sounding trumpets of our uplifted minds."[64] Referring to our liturgical and Biblical tradition, Papadiamandis asks those who disagree with him to consider the passage read during the Divine Liturgy of Great Saturday, in which Babylonian music is described as containing "trumpets and guitars, sambuca[xix] and harp, and all types of musical instruments" while it conversely describes the Three Children hymning God "the three as if from one mouth."[65] Papadiamandis also challenges those who, nostalgic for the Renaissance and the ancient Greek tradition, reject Byzantine music as supposedly not Greek. He argues that even if it were possible to scientifically prove that Byzantine music was identical to the music of the ancient Greeks, the reformers would still reject it. He continues by arguing that appreciation and feeling for something as graceful as Byzantine music only comes naturally to those who are either uncomplicated or refined. The Greek pseudo-aristocracy lost its simplicity long ago, while it never managed to reach some degree of refinement. Papadiamandis concludes that, "In any case, Byzantine music is as Greek as it needs to be. We neither want it to be, nor do we imagine it to be, the music of the ancient Greeks. But it is the only authentic [music] and the only existing [music]. And for us, if it is not the music of the Greeks, then it is the music of the Angels."[66]

[xix]A triangular musical instrument with four strings.

Originality in traditional ecclesiastical arts must be faithful to the first forms of this art. The development of the tradition does not need to result in its subversion and betrayal, nor does adherence to the tradition result in immobility. Rather, it is fullness of life. Papadiamandis knew this principle of art well. "The Church," clergy and laity, "has an accepted form, which no one is able to violate without being punished, and She categorically forbids every novelty, either in architecture and painting and in the rest of the church's decoration or in music and other [aspects] of the liturgy."[67] He cries out against the novelties that were occasionally made—and that would, later on, become a general phenomenon—in this exhortation: "Cultivate the dignified Byzantine tradition in worship, in the decoration of the churches, in music, and in painting."[68] This principle coincides with Plato's understanding of tradition and art.[xx] Unlike those then—and now—who admire and extol as "originality" the emergence of individuality and innovations, Plato counsels "do not innovate... against the order."[69] The self-effacement and humility that this conception of artistic creation requires coincides with Christ's admonition, "For whosoever will save his life shall lose it,"[70] and with the classic words of St. John of Damascus, "I say nothing from my own thoughts,"[71] while he was simultaneously making truly original compositions. Papadiamandis does not belong to the chorus of blind "lovers of Byzantine art,"[72] but to the liturgical tradition that this art serves. He does not have an aesthetic or emotional relationship to art, but a spiritual one, which is why he easily understands those things that others find difficult to comprehend—that "God is the Absolute Being and, as such, must necessarily be worshipped."[73]

[xx]For more on this, see Constantinos Cavarnos's book, *Plato's Theory of Fine Art.*

WITHOUT A WEDDING CROWN

Was she not also the mistress of her own house and courtyard? And had she not once been a young woman of breeding? She had been educated at schools. She had received her diploma from the Arsakeion young ladies' academy.

And she observed her social obligations and carried out her household tasks better than any other. Her house and her front door steps were models of cleanliness, and she was willing to whitewash and mop without ever feeling bored or showing that eccentricity which is common to all women who have an excessive love of cleanliness. And when Holy Week came around she doubled the amount of whitewashing and cleaning until the floor so shone that the walls were jealous of the floor.

Holy Thursday came and she lit her fire, set up her pot and dyed her Easter eggs deep red. Then she prepared her mixing bowl, knelt down, made the sign of the cross three times over the flour, then kneaded the round Easter loaves cleanly and with skill, pressing red eggs into them in the form of a cross.

And in the evening, when night had fallen, she did not venture out with the other women to listen to the service of the Twelve Gospels. She wished there could have been some way to hide behind the back of some tall, fat lady or at the tail end of that throng of women, hugging the wall, but she was afraid they would turn and stare at her.

Throughout all of Good Friday she daydreamed and cried to herself, lamenting her youth and the dear ones she had lost, and in a waking dream she considered going that evening, before the service began, to stealthily kiss the *Epitaphios*, just as that woman with an issue of blood had stolen her cure from Christ, and then to leave. But at the last moment, as darkness began to fall, she lost courage and decided not to go. Her heart began to beat quickly.

Late at night, when the holy procession with its crosses and banners and candles emerged from the church amid hymns and chanting and sounds of voices interwoven with the musical cries of the children from the Hatzikosta orphanage and the noise and the bustle of the crowds in the dimly-lit city, then Yiambis, the churchwarden, ran ahead to get to his house and donning his embroidered silk cap and holding his amber worry beads, went out onto the porch in the hope vainly entertained year after year that the priests would decide to stop below his porch and offer a prayer; then that poor Christina the Teacher (as she had, at one time, been called in the neighborhood) at the small window of her house, half-hidden behind a shutter, held up her diminutive wax candle, the light just filling the palm of her hand, and heaped frankincense onto the clay incense burner, offering from afar myrrh to Him who always has accepted the fragrances and the tears of the woman who was a sinner, even though she had not dared to draw close and kiss His immaculate, nail-driven and blood-drenched feet.

And on Sunday morning, long after midnight, again standing half-hidden behind her window, she held her superfluous and unchurched candle and listened to the joyful voices and the fireworks, and jealously watched from afar those women who were hurrying home from church, clothes rustling, carrying their lighted candles from the service, happy, intending to keep the holy light of the Resurrection burning for the entire year. And she wept and lamented her ruined youth.

Only on the afternoon of Easter Day, when the bells rang out for the Vespers of Love, the so-called Second Resurrection, only then did she venture out of her house, noiselessly and with a light step, scurrying from wall to wall, closely sticking to each as she went, carrying herself in such a way as if she were about to enter some neighboring woman's courtyard on an errand. And from wall to wall she arrived at the north side of the church and slipped furtively inside the small side door.

In Athens, as is well known, the First Resurrection is for the ladies and the second for the female servants. Christina the

Teacher was afraid to go to the church for the night service for fear of being stared at, but she wasn't afraid of being seen during the day. Because it was the ladies that stared at her while the maidservants merely looked. She found a great difference in that. She didn't want to, or couldn't relate to the ladies and therefore lowered herself to the servant class. That was her fate.

The spectacle was beautiful and very lively, picturesque and colorful: the candelabras all alight, the holy icons gleaming, the cantors singing the Paschal hymns, the priests standing with the Gospel Book and the icon of the Resurrection clasped to their breasts, celebrating the service of the Kiss of Peace.

The servants with their ribbons and white aprons cast glances right and left and chatted away to each other, paying no attention to the divine service. The nursemaids held three-year-old and five-year-old boys and girls by the hand; the children were clutching their colored candles and burning the gold paper with which they were decorated, playing and quarrelling with each other and trying to set alight the hair of the child standing in front. The shoeblacks tossed firecrackers into dark corners of the church and terrified the servant girls. The single policeman there chased them but they went out through one side door and came back in through the other. The churchwardens went about with collection plates and sprinkled the nursemaids with rosewater.

Two or three young mothers from the lowest social class and seven or eight nursemaids were holding five- or seven-month-old infants in their arms. These small creatures opened their sweet eyes in astonishment, gazing greedily at the light of the candles, the candelabras and the candle stands, the rings and clouds of smoke rising from the censers, the red and green light coming in through the glass of the church windows, the swirling cassock of the monk acting as sacristan who was running back and forth on various errands, the beards of the priests moving each time they inclined their heads, each time they moved their lips, to repeat to all that Christ had risen; gazing and marveling at everything they saw around — the polished buttons and the twirled moustache of the policeman, the white head scarves of the women, and the ranks of other children, all lined up, near and far — as they played with the curls of those holding them, lisping inarticulate, angelic sounds.

There were two eight-month-old infants in the arms of two young mothers who were standing shoulder to shoulder next to a column; once the infants saw each other they immediately became acquainted and established a relationship, and the one merry infant, so pretty and good, stretched out its tiny, tender hand to the hand of the other and drew it to him uttering incomprehensible, heavenly sounds.

But the voice of the child was ringing and could be clearly heard all around, and Yiambis, the churchwarden, did not like to hear noises. During all of the night services of Passion Week he had often entered the dense ranks of the women to reprimand some impoverished mother coming from the common folk because her child had whimpered. Now again he was hurrying to censure the poor mother over her infant's harmless cries.

Then Christina the Teacher who was standing a little further back, behind the last column and up against the wall, pressed into a corner, thought involuntarily — and she thought it not as a teacher but as an ignorant and silly woman that she was — that, as it seemed to her, no one, not even a churchwarden, had the right to reprimand a poor, young mother for the whimpering of her baby, just as he did not have the right to bar her from the church because she had an infant at the breast. Wasn't Holy Communion given to crying infants every day? Were they to be barred from Holy Communion because they were crying? How long was the strictness of "those in charge" to be directed against and taken out on only the poor and the humble?

This small incident was the reason Christina came to remember that one night many years ago, during the Exaltation of the Cross when she had gone to church at the chapel of Saint Elissaios, beyond the Market Gate, and as the lay reader was reading the lesson from the Apostle when he proclaimed the words *God has chosen the weak things of the world*,[1] suddenly, by a miraculous coincidence, an infant began to cry out in a powerful voice from the women's section, competing with the reader's voice. And what sweetness had that child's warbling! Just as beautiful must have been the *Hosanna*, which was chanted, in olden times by the children of the Hebrews to the coming Savior.[2] *Out of the mouth of babes and nursing infants You have ordained strength because of Your enemies, that You may silence the enemy and the avenger.*[3]

Such were Christina's reflections, thinking that no mother would be so lacking in self-respect as not to be troubled and not to quickly comfort her child and to beg for a door to open miraculously in the wall next to her so she could hurry it away more rapidly. Moreover, the admonishments of the churchwarden were useless and caused even more noise, and since all the ordinary means of persuasion are powerless to quiet a nursing infant, for only the mother possesses those other means of doing so, it is unnecessary for a third party to come over and remind her to use them. And then they say that men have more brains than women!

That was Christina's opinion. But what could she say? She wasn't asked for her opinion. She was Christina the Teacher, as she had once been called. She had no children so as to fear the reprimands of the churchwarden. She had buried her children without having given birth to them. And the man she had had was not her husband.

They were a couple without a wedding crown.

Without a wedding crown! How many instances there are!

But we are not going to make sociological observations today. Nevertheless, in the absence of forms of social welfare, Christian and ethical, if one is to be, at least, consistent and logical, it would be much better to vote in favor of civil marriage.

Ever since the time that she had needed the recommendations of party bosses in order to get an appointment as a teacher, one of those bosses, Panayis Delikanatas, a tavern keeper, had taken advantage of her. When the Ministry changed hands and he no longer had the influence to get her appointed, he said: "Come and live with me and I'll marry you later." When? In a few months, six months, a year.

And the years went by and his hair remained black while hers turned white. And he never married her.

She gave birth to no child. He also had other lovers. And he had children by them.

This wretched woman, in full knowledge of the situation, censured, protesting, patient, persevering, took the illegitimate children of her unwed man into her home. She warmed them in her embrace, showed them motherly affection, felt compassion for them. And she nurtured them and struggled to raise them. And when they got to be two or three and she felt as if they were her own children, Charon would come accompanied by scarlet fever, smallpox and other hideous companions . . . and tear them from her embrace.

Three or four children died in that way within seven or eight years.

And so she became bitter as the years passed. She grew old and white. She wept for her husband's illegitimate offspring as if they had been her own — those poor blessed things, soaring towards the flowers of Paradise, in the company of the angels dwelling there.

He didn't even talk to her about marriage anymore. And she didn't say anything either. She suffered in silence.

And she washed and tidied her house constantly. On Holy Thursday she dyed her eggs red. And on feast days she didn't have the courage to go to church.

Only on the afternoon of Easter Day, during the Vespers of Love, she furtively and timidly slipped into the church to hear the hymn "Day of the Resurrection" together with the servant girls and the nursemaids.

But He, who had risen *for the oppression of the poor, for the sighing of the needy,*[4] who accepted the myrrh and the tears of the woman who was a sinner and the thief's remember me,[5] will also accept the repentance of this poor woman and will give her a place of green pasture and comfort and refreshment in His eternal kingdom.

Translated by Philip Ramp

From *The Boundless Garden*, Selected Short Stories, Vol. II (forthcoming) (Limni, Greece: Denise Harvey).

A VILLAGE EASTER

Memories of Childhood

Uncle Milios never spoke a truer word, when he said the good Christians living outside the town might end up having to celebrate Easter that year without a liturgy. In fact no prophecy was ever closer to fulfilment, for it almost came true twice—but happily God made the authorities see the light, and in the end the poor villagers, local shepherd-farmers, were judged worthy to hear the Word of God and eat the festive eggs.

The cause of all this was the busy little coaster that (supposedly) linked those unhappy islands to the inhospitable shore opposite, and which twice a year, when the season changed in spring or autumn, would almost invariably sink, and as often as not take the whole crew down with it. They would then put the post of captain up for auction, and each time some poor wretch, undaunted by the fate of his predecessor, was found to undertake this most perilous task. And on this occasion, at the end of March, as winter was taking its leave, the coaster had gone down again.

The parish priest, Father Vangelis, who was also the abbot (and only monk) of the small monastic establishment of St. Athanasios, had been appointed by the bishop to take charge of the villages on the opposite shore. Though already an old man, he would take the boat across four times a year, during each of the main fasts,[1] to hear the confessions of his unfortunate parishioners—the "hill-people" or "mountain-scarecrows" as they were called— and give them some spiritual instruction, before he hastened back to his monastery (if it was during Lent) to celebrate Easter there. But that year, as we have said, the coaster had sunk, the islands were cut off for several days, and Father Vangelis was reluctantly obliged to stay and celebrate Easter on the far shore of the billowing, storm-tossed sea. It seemed as though his little flock in Kalivia, whose homes clustered around the monastery of St. Athanasios, would end up not having any liturgy at all.

Some of them thought they should take their wives and children down into the town, to hear the Resurrection proclaimed and attend the liturgy there, but Uncle Milios, the village elder of Kalivia, wished to celebrate Easter the way he always had; Sevenmonth (so called because he'd been born premature) didn't want his wife being stared at by the townspeople; and Uncle Anagnostis, an old villager who knew the Easter service by heart, but couldn't actually read a word of it, longed to chant "Receive the body of Christ" himself. All three insisted (and many agreed) that at all costs they must get one of the priests in town to come up to Kalivia and celebrate the liturgy for them there.

Everyone felt the best choice would be Father Kyriakos: he wasn't of a particularly good family (he was even related to one or two of the villagers himself) and he didn't look down on them. He was even said to have some Albanian blood in him. He certainly wasn't stand-offish—in fact it was rumoured here and there that the priest had a habit of "finishing off the husband's procreation duties" with his female parishioners. But that was just the idle talk of mischief-makers and grudge-bearers, and only fools paid any attention to it. Like most of the true clergymen of the Greek Church (with one or two exceptions), the priest was by and large of blameless character.

Though this is true, the fact remains that married priests are usually out of pocket and out of luck, and, being forever burdened by the need to feed their offspring, they can appear to be grasping individuals, who don't even trust their own colleagues fully. This was the case with Father Kyriakos, who was perfectly willing to go and celebrate Easter for the villagers, as he had a generous heart and would have liked them to enjoy Easter and the arrival of spring along with everyone else, but he had his suspicions about the other parish priest, and was reluctant to leave him in charge of the parish, especially on that day. Father Theodore, however, the other priest, who was known as "the Whirlwind," urged him to go, saying it would be a pity to lose the income from Kalivia, and suggesting that they share the receipts from the parish and the village equally between them.

This did not reassure Father Kyriakos at all: in fact it made him even more suspicious. However, as he had already more or less made up his mind to go to Kalivia when he asked his colleague for his opinion, he told his son Zachos—who pulled a face and grumbled—to stay in the church sanctuary as a spy, collect his half of the offerings and the priest's fee, and only come and join him in Kalivia at sunrise, when the liturgy had ended.

*   *   *

It was four hours before dawn, and the Evening Star was already high in the night sky. Uncle Anagnostis woke the priest, and before they entered the little church of St. Demetrios he improvised a bell out of a solid piece of walnut wood and a stick, and walked through the village, banging noisily to wake the sleeping inhabitants.

One after another the villagers arrived, accompanied by their wives. All were dressed in their best clothes.

The priest gave the blessing.

Uncle Anagnostis began to recite from memory, beginning with the preliminary prayer and the canon, "On the Waves of the Sea."

Father Kyriakos appeared at the sanctuary doors, chanting, "Come, receive the Light."[2]

When they had all lit their candles, they filed out into the open air to hear the Resurrection gospel. A sweet, contemplative Resurrection, amid the blossoming trees, the fragrant bushes swaying in a gentle breeze, and the white flowers of the wild clematis, "neige odorante du printemps."[i]

They sang "Christ is risen," and all went back into the church. Men, women and children: no more than seventy souls, all told.

Uncle Anagnostis began to chant the Easter canon, and the priest himself (as there was no one else to do so) gave the responses from the sanctuary. He was about to come out and say

[i]"fragrant snow of spring" : V. Hugo, *Les Orientales*, xxxiii, 10.

the preparatory prayer, kiss the icons and begin the liturgy, when a rather tall twelve-year-old boy, flushed and panting, followed by two other boys of about the same age, suddenly walked, or rather burst, into the church. It was Zachos, Father Kyriakos's son. He rushed into the sanctuary, gasping for breath, and began addressing the priest. Though the congregation could hear his voice, they couldn't make out a single word of it.

This is what he was saying:

"Papa, Papa!" (the children of priests also usually address their father as "Papa"). "Papa, Papa!....Father Whirlwind.... by the back door....the oblations....from the sanctuary...his mother-in-law...and his wife....carrying....by the back door... the oblations....I saw them....by the back door....the oblations... from the sanctuary....and his mother-in-law...and his wife..."

Father Kyriakos was the only person who could have made any sense of his breathless son's disjointed words. He understood from them that Father Theodore, the Whirlwind, the other parish priest, was stealing the collection and passing it out to his wife and mother-in-law through the back door leading from the sanctuary.

Perhaps things were not exactly as Zachos suggested. Like all young boys, he loved the countryside and he loved having fun, and he had found it very difficult to obey his father's orders and stay behind in the town. He would have jumped at any excuse to get away and set off on a nocturnal jaunt to Kalivia, especially as he hadn't had any difficulty finding some friends to come along with him.

But Father Kyriakos did not stop to think. He went red and flew into a rage. In a word, he sinned. Rather than giving his son a good box around the ears and calmly proceeding with his duty, he immediately stripped off his stole, removed his surplice and strode down the nave and out of the church—averting his eyes from his wife's face as she stared at him in alarm.

Uncle Milios, however, had an idea about what might have provoked this behaviour, and went out after him. A short distance from the church, between three trees and two stretches of fencing, the following conversation took place:

"Papa, Papa, where are you going?"

"Don't worry—I'll be back straightaway."

He didn't know what to say. The fact is that he had resolved to go back down to the town and confront the other priest about the theft. He honestly believed he had enough time to get back and celebrate the liturgy before the sun rose.

"Where are you going?" insisted Uncle Milios.

"Get Anagnostis to read the Acts of the Apostles. I'll be right back."

He had forgotten that Uncle Anagnostis couldn't read anything, unless he already knew it by heart.

"After all, I'm leaving my wife here!" he added, unable to think of anything else to say. "I'm leaving my wife here with you!"

And with these words he was gone.

Uncle Milios walked gloomily back into the church.

"I knew it," he muttered to himself.

*   *   *

In the church great astonishment held sway. The villagers stared at each other in bewilderment. Some were whispering. The women were asking the priest's wife to tell them what was going on—but she was even more at a loss than they were.

Meanwhile, the priest ran and ran. The cold night air cooled his brow a little.

"And how am I supposed to feed all these children? Eight of them, God forgive me: the wife makes nine, and me—ten! They'll rob you as soon as look at you!..."

Five hundred paces from the church the path began to descend, and led down into a lovely valley. There was a watermill standing on the slope, by the side of the road. As the priest listened to the gentle murmuring of the stream and felt the cool breeze against his face, the fact that he was going to celebrate the liturgy (let alone how or where he was going to celebrate it) was swept completely from his mind, and he stooped down to drink. But his lips had not yet touched the surface of the water, when he suddenly remembered, and realized what he was doing.

"I have to celebrate the liturgy," he exclaimed, "and I'm drinking water...?"[ii]

And he didn't drink.

Then he pulled himself together.

"What am I doing?" he said, "Where am I going?"

He made the sign of the cross.

"I have sinned, Lord. I have sinned! Do not hold me to account!"

He resumed: "If he is a thief, it is for the Lord to...forgive him...him and me. I must do my duty."

He felt a tear run down his cheek.

"Oh Lord," he exclaimed with all his heart, "I have sinned, I have sinned! You gave yourself up for our sins, and in return we crucify you daily!"

He turned around and hurried back up towards the church to continue the service.

And I was actually going to drink water! I am not fit to celebrate! But what can I do? I can't take communion! I shall say the office without taking communion ? I am not worthy! 'Behold the first fruits of the vine!'[iii] I am not worthy!"

He re-entered the church, and the villagers greeted his return with joy.

He celebrated the divine mystery and administered the Holy Communion to the faithful, taking care that every last drop from the chalice passed through their lips. Himself, he abstained, vowing to tell all to his confessor—and ready to accept whatever penance he might impose.

*   *   *

Around noon, after the service of the Second Resurrection,[3] the villagers laid out the feast under the plane trees by the cooling spring. For a carpet they had the grass and the meadow flowers and for a table they used ferns and rushes. The cool breeze rustled in

---

[ii]All communicants, including the celebrant, refrain from both food and drink prior to communion.

[iii]John of Damascus, Canon on the Sunday of Easter, ode 8, troparion 1.

the trees, while Sevenmonth responded with sweet sounds from his lyre. The lovely Xanthe, his wife, sat between her mother Melachro and Aunt Kratira, her mother-in-law, taking care to keep her cheeks partially covered with her headscarf and staring pointedly at the trunk of the great plane tree so that the men would not look at her and arouse her husband's jealousy.

Her sister, Atho, fifteen years old and still unmarried, without a care in the world and no less of a beauty herself, kept teasing her, saying: "Silly girl, what did you see in him? I wouldn't have him if you offered me the heavens and the stars...I'd rather be a nun!"

It was true that Sevenmonth was not much to look at in terms of appearance or size, but he made up for these shortcomings with agility of body and mind, and a cheerful and good-natured disposition.

Father Kyriakos presided over the feast. His wife sat opposite him, an irreproachable dark-haired woman, stocky and round-faced, who once a year, almost without fail, would innocently hatch out another little priest-child—without bothering with all those herbs (whether for getting a child or for preventing one) that fill the minds of other women.

To the right of the priest sat Uncle Milios, the village elder, and devoted servant of his little community. He knew better than anyone how the lamb should be roasted, carving it carefully so that everyone got his share, and proposing toasts as he tucked into his food. His toasts were unrivalled. After the priest had made a short formal toast of his own, Uncle Milios, clutching an enormous seven-oka cask, stood up and began to greet the company one by one:

"Christos Anesti! Christ is risen! Truly the Lord is risen! He lives and reigns throughout the ages!"

After this preamble, he got down to business:

"Health to us all! Good health! Prosperity! Good cheer! Papa! May your vocation bring you joy!" And to the priest's wife: "May your husband and all your little ones bring you joy! Cousin Theodore! Long life and happiness! Godfather Panayiotis! Just as you baptized us with oil, may you also crown us with wedding wreaths of vine.[4] Kratira, my in-law! May God grant you a fine husband for your daughter! George, my nephew! May you make an honourable marriage, and may we rejoice on your wedding-day! Aunt Kyparissou! May your son marry a good woman, and gladden your heart! Raise your glasses! Cheers! Here's to us all! Your health! Cousin Xanthe! May good omens accompany the birth of your child! Your health! Here's to us all! May life be good to us, now and always!"

And the amount he drank depended on whom he was toasting.

Little Sevenmonth also wanted to propose a toast, but a more tender one. He hoped to touch his wife's heart and make her answer him:

"What's up?"

"Drink up, and pass the cup!"

"What, with wine?"

"I drink to you, O darling mine!"

When he had drunk, he passed the cask to his lovely Xanthe, and she moistened her lips.

Then they began to sing. First of all "Christ is risen," followed by popular songs. When Uncle Milios tried to sing "Christ is risen," it either became a slow Anatolian lament, or else a heroic ballad, but the most original singer of all was Uncle Kitsos, an aged gendarme from Northern Epirus—an old regular, who had been left stranded on the island since King Otho's reign. [iv] He wasn't even sure whether his name was still in the official register—at times he received his pay, and at other times he didn't. He wore an open-sleeved tunic, short knee breeches and greaves around his shins. The mayor (there was also a mayor, alas!) had sent him to Kalivia for Easter, supposedly to maintain law and order, although there wasn't actually any need for it to be maintained. The truth is that he had sent him off to enjoy himself with the good-hearted country people, whose company Uncle Kitsos liked, even though he would call them "poor wretches"

[iv]Otho of Bavaria was appointed as the first king of independent Greece by the European powers after the Greek War of Independence. He reigned from 1832 to 1862.

or "tinkers." It is also true that if he had stayed in the town, the mayor would have been under an obligation to entertain him, for Uncle Kitsos had been spoilt by the previous mayors and treated to cakes and eggs at Easter. What customs...!

After kissing the cask three or four times, Uncle Kitsos began to chant "Christ is risen" after his own fashion, as follows:

> Crisis lads, Crisis risen
> from the dead by death
> chomping down death
> and to those, those in the tombs
> life most blessed![5]

And yet, despite its singularity, no one ever sang a sacred song with more Christian feeling and enthusiasm, with the possible exception of that worthy old Cretan, long-famed in Athens, who sang the "Dumb are the lips of the impious"[6] with his own interpolation: "Dumb are the lips of the impious and profane, the scoundrels!, at your revered image...."

Ah, the true Orthodox Greeks!

*   *   *

As the shadows lengthened, the men began to dance the *klephtiko* (the women waited till Monday and Tuesday before dancing the *syrtos* and the *kamara*),[7] and Father Kyriakos, his wife, and young Zachos, whom his father had let off in view of the special day (he had decided that his son was actually to blame for all the confusion), took leave of the company and went back down to the town.

Father Kyriakos gave his fellow priest his full share of the collection from Kalivia, and did not even bother to raise the subject of the supposed theft. As it was, Father Theodore himself told him that his share of the parish receipts was in his own (Father Theodore's) house. He had thought it best, he said, to take both shares out through the back door of the sanctuary, so as to keep them from the eyes of gossips with nothing better to think about, who might otherwise kick up a fuss about all the money priests receive. "On the rare day," he said, "that we actually get something in the collection box, everyone has plenty to say about it—but they never stop to consider all the weeks and months that go by without harvest!"

So that was why Zachos had got it wrong.

(1890)

Translated by Andrew Watson

From *The Boundless Garden*, Selected Short Stories, Vol. I (Limni, Greece: Denise Harvey, 2007).

ENDNOTES

Introduction

[1] Romans 12:1–2.
[2] 1 Corinthians 14:15.

Chapter 1

[1] Papa-George Rigas related the facts concerning Papadiamandis's birth and Baptism to the publisher Elias Dikaio. See Octave Merlier, "A. Papadiamánti Grámmata" in *Vivliopoleíon N. Sidéri*, (Athens 1934), 228. See also Nicholas D. Triandaphilopoulos, ed. *Alexándrou Papadiamánti Allilographía* (Athens: Domos Publications, 1992), letter #287, 216–217.

[2] Nicholas D. Triandaphilopoulos, ed. "Papa-Adamantios Oikonomos," *Aléxandros Papadiamántis Ápanta*, critical edition (Athens: Domos Publications, 1982) vol. 5:332. All citations to Papadiamandis's works refer to this edition. English translations of the titles of Papadiamandis's works appear throughout the text and in the footnotes. In Appendix 1, there is an index of Papadiamandis's works arranged alphabetically giving the transliterated Greek title opposite their English translation.

[3] "Biography of Al. Papadiamandis," *Ápanta*, vol. 5:319.

[4] For more regarding this movement, see Archimandrite Amphilochios Radovits (now Metropolitan of Montenegro), *I Filokalikí Anagénnisi toú XVIII kaí XIX ai. Kaí oi Pneumatikoí Karpoí tís* (Athens: Goulandri-Horn Institute Publications, 1984); for Papadiamandis's relationship with monasticism and the *Kollyvádes*,

see George Veriti, "Tó Anamorfotikó Kínima tón Kollyvádon kaí oi dúo Aléxandroi," *Aktínes*, 36 (1943):99–110, and Nicholas D. Triandaphilopoulos, *Daimónio Mesimvrinó* (Athens: Grigori Publications, 1978), 94–103.

[5]"Hazopoulo," *Ápanta*, vol. 4:419–420.

[6]Ibid.

[7]"Years later, after Demetrios...had spent some years in the Russian monastery on Athos, he returned to the land of his fathers. He would eventually become famous as the Elder Dionysios and as a spiritual father." See "The Black Stumps," *Ápanta*, vol. 4:478–479.

[8]"The Quintals," *Ápanta*, vol. 4:407.

[9]"The Monk," *Ápanta*, vol. 2:325–326. [*The Boundless Garden*, Lambros Kamperidis and Denise Harvey, ed., David Connolly, Elizabeth Key Fowden, Garth Fowden, et al., translators, Evia, Greece: Denise Harvey (Publisher), 2007, 159.]

[10]"Papa-Adamantios Oikonomos," *Ápanta*, vol. 5:332–333.

[11]"Easter Chanter," *Ápanta*, vol. 5:515. [*The Boundless Garden*, 265.]

[12]*Ápanta*, vol. 5:35. This poem's subtitle is from the Psalms, "O spare me, that I may recover strength, before I go hence, and be no more." Psalm 38(39):13.

[13]Triandaphilopoulos, ed. *Alexándrou Papadiamánti Allilographía*, letter #287:219. It is significant that he sang this troparion, in anticipation of the feast of Theophany. [Tr.]

[14]Luke 2:34.

[15]See, for example, K. T. Dimaras, *Istoría tís Neoellinikís Logotechnías*, 1st ed., vol. 2 (Athens, 1949). For these positions see also K. Stergiopoulos, "Papadiamántis Símera—Diaíresi kaí Haraktiristiká tís Pezographías tou," *Diavázo*, November-December 1977, no. 9.

[16]See Demetrios Balanos, "Papadiamántis, Thrýlos kaí Pragmatikótis," *Néa Estía*, no. 55:24–28.

[17]"Énas Orismós toú Solomoú giá tó Ýphos (stile)," *Melétes*, (Athens: Galaxías Publications, 1967), 210.

[18]*Íkaros* Publications, 1985 (14), 54.

[19]See "Mnimósino Papadiamánti," *Néa Estía—Aphiéroma stón Papadiamánti*, Christmas 1941, 2-3.

[20]See *Néa Zoí* [Alexandria], April 1908.

[21]"Easter Chanter," *Ápanta*, vol. 2:524. [*The Boundless Garden*, 274.]

[22]He confesses, "All these thoughts, it is true, did not pass unaided through Father Samuel's head, but then, was there ever a writer who did not from time to time substitute his own cogitations for those of his hero?" ["The Monk," *Ápanta*, vol. 2:329.] [*The Boundless Garden*, 164.]

[23]"Easter Chanter," *Ápanta*, vol. 2:517. [*The Boundless Garden*, 267.]

[24]"Final Response to *The Word*," *Ápanta*, vol. 5:165.

[25]*Ápanta*, vol. 2:524–525.

[26]See "Pós Vlépoume Símera tón Papadiamánti," *Archeío Euvoikón Meletón*, vol. 2:60-121.

[27]See Nicholas D. Triandaphilopoulos, "Prologue," *Aléxandros Papadiamántis—Eíkosi Keímena giá tí Zoí kaí tó Érgo tou* (Athens, 1979), 9–10.

[28]Ibid., 10.

[29]"Great Week in Athens," *Ápanta*, vol. 5:96

Chapter 2

[1]See Canons 24 of Antioch and 12 of Sardicea, in P. Akanthopoulos, *Kódikas Ierón Kanónon kaí Ekklisiastikón Nómon*, 2nd ed. (Thessalonica: Kyriakidis Publications, 1991), p. 246 and 262 respectively.

[2]Canon of Carthage, ibid. 426.

[3]See the "Prayer of the Cherubic Hymn" in the Divine Liturgy of St. John Chrysostom.

[4]See Ignatios of Antioch, *Letter to the Ephesians*, IV, PG 5, 736A.

[5]John 21:16.

[6]John 10:14.

[7]See Adamantios Korais, *Papatréchas*, ed. Alkis Angelos, (Athens: Ermís Publications, 1978), where the hero of the story is presented as a characteristic model embodying the "ideal" priest, who wields legislative and governing capabilities, and whose responsibilities require that he be well-educated and conversant in classical education. Pertinent to this point, see the study, "Oi iereís toú Papadiamánti í I schési tís paideías mé tó ieratikó íthos," *Praktiká A' Diethnoús Synedríou giá tón Aléxandro Papadiamánti* (Athens, 1994).

[8]*Ápanta*, vol. 3:528.

[9]Easter Sermon of St. John Chrysostom.

[10]*Ápanta*, vol. 2:125. [*The Boundless Garden*, 21.]

[11]Romans 12:15.

[12]See "The Godmother," *Ápanta*, vol. 3:586.

[13]See "The Stricken One," *Ápanta*, vol. 2:136. Likewise, when Asiminas "considered [her daughter Aphendra] to be spastic and neurasthenic...she summoned the priest one evening, and he began to read the four gospels above her head." "Fortune from America," *Ápanta*, vol. 3:337.

[14]See "The Whorehouse," *Ápanta*, vol. 4:569–572.

[15]See Papa-Nicholas as a "type" of Papadiamandian priest in D. Bosinaki, *Monódromos* (Dodóni Publications, 1984), 14–20.

[16]"Fortune from America," *Ápanta*, vol. 3:341.

[17]See, "The Gleaner," *Ápanta*, vol. 2:121.

[18]*Ápanta*, vol. 2:520. [*The Boundless Garden*, 271.]

[19]Psalm 125 (126):5: "They that sow in tears shall reap in joy."

[20]See First Antiphon of the Hymns of Ascent, third tone.

[21]John 12:24.

[22]*Ápanta*, vol. 2:521; Compare John 11:25. [*The Boundless Garden*, 271.]

[23]*Ápanta*, vol. 2:277. [*The Boundless Garden*, 106.]

[24]St. Gregory of Nyssa, *Homily on the Song of Songs*, 4, PG 48, 845D.

[25]See *Ápanta*, vol. 5:194–195.

[26]Ibid., 197.

[27]Ibid., 197–198: "But all these things have only relative value. Of much more substance and benefit are other things, which do not enter the sphere of legislative provision, but that are wholly ethical and for this reason cannot be imposed."

[28]See "A Pilgrimage to the Kastro," *Ápanta*, vol. 2:295. [*The Boundless Garden*, 126.]

[29]"Theophany," *Ápanta*, vol. 5:140–141.

[30]Ibid.

[31]"Priests of the Cities and Priests of the Villages," *Ápanta*, vol. 5:195: "Among our priests there are still many who are virtuous and good, in the cities and in the villages. They are simple folk, salutary, worthy of respect. It doesn't matter that they don't give sermons. They find other ways of teaching their flock."

[32]"Priests of the Cities and Priests of the Villages," *Ápanta*, vol. 5:195-196.

[33]1 Peter 5:2-3.

[34]A prayer during the ordination of a deacon, *Evchológion tó Méga* (Athens: Astír Publications, 1970), 187.

[35]See Nicodemos Milas, *Tó Ekklisiastikón Díkaion* (Athens, 1906), 593–594.

[36]*Ápanta*, vol. 4:494.

[37]Ibid., 495.

[38]*Ápanta*, vol. 4:503.

[39]*Ápanta*, vol. 2:126. [*The Boundless Garden*, 22.]

[40]Ibid. [*The Boundless Garden*, 30.]

[41]"A Village Easter," *Ápanta*, vol. 2:133. [*The Boundless Garden*, 30.]

[42]"Reverie of the Fifteenth of August," *Ápanta*, vol. 3:88.

[43]See "The House of Kokonos," *Ápanta*, vol. 2:642.

[44]See "The Godmother," *Ápanta*, vol. 3:586.

[45]See "Easter Chanter," *Ápanta*, vol. 2:521. [*The Boundless Garden*, 272.]

[46]"The Monk," *Ápanta*, vol. 2:327. [*The Boundless Garden*, 161.] The same hunger for parishioners' gifts, accompanied by haste in the performing of the services and an absence of the liturgical ethos may be noted in the "professional" priests of Athens and is described later in the same story: "Another kind of noisy *havra* could be witnessed when they went to perform the service of Anointing of the Sick in some home: prayers, litanies and scripture readings would be gabbled by all four at the same time, as if they were in a hurry to finish with the sick person as quickly as possible." Derisive criticism regarding the gifts may be found in another Athenian story as well, "The Suicide." There, however, they are not expressed as the opinions of the author, which suggests that he does not accept them. Rather, they are presented as the thoughts of a lonely figure, Sakellarios, who was in despair and was considering suicide: "When the prayers are commodities, perhaps they have no other value than that of money? Perhaps Paradise can also be bought, like everything else?" *Ápanta*, vol. 4:633–634.

[47]"The Monk," *Ápanta*, vol. 2:325. [*The Boundless Garden*, 159.]

[48]"Priests of the Cities and Priests of the Villages," *Ápanta*, vol. 5:193.

[49]These views of his are recorded in his story, "The Monk." *Ápanta*, vol. 2:315–342.

[50]*Ápanta*, vol. 4:397.

[51]*Ápanta*, ibid.

[52]"The Quintals," *Ápanta*, vol. 4:407.

[53]See "Father Dionysios," *Ápanta*, vol. 5:330.

[54]Ibid., 329.

[55]"Papa-Adamantios Oikonomos," *Ápanta*, vol. 5:332–333.

[56]"The Monk," *Ápanta*, vol. 2:329–330. [*The Boundless Garden*, 164.]

[57]See *Ápanta*, vol. 4:131–134.

[58]See G. Patronos, *Ekklisía kai Kósmos* (Athens, 1983), 26–27.

[59]"The Little Star," *Ápanta*, vol. 4:308.

[60]Ibid.

[61]*Ápanta*, vol. 4:350.

[62]See Matthew 20:25-28: "You know that the rulers of the Gentiles lord it over them, and those who are great exercise authority over them. Yet it shall not be so among you; but whoever desires to become great among you, let him be your servant. And whoever desires to be first among you, let him be your slave—just as the Son of Man did not come to be served, but to serve, and to give His life a ransom for many."

[63]See, in particular, the stories to which we referred above, "The Monk" and "The Visit of the Holy Bishop."

[64]2 Timothy 2:15.

[65]"Attend, O Lord Jesus Christ our God, out of Thy holy dwelling-place, from the throne of glory of Thy Kingdom; and come to sanctify us, O Thou who sittest on high with the Father, and art here invisibly present with us," Prayer, after the diptychs of the Divine Liturgy of St. John Chrysostom (South Canaan, Pa: St. Tikhon's Seminary Press, 1977), 75.

[66]St. John Chrysostom, *Commentary on the Epistle to the Philippians*, PG 62, 204.

[67]Ibid.

[68]John 21:16.

[69]*Merchants of the Nations, Ápanta*, vol. 1:139.

[70]See "Holy Week in Athens," *Ápanta*, vol. 5:332–333.

[71]In the story, "Songs of God," during the funeral of Nicholas Boukas's child Koula, these professional priests "chanted

customarily from the hymn 'Blameless in the way' up until the 'last kiss' [as at a normal service for an adult]. Only Papa-Nicholas, from St. John's in the field from Naxos, seemed to do be doing a separate service; he whispered to himself, and his eyes appeared to be full of tears." That is to say, he recited the appropriate service for the repose of children. See *Ápanta*, vol. 4:393–394.

[72]Matthew 9:36.

[73]"Theophany," *Ápanta*, vol. 5:140–141.

[74]"Fey Folk," *Ápanta*, vol. 2:499. [*The Boundless Garden*, 248.]

Chapter 3

[1]St. John Chrysostom, *Homily on the Ascension of Christ*, 12, PG 52, 784D.

[2]St. John Chrysostom, *Homily on Second Corinthians*, 5, PG 61, 427D–428A.

[3]See John Karmiris, *Í Thésis kai i Diakonía tón Laikón en tí Orthodóxo Ekklisía* (Athens, 1976), 36.

[4]See, relatedly, I Corinthians 12:18-31.

[5]Clement of Rome, *1 Letter to the Corinthians*, 40, 75–76, PG 1, 289A.

[6]Romans 12:4-5.

[7]*Oration*, 32, 11, PG 36, 185B.

[8]"A Pilgrimage to the Kastro," *Ápanta*, vol. 2:284. [*The Boundless Garden*, 114.]

[9]"Poor Saint," *Ápanta*, vol. 2:213.

[10]"Easter Chanter," *Ápanta*, vol. 2:518. [*The Boundless Garden*, 269.]

[11]Ibid., 524. [*The Boundless Garden*, 274.]

[12]"Sweet Kiss," *Ápanta*, vol. 3:77-78.

[13]"*Parakolouthoúnton*": The replacement of the participle "ones approaching" ("*proselthónton*") or "ones participating" ("*metechónton*") with the participle "ones following/watching" ("*parakolouthoúnton*") in the commemoration during the Great Entrance of the Divine Liturgy is not only anti-canonical (see John Foundoulis, *Apantíseis eis Leitourgikás Aporías III* [Thessalonica, 1976], 90–91), but also displays a mistaken understanding of the place of laymen in the Church and a distortion of our understanding of the Divine Liturgy.

[14]"Halasohorides," *Ápanta*, vol. 2:425. In another place in the story, it is recorded that "Uncle Anagnostis had not ceased concelebrating with Papa-Soteris for fifty years." Ibid., 426.

[15]"Easter Chanter," *Ápanta*, vol. 2:517. [*The Boundless Garden*, 268, 273.]

[16]Ibid., 528. [*The Boundless Garden*, 273.]

[17]Ibid., 522. [*The Boundless Garden*, 273.]

[18]Ibid., 523. [*The Boundless Garden*, 274.]

[19]Ibid., 513. [*The Boundless Garden*, 263.]

[20]"A Village Easter," *Ápanta*, vol. 2:126. [*The Boundless Garden*, 22.]

[21]"Roman Easter," *Ápanta*, vol. 2:178.

[22]"A Village Easter," *Ápanta*, vol. 2:132–133. [*The Boundless Garden*, 29.]

[23]Ibid. [*The Boundless Garden*, 29.]

[24]Ibid. [*The Boundless Garden*, 29.]

[25]It is from the katavasia of the third canticle of the Canon of Nativity, a poem of Cosmas, bishop of Maïoumas.

[26]From the same canon, canticle eight, fourth troparion.

[27]"A Pilgrimage to the Kastro," *Ápanta*, vol. 2:287.

[28]"Reverie of the Fifteenth of August," *Ápanta*, vol. 4:92.

[29]"At Saint Anastasa's," *Ápanta*, vol. 2:346. [*The Boundless Garden*, 182.]

[30]"The Monk," *Ápanta*, vol. 2:327-328. [*The Boundless Garden*, 162.] This is the situation today in many communities outside Greece, while in Greece it has been addressed. That said, the vainglory and vanity that Papadiamandis discerned in his day continues to characterize the ethos of many wardens today.

[31]"Holy Week in Athens," *Ápanta*, vol. 5:99–100.

[32]"Without a Wedding Crown," *Ápanta*, vol. 3:134.

[33]"The Epitaphios and the Resurrection in the Villages," *Ápanta*, vol. 5:119.

[34]"Ecclesiastical Discourses and Studies," *Ápanta*, vol. 5:143–144.

[35]References to co-workers in the pastoral service of the Church are found especially in the Apostle Paul, particularly in his Letter to the Romans 16:3, 9, and 21.

[36]"The Last One Baptized," *Ápanta*, vol. 2:89–90.

[37]"The Unchurched," *Ápanta*, vol. 3:527.

[38]Ibid.

[39]Ibid., 528.

[40]"The Teacher," *Ápanta*, vol. 4:147.

[41]Ibid., 148.

[42]Ibid.

[43]Ibid., Compare 1 Timothy 6:5.

[44]Ibid.

[45]It is worth noting that Papadiamandis refers to a few such laymen: G. Laganopoulos, "who seems to have a gift of rhetoric, and who, if he looked into the study of the great Fathers, would become distinguished" (see "Great Week in Athens," *Ápanta*, vol. 5:177-178), and also Ignatius Moschakis, distinguished preacher of the divine word, whom Papadiamandis recommends to the church council of the church of St. Eirini in Athens, to take on as a regular preacher. See "Ecclesiastical Discourses and Studies," *Ápanta*, vol. 5:143.

[46]Metropolitan Dionysios (Psarianos) of Kozani, *Oikodomí* (Kozani, 1964), 29–30.

[47]See *Ápanta*, vol. 3:575-576.

[48]In a series of articles entitled "Holy Week in Athens," which were first published in the Spring of 1892 in the newspaper *Akrópoli*, Papadiamandis alludes to certain "prominent theologians, who transferred the religious gatherings to an auditorium of a brotherhood." *Ápanta*, vol. 5:178.

[49]Ibid., Compare Metropolitan Dionysios (Psarianos) of Kozani, (in: *Oikodomí*, 4th year [1962], booklet 37) where seventy years later, using the same ecclesiastical criteria, the same conclusions are reached, "Many powerful things are taught in the brotherhoods, most of them, however, are outside the spirit, the tradition, the worship, and the experience of the Church, which is the experience of Saints, of obedience, and hardship."

[50]"The Lady Supporter of Makrakis," *Ápanta*, vol. 4:158.

[51]Ibid., 160.

[52]Ibid.

[53]The first, called "The Makrakian Episode in Skiathos," was published without his signature in the newspaper Akrópoli on July 30, 1891, while the other, "Final Response to *The Word*" was published in the August 20-21, 1891 edition of the newspaper *Tó Ásty* with the signature, "Alex. Papadiamandis."

[54]Apostolos Makrakis is characterized as "a silver-tongued sophist," "a deceitful orator," and "a quick-witted chatterbox." See *Ápanta*, vol. 5:163–164.

[55]Panagiotis Moullas gives this interpretation in *A. Papadiamánti, Autoviographiká* (Athens: Érmi Publications, 1974), 61–62.

[56]See Nicholas D. Triandaphilopoulos, *Daimónio Mesimvrinó, Énteka Keímena giá tón Papadiamánti* (Athens, 1978), 36.

[57]"Final Response to *The Word*," *Ápanta*, vol. 5:165. Compare John 8:7 and St. John Chrysostom, *Commentary on St. Paul's Letter to the Ephesians*, Preface, PG 62, 10.

[58]"Fey Folk," *Ápanta*, vol. 2:499. [*The Boundless Garden*, 248.]

[59]"Ecclesiastical Discourses and Studies," *Ápanta*, vol. 5:144. Compare Christos Yiannaras, *Orthodoxía kaí Dýsi stí Neóteri Elláda* (Athens: Dómos Publications, 1992), 355.

[60]Ibid.

[61]St. John Chrysostom, *Homily on St. Paul's First Letter to the Corinthians*, 1, 1, PG 61, 13.

[62]*Ápanta*, vol. 4:317.

[63]*Ápanta*, vol. 4:319.

[64]"Ecclesiastical Rhetoricians and the Holy Synod." *Ápanta*, vol. 5:147–148.

[65]Ibid.

[66]"Theophany," *Ápanta*, vol. 5:140–141.

[67]Romans 1:7.

[68]See George Mantzaridis, *Christianikí Ithikí*, 3rd ed. (Thessalonica, 1991), 147.

[69]*Petition of Completion*, in the Divine Liturgy.

[70]This is a theme that is repeated throughout the services of the *Triodion*, which is used during the penitential services of Lent.

[71]Matthew 13:47.

[72]See paragraph 6, PG 2, 1176A-C.

[73]See *Mystagogy*, 2, PG 91, 668C, where the Church is type and image "of the whole world, which consists of beings seen and unseen."

[74]"At Saint Anastasa's," *Ápanta*, vol. 2:353. [*The Boundless Garden*, 190.]

[75]St. John Chrysostom, *Homily on St. Paul's Letter to the Ephesians*, 9, 3 PG 62, 72.

[76]"Watchman at the Quarantine Colony," *Ápanta*, vol. 2:576.

[77]"Without a Wedding Crown," *Ápanta*, vol. 3:133.

[78]"The Wedding of Karahmet," *Ápanta*, vol. 4:507.

[79]"Humble Saint," *Ápanta*, vol. 2:221, 225.

[80]"The Witches," *Ápanta*, vol. 3:240.

[81]"A Drop of Water…," *Ápanta*, vol. 4:123–124.

[82]See "Disenchantress," *Ápanta*, vol. 3:307. In a similar way, Papadiamandis also accepts the guileless Apostolos ("Kakomis," *Ápanta*, vol. 3:557–564).

[83]"Lights All Alight," *Ápanta*, vol. 3:39.

[84]"The American," *Ápanta*, vol. 2:259–260. [*The Boundless Garden*, 88.]

Chapter 4

[1]*Apparatus fontium or testimonia*, as they have come to be called.

[2]See Nicholas D. Triandaphilopoulos, "Prologue," *Ápanta*, vol. 1:xxii.

[3]It is rightly pointed out by his publisher that "he knew these things better than he knew the palm of his hand," *Ápanta*, vol. 1:xvii. For more regarding the use of Holy Scripture in the texts of Papadiamandis, see Apostolos Zorba's unpublished doctoral dissertation, *I Glóssa tís Agías Graphís kaí tón Leitourgikón Vivlíon stó Érgo toú Papadiamánti* (Athens, 1991).

[4]1 Kings 18:26.

[5]"The Witches," *Ápanta*, vol. 3:243.

[6]See, characteristically, "Holy and Great Week," *Ápanta*, vol. 5:90.

[7]An example is found in *Merchants of the Nations*, where he refers to a large section of the Six Psalms. (The Six Psalms are composed of Psalms 3, 37, 62, 87, 102, and 142, and are read daily at the beginning of Matins. [Tr.]) *Ápanta*, vol. 1:320, 321, and 323. Regarding the publishing difficulties concerning these verses in the first publications, as well as in earlier editions, see Nicholas D. Triandaphilopoulos, "Mikrí Simeíosi giá tón Exápsalmo stoús Empórous tón Ethnón," *Epopteía*, December 1979, 997. Regarding the similar corruption of the passage "Give instruction to a wise man, and he will be yet wiser," from Proverbs 9:9, which is recorded in the story, "The Hidden Wall" (*Ápanta*, vol. 4:167), see also Triandaphilopoulos, "Prologue" *Ápanta*, vol. 1:xviii, xix, where it is characteristically pointed out that Papadiamandis "was a chanter from his childhood years and had read [this passage] in the readings of Vespers an infinite number of times."

[8]*Ápanta*, vol. 2:569.

[9]Mark 12:9 and Luke 20:16.

[10]*Ápanta*, vol. 2:572.

[11]Matthew 12:45 and Luke 11:26.

[12]See Mark 3:4 and Luke 6:9.

[13]"Haramados," *Ápanta*, vol. 3:657. Compare Matthew 12:8, Mark 2:28, and Luke 6:5.

[14]With the ease of a masterful piper, he acts as does his hero— "he took out his pipe and began to play whatever tune came immediately to mind." ("The Fallen Dervish," *Ápanta*, vol. 3:114.) The flute, "by two specks, is different, from the 'Yes,' which Christ said. The 'Yes': gentle, humble, meek. The 'Yes':...the one that loves man." (*Ápanta*, vol. 3:115.) (Papadiamandis is making a play on words here, as the word for flute in Greek, *náï*, and the word for yes, *naí*, are very close. [Tr.]) This is unquestionably a reference recalled from the Gospel (Luke 10:21, "even so [*naí*], Father; for so it seemed good in thy sight.") and from the Apostle Paul (2 Corinthians 1:19, "For the Son of God, Jesus Christ, who was preached among you by us...was not yea and nay, but in him was yea.") The "gentle, humble, meek...'Yes' of love for man" refers to the loving answer of the One Who "emptied himself," "humbled himself, and became obedient unto death, even the death of the cross." (Philippians 2:8.) He is meek, as He who said to the wearied and heavily burdened, "Learn of me; for I am meek and lowly in heart." (Matthew 11:29.) Undoubtedly, He is the Lover of man, for with Christ's affirmation to the plan of salvation, the theosis of man is realized.

The comparison of the "flute" (*náï*) with the "yes" (*naí*) of Christ is a classic example of Papadiamandis's assimilation and use of Holy Scripture and creates an opening in his text through which his liturgical and truly traditional wealth of knowledge and experience flows. The text continues as follows:

Down in the depths, in the pit, in the gulch, as the murmur of a stream in the current, a voice rising from the deep, as myrrh, as dew, as mist, lamentation, pathos, melody, arising on a downy evening breeze, raised up enchantment, meek, smooth, guileless, a whisper, supple, climbing to the gusts, attuned to the winds, reflecting the vastness, beseeching the infinite, childlike, innocent, twisting, the voice of a virgin singing dirges, a whimpering fowl in agony, yearning for the return of Spring. ("The Fallen Dervish," *Ápanta*, vol. 3:115.) The depths, the pit, and the gulch recall the descent into Hades, to the kingdom of death, into which Christ descended so as to pull up fallen Adam, man. Many of the characterizations given to the voice rising from the deep—as lamentation, pathos, and the voice of a virgin singing dirges—seek to evoke the same imagery of Christ's descent. Even the whimpering fowl in agony, yearning for the return of Spring is not so very different from the voice of the turtledove of the Song of Solomon, [Song of Solomon 2:11-12] or from the sweet spring of the *Lamentations* of the *Epitaphios Lamentation* (the service of lamentations sung around Christ's funeral bier by Orthodox Christians on Holy Friday. [Tr.]) (For all these aspects, see Kaitis Chiotellis, "Synomilóntas mé tón 'Xepesméno Dervísi,'" *Phóta Olóphota*, ed. Nicholas D. Triandaphilopoulos (Athens: E.L.I.A. Publications, 1981), 364–365, where along with this he also sees a possible reference to Oedipus on the Column. See also, Lampros Kamberidis, "Ávras Leptís Enkálesma," ibid., 207-231 and Lampros Kamberidis, *Tó Náï, tó Glykí, tó Práon* (Athens: Dómos Publications, 1982.)

[15]"The Gypsy Girl," *Ápanta*, vol. 1:497.

[16]"Athens as an Eastern City," *Ápanta*, vol. 5:272.

[17]Ibid.

[18]*Address to Evtropios*, PG 52, 391D. He refers to the same text in the story, "Social Harmony," *Ápanta*, vol. 4:142.

[19]"The Monk," *Ápanta*, vol. 2:318.

[20]"Reverie of the Fifteenth of August," *Ápanta*, vol. 4:90. He also makes reference to the words of St. Gregory the Theologian's *Epitaphios Address for Basil the Great* (see "Black Scarf Rock," Ápanta, vol. 2:166).

[21]"My St. George!" *Ápanta*, vol. 5:188–189.

[22]Compare *Néos Evergetinós*, by Archimandrite Gabriel of Dionysiou, Volos, 1954, second edition, 9-10.

[23]"Love on the Precipice," *Ápanta*, vol. 4:486.

[24]*Ápanta*, vol. 2:611.

[25]"Holy and Dead," *Ápanta*, vol. 3:123.

[26]"Lonely Tomb," *Ápanta*, vol. 4:363; see also the entries in the *Synaxarion* for Saints Andronicos and Athanasios (*Menaion*, 9th of October).

[27]Some of these stories include "Sweet Kiss," "Homesick," and, particularly, "Eros-Hero." The latter, in fact, describes the battle of St. George with the demon and reminds the reader of similar battles fought by the desert fathers, recorded in the *Gerontikon*, the *Lausiac History*, the *Spiritual Meadow*, and the *Evergetinos*.

[28]"The Furnace," *Ápanta*, vol. 4:206.

[29]Ibid., 207. Compare *Parakletike*, Mode 1, Friday morning, Canon of the Cross and Resurrection, hirmos, 7th canticle.

[30]Ibid.

[31]"The Fairy in the Tree," *Ápanta*, vol. 4:211. Compare 3rd Hour, Great Friday, second idiomelon.

[32]Ibid., 214; see also the Canon of Easter, 3rd canticle, 2nd troparion.

[33]*Ápanta*, vol. 2:330-32, 340. In a similar way, in "A Different Type" Papadiamandis adapts and imbeds passages from the Psalms and hymns of the Church into his narratives (*Ápanta*, vol. 3:595). A deep knowledge of hymnology and ecclesiastical language is confirmed in all the works of our author, particularly in his three articles entitled, "Ecclesiastical Editions in Athens," *Ápanta*, vol. 5:215–225.

[34]Considering, for example, the hymnology of Nativity, he determines the antiquity of the feast from the influence that texts of the Fathers had on the festal hymns prior to St. John Chrysostom. For example, he refers to the hymn, "Christ is born, glorify Him, Christ from the heavens, meet Him, Christ on earth, let us arise," which is taken word for word from the festal sermon of St. Gregory the Theologian for this feast. See "Nativity," *Ápanta*, vol. 5:134.

[35]*Ápanta*, vol. 4:390–391.

[36]Ibid.

[37]Ibid.

[38]"Holy and Great Week," *Ápanta*, vol. 5:90. Compare Prodromos Akanthopoulos, *Kódikas Ierón Kanónon*, 40, 150.

[39]*Ápanta*, vol. 5:90.

[40]*Ápanta*, vol. 2:85.

[41]This issue appears in "The Widowed Priest's Wife," where the authority of the folk tradition overshadows that of the Church's

canonical tradition. "It seems certain that no canon is recorded in *The Rudder* that forbids widowed priests' wives to re-marry. But [the people] regarded the superstition and the tradition, both composed together, as having essentially equal weight as an apostolic or synodal canon." *Ápanta*, vol. 2:85.

[42]"The Widowed Priest's Wife," *Ápanta*, vol. 2:86.

[43]"At St. Anastasa's," *Ápanta*, vol. 2:353. Papadiamandis's position regarding the canons also appears in his stories "The Orphan," "Alone Among Strangers," and "The Promiscuous One." See *Ápanta*, vol. 4:59, 83-84, and 350, respectively. [*The Boundless Garden*, 190.]

[44]See "Carnival Night," *Ápanta*, vol. 2:310–311.

[45]He addresses this, for example, through the events of the service of the submerging of the Venerable Cross on the day of Theophany, which are recounted in "The Invalid," *Ápanta*, vol. 2:111.

[46]"St. Basil's Day," *Ápanta*, vol. 5:137.

[47]In this work of St. Basil's, among other things, he encourages young people to take their studies seriously, so that they might become useful members of the Church and society. [Tr.] Ibid., 137-138. Compare Basil the Great, *Admonition To Young People, That They Might be Benefited by Greek Letters*, PG 31, 564-569.

[48]Ibid.

[49]In his analysis of the phrase "the rising of all risings" [literally, "the east of easts," where "east" in Greek refers to the rising of the sun [Tr.]] that is found in the exaposteilarion of Nativity, he writes, "I have heard that this final phrase, written in few letters, was privileged to inspire great enthusiasm in our friends in Caesarea of Cappadocia, who though they had lost the purity of their language, in their heart and *phrónima* were Greek, and were justifiably proud saying that 'the light comes from the East.'" "Nativity," *Ápanta*, vol. 5:134.

[50]If the story "The Reverberation of the Mind" is presented as a challenge to our general convictions as regards Jewish people, "The Fallen Dervish" will touch the bounds of impiety, if the story is studied based on a conception of "patriotic" or "religious" piety and tradition that is not Orthodox. From the perspective of chauvinistic patriotism, the story—and it is not the first time in Papadiamandis's writing—offers some Cavafian

sarcasm regarding the rhetorical patriotism of the nationalism of the time, when he makes Theseus recognize the love song of the Dervish as his own song, both from "the centuries of slavery," as well as "from the years of prosperity." (*Ápanta*, vol. 3:115) "The heavy walls and the thick columns of Theseus, the magnificent roof, were not startled by the voice, from that tune. They remembered the voice; they recognized it. And they had once heard it. Both during the centuries of slavery and during the years of prosperity." Compare Nikos Fokas, "I Anorthódoxos Klímaka," *Mnimósino toú Aléx. Papadiamánti* (Athens, 1971), 163. For "The Reverberation of the Mind" see *Ápanta*, vol. 4:367–380. The story is half-finished, however, and for this reason whatever reference to, or even more, whatever conclusion as to its general tone should be formulated with a certain reservation.

[51]The heretics who take advantage of this situation are "grazing on the scarred and wounded body of the East." See "The Monk," *Ápanta*, vol. 2:335. Elsewhere, with overflowing sadness he sums up the wretched situation and the heresies riddling the East: "The destitute East existed then, as now, and always…as a fenceless vineyard." ("The Watchman at the Quarantine Colony," *Ápanta*, vol. 2:569.)

[52]"Nativity," *Ápanta*, vol. 5:133 Compare PG 49, 351–362.

[53]Ibid.

[54]"Great Week in Athens," *Ápanta*, vol. 5:181.

[55]*I Pápissa Ioánna* (Galaxias Publications), 55.

[56]"The Dance at Mr. Periandros's," *Ápanta*, vol. 4:14-15.

[57]*Ápanta*, vol. 4:429.

[58]*Ápanta*, vol. 2:516. [*The Boundless Garden*, 266-267.]

[59]8th canticle, 3rd troparion, *Ápanta*, vol. 5:48.

[60]*The Gypsy Girl*, *Ápanta*, vol. 1:496. For more, see Zisimos Lorenzatos, "Aléxandros Papadiamántis–Penínta Chrónia apó tó Thánató tou," *O Tachidrómos* 7, no. 1 (1961), which was re-published in a revised form in the volume, *Aléxandros Papadiamántis*, prologue and ed., Nicholas D. Triandaphilopoulos (Athens, 1979), 214.

[61]Athanasios of Paros, one of the most important *Kollyvádes* Fathers and a nourisher of the Skiathan scribe, is an example of a person who knew how to discern the things of Europe. The titles of two of his works are characteristic: "Response to the illogical zeal of those philosophers coming from Europe" [*Antiphónisis*

prós tón Parólogon Zílon tón apó tís Evrópin Erchoménon Filosóphon] and "Very beneficial admonition to those knowingly sending their sons to Europe for financial gain" [*Paraínesis ophelimotáti prós toús Adeós Pémpontas toús Yioús ton eis tín Evrópin Xárin Pragmateías*].

[62]"The Two Monsters," *Ápanta*, vol. 4:317.

[63]See, written by the first, *Istoría Ellinikís Logotechnía*, and by the second, "Papadiamántis, Thrýlos kaí Pragmatikótis," *Aphiéroma Néas Estías stón Papadiamánti* (Christmas 1941), 24–28. Compare Nicholas D. Triandaphilopoulos, *Daimónio Mesimvrinó* (Athens, 1978), 37.

[64]"At St. Anastasa's," *Ápanta*, vol. 2:347. [*The Boundless Garden*, 183-184.]

[65]Compare *The Iliad*, 600:60.

[66]Psalm 71(70):9, 18.

[67]"Reverie of the Fifteenth of August," *Ápanta*, vol. 4:97.

[68]Ibid.

[69]See *Menaion* for August 29, Canon of the feast (of the beheading of the Honorable Forerunner) canticle 9, troparion 3.

[70]"A Drop of Water…," *Ápanta*, vol. 4:125. Compare *The Iliad*, 600:29-31. The same fantastic synthesis and personal experience of the diachronicity and unity of the tradition in Papadiamandis is witnessed to by the following passage from the story "The Rose-Tinted Shores," *Ápanta*, vol. 4:226, "And the gates of heaven bellowed as they flew open of their own accord—gates over which the Hours preside" (trans, Samuel Butler, University of Chicago, *Encyclopedia Britannica* 1952, 37.) (*The Iliad*, Book 5, 749, Th. 393). Let us leave the ancients, and let us chant with Cosmas the divinely sweet, "The seasons bowed down before Thy face: for at Thy feet the sun laid its light…O Christ" (Cosmas of Maïoumas, Canon for the Transfiguration of Christ, canticle 5, canon 1, troparion 1) (*The Festal Menaion*, trans. Mother Mary, Archimandrite (now Metropolitan) Kallistos Ware [South Canaan, PA: St. Tikhon's Seminary Press, 1990]).

[71]"Most wonderful hymns [more wonderful than any musical instrument]

Which God, which hero,
Which man shall we glorify?"

["*Anaxiphórminges ýmnoi,
tína Theón, tín' íroa
tín ándra keladísomen?*"

Pindar Olymp. 2, 1-2 (Snell).]

[72]"Voice of a Subtle Breeze," *Ápanta*, vol. 5:233.

[73]Ibid.

[74]From the newspaper, *Tó Ásty*, March 26-27, 1893. It was reprinted in G. K. Katsimbalis, *Aléxandros Papadiamántis: I. Prótes Kríseis kaí Plirophoríes II. Symplíroma Vivliographías* (reprint) (Athens: E.L.I.A. Publications, Athens, 1991, 38-39.)

[75]"Language and Society," *Ápanta*, vol. 5:296.

[76]G. Baleta, *Ápanta*, vol. 5:648.

[77]Demetrios Balanos, for example, is scandalized—completely unjustifiably for a Patrologist—by Papadiamandis's referral to St. Kyriakos as a "three-year old child" [*trietízon paidíon*] in the story "A Pilgrimage to the Kastro." See *Ápanta*, vol. 2:294. Balanos forgets that Papadiamandis's linguistic boldness echoes the much greater boldness of the hymnographer, who refers to the Panagia as a "three-year old girl." See the *Menaion*, November 21.

[78]See Nicholas D. Triandaphilopoulos, *Daimónio Mesimvrinó* (Athens, 1978), 45. The same spiritual ancestry, Byzantine, is brought into our literary world by N. Eggonopoulos and Nicholas G. Pentzikis, and this ancestry characterizes their expression.

[79]See, *Tó Ágion Óros kaí i Paideía toú Génous mas* (text of the Holy Community of the Holy Mountain) (the Holy Mountain, 1984), 18.

[80]In the stories "The Fallen Dervish" and "My Living Coffin," we see the etymological meeting of *The Iliad* and works of Evstathios of Thessalonica with Sanskrit and Indo-European sources. [See *Parekvolés stín Iliáda*] (1483, 48), where it is noted that "the place where the wind passes through is called a courtyard," and where the flute [*avlós*] is referred to as "an instrument by which spirit passes through." The Aeolian "*ávpr*" (*ávra, avlí, avlós*) –*aír*, derives etymologically from the Sanskrit particle "va," which basically means air and wind. The meanings of *ávra, avlós*, and *avli* are contained one within the other, while the musical affinity that unites them is self-evident to Papadiamandis, knowledgeable as he was of cryptic interrelations. We encounter similar analogous interrelations in Seferis. In "Cappadocian Monasteries Cut from Stone," Papadiamandis mentions that he saw shepherds playing their pipes at the birth of Christ, as in the iconography of Nativity. The iconographer, in his ignorance or wisdom, translates "*agravloúntes*" ["those living in the field"] from the canticle, which

originally meant "*avlízomai*" in the fields, that is to sleep outdoors, with "*avlízoun*," to play their pipes in the fields. The iconographer shared Papadiamandis's desire to glorify God in song, as expressed in lines from "Sweet Kiss" commemorating the courts of the Lord. (See Lampros Kamberidis, "Ávras Leptís Engálesma," 228-229.) In a paraphrase of the Psalms of David, he mentions these courts of the Lord:

> And again I made as though to come my Christ, to Thy courts,
> To duck into Thy thrice-beloved threshold,
> Which my soul insatiably desires.
> ...
> My flesh and heart glory in being near Thee.
> The nightingale found a nest, the tortoise a shelter,
> In which to put their young. The poor ones are put down on
> Thy sacred altar, my eternal Christ.
> ...
> Better a day in Thy courts, than thousands
> In the shadow; may I be as a cast-out from Thy temple,
> Better, than to live in a sinful dwelling.
> (*Ápanta*, vol. 3:74–75.)

The source of inspiration is noted by its own creator, "All the lines are a paraphrase from the Eighty-Third Psalm, which begins, 'How cherished art Thy dwellings, O Lord of hosts; my soul longeth and fainteth for the courts of the LORD'" (*Ápanta*, vol. 3:74–75.] It is a Psalm that was very familiar to the faithful Skiathan churchgoer, as it is read in church every afternoon during the 9th Hour, before Vespers.

[81]See Kamberidis, Ibid., 228-229.

[82]All three are found in Volume 1 of *Ápanta*.

[83]Compare the *Menaion* of December 25, Doxastikon of Vespers.

[84]"Priests of the Cities and Priests of the Villages," *Ápanta*, vol. 5:198.

Chapter 5

[1]2 Timothy 2:10.

[2]1 Corinthians 13:12.

[3]1 Corinthians 14:40.

[4]See *Triodion*, apolytikion of Matins, Monday of the first week of the fast.

[5]This Athonite liturgical typicon had the Jerusalem typicon of St. Savvas as its foundation and starting point.

[6]*Ápanta*, vol. 4:419-420.

[7]*Ápanta*, vol. 4:478-479.

[8]*Ápanta*, vol. 2:325-326. [*The Boundless Garden*, 159.]

[9]"Easter Chanter," *Ápanta*, vol. 2:325-326. [*The Boundless Garden*, 285.]

[10]*Ápanta*, vol. 2:529, 534. [*The Boundless Garden*, 285.]

[11]See "Fey Folk," *Ápanta*, vol. 2:496-497. [*The Boundless Garden*, 245.]

[12]Ibid.

[13]"The Watchman at the Quarantine Colony," *Ápanta*, vol. 2:496-497.

[14]Ibid.

[15]See John Foundoulis, "Leitourgikí Zoí," *Simonópetra*, (Athens: ETBA Publications, 1991), 132.

[16]"Burdened Bones," *Ápanta*, vol. 4:221. Compare, in the *Pentekostarion*, Saturday of the Souls before Pentecost, Service of the All-Night Vigil, canticle 1, troparion 1.

[17]*Ápanta*, vol. 2:127.

[18]*Ápanta*, vol. 3:644.

[19]See the stories, "A Pilgrimage to the Kastro," "Fey Folk," and, "Delisiphero."

[20]"A Village Easter," "The Unchurched," "At St. Anastasa's," and "Easter Chanter." It is characteristic that in two of these, "A Village Easter" and "The Unchurched," Papadiamandis speaks of the "Good Word," meaning the *Catechetical Sermon* of St. John Chrysostom, which is read during the Easter Divine Liturgy.

[21]"Fey Folk," *Ápanta*, vol. 2:497. [*The Boundless Garden*, 246.]

[22]Ibid. [*The Boundless Garden*, 246.]

[23]*Ápanta*, vol. 4:528-529.

[24]*Ápanta*, vol. 4:91-92.

[25]*Ápanta*, vol. 4:92-95.

[26]"A Different Type," *Ápanta*, vol. 3:591.

[27]*Ápanta*, vol. 4:610.

[28]It was first published in the newspaper, *Akrópoli*, 28 March 1894, and was reprinted in *Néa Estía*, Christmas 1934, and was also included in *Aléxandros Papadiamántis*, Prologue and Selection

by Nicholas D. Triandaphilopoulos (Athens, 1979), 17-23.

[29]Nicholas D. Triandaphilopoulos, "Prologue," 10.

[30]See "Gerasimos Vokos, Agrypmnía eis tón Ágion Elissaíon," *Aléxandros Papadiamántis* (Athens, 1979), 18-19.

[31]It was first published in the newspaper *Phórminx*, 15-31 March 1908, and was reprinted in 1979 in the same volume as above, on pages 53-55.

[32]"*Aléxandros Papadiamántis*, Prologue and Selection" by Nicholas D. Triandaphilopoulos (Athens, 1979), 53.

[33]It was first published in the newspaper *Phórminx*, 15-31 December 1910. The beginning of the article witnesses to the fact that it was written after the repose of Papadiamandis (3 January 1911). Apparently the printing of the newspaper was late. It was reprinted in 1979 in the above volume, 59-63.

[34]Ibid., 61.

[35]The opinion that Papadiamandis most likely knew Byzantine music [that is, not only practically, but theoretically, with the ability to read Byzantine music notes] was developed by Angelos Mantas, with his presentation (not yet published) at the Conference: *Aléxandros Papadiamántis kaí i Epochí tou*, 4 and 5 May 1989, organized by the Greek Ministry of Culture within the framework of the exhibitions of *Politistikó Aigaío III*.

[36]St. Nicholas Kavasilas, *On the Life in Christ*, 4, PG 150, 581A.

[37]See the Prayer of the Bowing of the Head after the sanctification of the holy gifts. "Do Thou, o Lord, make the present offering, to ease the path of each of us toward the good, each according to his need; sail with those who sail, accompany those that travel, heal the sick, Thou Who art the Physician of our souls and bodies."

[38]See, for example, Cyril of Jerusalem, *Catechisms* 10, PG 33, 665AB, "But the Savior comes in various forms to each man for his profit. For to those who have need of gladness He becomes a Vine; and to those who want to enter in He stands as a Door; and to those who need to offer up their prayers He stands as a mediating High Priest. Again, to those who have sins He becomes a Sheep, that He may be sacrificed for them. He is made all things to all men, remaining in His own nature what He is." [Translation: *The Nicene and Post-Nicene Fathers*, Second Series, ed. Philip Schaff, trans. Edward Hamilton Gifford (Peabody, MA: Hendrickson Publishers, 1995), vol. 7:58]

[39]Doxastikon of the Praises, *Menaion* of December 6. See also, Hieromonk Gregory, *I Theía Leitourgía, Schólia*, 2nd ed. (Athens: Domos Publications, 1985), 315–316. The same connection between material and spiritual petitions is expressed in the Prayer of the Bowing of the Head at the end of Matins, where the faithful ask God to give them "His worldly and otherworldly good things."

[40]*Mystagogy*, 1, PG 91, 668B.

[41]See, "Under the Royal Oak," *Ápanta*, vol. 3:328.

[42]Compare St. John Chrysostom, *Homily on the Gospel of St. John*, 46, PG 59, 260 and Cyril of Alexandria, *Interpretation of the Gospel of St. John* XI, 11, PG 74, 560.

[43]A great variety of liturgical references in Papadiamandis's works may be found in many of his stories. In "The Godmother" a Baptism is described and, later on, a funeral service for infants. [See *Ápanta*, vol. 3:588 and 590, respectively.] In "The Watchman at the Quarantine Colony" [*Ápanta*, vol. 2:551] and "Lonely Tomb" [*Ápanta*, vol. 4:361] the typicon of the burial service is recorded, while in "Sweet Kiss" mention is made of the Small Supplicatory Canon [*Ápanta*, vol. 3:87]. In "The Miracle of Kaisariani" the service of the blessing of the waters is mentioned [*Ápanta*, vol. 3:357], while "The Monk" provides nearly the whole service of monastic tonsure [*Ápanta*, vol. 2:317 and 331]. One last example is from the story "Holy and Dead," where the typicon of the blessing of the *kóllyva* "in honor of and in memory of the Saints [whose day was] being celebrated" [*Ápanta*, vol. 3:123–124] is described in great detail.

[44]*Merchants of the Nations, Ápanta*, vol. 1:229.

[45]Ibid.

[46]Ibid., 230. Similarly bold is his recommendation for the institution of the political marriage, when the necessary presuppositions for the reception of the grace of God, bestowed in the Mystery of marriage, are absent. See "Without a Wedding Crown," *Ápanta*, vol. 3:136, "But we aren't about to speak about society today. However, in the absence of another provision, Christian and ethical, at least to be consistent and logical, it is incumbent upon them to vote for the political marriage."

[47]Ibid., 230–231.

[48]See "Fortune from America," *Ápanta*, vol. 3:333, "Papa-Makarios the spiritual father suffers the same things on the eves of Nativity and Great Week.... Can a priest manage, as much strength as his prayer might have, to absolve them all from their sins with one prayer?"

[49]"Oh! The Little Heartbreakers," *Ápanta*, vol. 3:11–12.

[50]"A Village Easter," *Ápanta*, vol. 2:125. [*The Boundless Garden*, 21.]

[51]"The Death Agony," *Ápanta*, vol. 4:397.

[52]Ibid., 399.

[53]Ibid., 400–401.

[54]"Fey Folk," *Ápanta*, vol. 2:493.

[55]Ibid., 494.

[56]We could refer to other examples as well. For example, in the story "The Fairy in the Tree," the penance that Papa-Hesychios gives to Granny Kontonikaina is directed at her reunification with a certain Michael, whom she had cursed. [*Ápanta*, vol. 4:215.] This is also the goal of Aphentra's words to Granny Molota when the latter reveals, in confidence, her old—innocent—relationship with Uncle Kolia, the "unchurched one." Aphentra counsels her, "Ah, all right, you have found him now, at Easter. It's the hour of embracing, of love. May you be forgiven, tell it to the priest and he will let you partake [of Holy Communion]." ["The Unchurched," *Ápanta*, vol. 3:530.]

[57]"Delisiphero," *Ápanta*, vol. 3:643–644.

[58]*Ápanta*, vol. 4:530–531.

[59]*Ápanta*, vol. 3:596.

[60]"A Different Type," *Ápanta*, vol. 3:596.

[61]"The Hushing Up," *Ápanta*, vol. 4:593.

[62]Ibid.

[63]Ibid.

[64]See "Without a Wedding Crown," *Ápanta*, vol. 3:136.

[65]"The Visit of the Holy Bishop," *Ápanta*, vol. 4:132–133.

[66]Ibid., 133.

[67]See more on this topic in: Mantzaridis, *Eisagogí stín Ithikí* (Pournaras Publications, 1990), 118–119. See also Anastasios of Sinai, *Guide*, PG 89, 77C.

[68]Mantzaridis, Ibid., 119.

[69]Mark 2:27.

[70]See *Ápanta*, vol. 2:525–526. We also have a description of the priestly vestments in the story "Sweet Kiss," *Ápanta*, vol. 3:73.

[71]*Ápanta*, vol. 2:526. [*The Boundless Garden*, 277.]

[72]Ibid. [*The Boundless Garden*, 277.]

[73]*Ápanta*, vol. 3:584–585. Also see Hieromonk Gregory, *Tó Ágion Váptisma: Schólia*, (Athens, 1989), 60.

[74]"By and large, the directions of the typicon are not strictly kept in Athens." "Great Week in Athens," *Ápanta*, vol. 5:99.

[75]Ibid.

[76]"Great Week in Athens," *Ápanta*, vol. 5:99.

[77]Uncle Mark, in "A Different Type," had been a sea captain. He was the administrator of a small church in Athens and would read the Six Psalms, the fifteenth Psalm, the Creed, and so on. However, Papadiamandis expresses reservations as regards the authenticity of his reading tone: "He would read slowly, with measured emphasis, with seeming compunction and affliction. It was far from genuine however, far from the simple and plain ecclesiastical tone—an ancient tone reminiscent of the ancient Greek simplicity—which is cultivated on the Holy Mountain...." See *Ápanta*, vol. 3:592.

[78]"Only the wardens of the churches asserted their will, while the priests and chanters would disappear before them." See "Great Week in Athens," *Ápanta*, vol. 5:99.

[79]"The Epitaphios and the Resurrection in the Villages," *Ápanta*, vol. 5:120.

[80]Ibid., 121.

[81]Ibid.

[82]For example, we could recall the following verses: "I will never forget thy precepts: for with them thou hast quickened me. I rejoice at thy word, as one that findeth great spoil. Therefore I love thy commandments above gold and topaz. How sweet are thy words unto my taste! Yea, sweeter than honey to my mouth!" See Psalm 118 (119), verses 93, 162, 127, and 103, respectively.

[83]"Religious Celebrations," *Ápanta*, vol. 5:159.

[84]See *Ápanta*, vol. 2:130. [*The Boundless Garden*, 26-27.]

[85]See John Moschos, *Spiritual Meadow*, PG 87G, 2873B–D.

[86]"For Pride," *Ápanta*, vol. 3:212.

[87]This is the case with the Uniates, who keep the typicon of the Eastern Church but commemorate and commune with the Pope. While they appear to be Orthodox during the performance of the Divine Liturgy, their faith and life are far from the faith and ethos of Orthodoxy. "Papism, with hypocritical zeal and political calculation, proudly professes that, through its Uniate and other communities, it preserves the orthodoxy of faith and worship of the East with great care and zeal—communities that at the same time agree to commemorate the Pope." ["Great Week in Athens," *Ápanta*, vol. 5:181.] Papadiamandis denounces this position as schizophrenic, for he well knows where truth and substance lie and where the form becomes useless. Beyond the falsity and hypocrisy created by the practical absence of meaning and substance in the worship of the Uniates, another division prevailing in the West is revealed. This division is primarily expressed in Western theology and extends to their ethos of daily life. While there is an abundance of "eucharistic piety" in the West, there is, simultaneously, a difficulty in expressing the Eucharist theologically.

[88]The romantic and secretive character of worship found in the West is a result of its culture and its way of approaching God. This romanticism is foreign to Orthodox worship and to the architecture and adornment of Orthodox churches.

[89]"The Memorial Services and the Purgatorial Fire," *Ápanta*, vol. 5:167.

[90]Ibid.

[91]In the better known of these, such as "A Pilgrimage to the Kastro," "The Richly Decorated Icon of the Mother of God," "Reverie of the Fifteenth of August," "A Village Easter," "Easter Chanter," "At St. Anastasa's," and "Fey Folk," we can see justification for this characterization. The same is true of many of his lesser-known works, both short stories and articles.

[92]"Kosmolaitis," *Ápanta*, vol. 3:533.

[93]*Merchants of the Nations, Ápanta*, vol. 1:319.

[94]Psalm 33:9. Classic examples of the Church's approach to catechism through the liturgical life are the ancient mystagogical catechisms, which opened up their liturgical form for people who had first believed and known the actions of the divine worship

through personal participation. For this reason not only the form/symbol was offered, but also the meaning hidden within, "the mind [nous] of the service." The same method is followed by later Fathers and ecclesiastical writers with their commentaries on divine worship, such as Herman of Constantinople (*Oration 9*, PG 98, 221–383), Theodore of Anthidos (*Liturgical Commentary or On the Symbols and Mysteries of the Divine Liturgy*, PG 140, 417–468), St. Nicholas Kavasilas (*Interpretation of the Divine Liturgy*, PG 150, 368, and following), St. Mark Evgenikos of Ephesus (*On the Holy Eucharist*, PG 160, 1080, and following, and *Explanation of the Ecclesiastical Service*, PG 160, 1164, and following) and so on. The Fathers would begin from this well-known model, which is learned experientially through the life of the Church and move on to that which is symbolized. St. Symeon of Thessalonica is a characteristic example of a Father with the gift for teaching the theory and description of the form while offering an interpretation, so as to plumb the deeper meaning of our liturgical inheritance. (See his works, *Dialogue Against All Heresies*, PG 155, 33D–176C; *On the Holy Services*, PG 155, 176D and following; *On the Divine Liturgy*, PG 155, 253, and following; and *Responses*, PG 155, 829, and following.)

[95] *Ápanta*, vol. 5:80.

[96] In English this week is usually called "Bright Week." [Tr.] See "Bright Week," *Ápanta*, vol. 5:94.

[97] Ibid., 95.

[98] See "Great Week in Athens," *Ápanta*, vol. 5:97, where he explains why, from Great Monday on, "the book of Job begins to be read" during the Presanctified Liturgies.

[99] "Great Week in Athens," *Ápanta*, vol. 5:102.

[100] Ibid., 104.

[101] Ibid., 101.

[102] Ibid., 114–118.

[103] "Holy and Great Week," *Ápanta*, vol. 5:90.

[104] Ibid., 88.

[105] See Alexander Schmemann, *Introduction to Liturgical Theology* (Crestwood, NY: St. Vladimir Seminary Press, 1986) 9.

[106] Ibid.

Chapter 6

¹*Ápanta*, vol. 3:73–74.

²"At the Panagia of Kechrea," "To the Panagia of Kounistra," "To the Panagia of Doman," and "To the Little Panagia in the Turret," see *Ápanta*, vol. 5:30–35.

³"Sweet Kiss," *Ápanta*, vol. 3:75.

⁴Osios Poemen the ascetic is also there, whom the iconographer presented as holding a scroll, where the following words are written, "Poemen did not give birth to children," as well as his answer to Anthipatos, before he judged as regards the innocence or fatal judgment of his innocent nephew, "If you find him guilty, punish him; though if innocent, do as you like" [With the sense, "do as you should, I will not demand it," thus leaving the correct action to the conscience of the person. [Tr.]] Both are taken from the entry in the *Synaxarion* of the Saint (*Menaion*, August 27) and reveal the profound relationship between Orthodox iconography and the synaxarian tradition. In the consciousness of the faithful, in particular those of Skiathos, Osios Poemen was the guard of the innocent and of children.

⁵*Menaion*, August 29.

⁶Matthew 2:16.

⁷See "Sweet Kiss," *Ápanta*, vol. 3:76. Compare the *Menaion* of December 26. The relationship between hagiography and iconography, as well as between the *Synaxarion* and iconography, emerges in another of Papadiamandis's descriptions as well, where where we find the description of a "sweet and most pleasing icon of St. Kirykos, a three-year-old child held by the hand of his mother, St. Ioulitta." The persecutor, Alexandros, tries to tempt the child with gifts and sacrifices and, through the child, his mother. The child, however, shouting at his mother, spits in the face of the tyrant, stammering through his lips the name of Christ. Then the tyrant, furious, throws him from the marble stairs and "shattered his tender head, created to bear a martyr's crown." [See "A Pilgrimage to the Kastro," *Ápanta*, vol. 2:294.]

⁸Mantzaridis, Ibid., 255.

⁹See more on this question in Constantine Kalokyris, *I Ousía tís orthodóxou Agiographías*, (Athens, 1960), 15.

[10]Mantzaridis, Ibid., 255.

[11]"A Pilgrimage to the Kastro," *Ápanta*, vol. 2:293–295. [*The Boundless Garden*, 124-127.]

[12]See Demetrios D. Triandaphilopoulos, "*O Aléxandros Papadiamandis kaí i Téchni tís Orthoxías*," in the vol., *Phóta Olóphota* ed. Nicholas D. Triandaphilopoulos (Athens: Ellinikó Logotechnikó kai Istorikó Archeío, 1981), 83.

[13]St. Nicholas Kavasilas, *Interpretation of the Divine Liturgy*, PG 150, 372B.

[14]Diadochos Photikis, *Visions*, 56, SC 5, 177.

[15]"Fey Folk," *Ápanta*, vol. 2:491. [*The Boundless Garden*, 240.] For a similar description of the same icon see the story "The Happenings at the Mill," *Ápanta*, vol. 4:520–521.

[16]"The Epidemics," *Ápanta*, vol. 3:549.

[17]Compare Cosmas Maïoumas, Canon for the Dormition of the Theotokos, canticle 1, hirmos, which begins with the words, "Thy sacred and renowned memorial, O Virgin, is clothed in the embroidered [*pepoikilméni*] raiment of divine glory...." [Translation: Mother Mary, Ware, 514.]

[18]The one begins, "*Gynaíká se thnitín, all' yperphyós kaí Mitéra Theoú*," and the second, "*Axíos os émpsychón se ouranón ypedéxanto...*" "The Richly Decorated Icon of the Mother of God," *Ápanta*, vol. 4:333. Compare John of Damascus, Canon for the Dormition of the Theotokos, canticle 1, troparion 2.

[19]See, "The Christmastide Hobgoblin," *Ápanta*, vol. 4:545. In addition, for the icon as a means of the expression of the faith and life of the Church, as well as for its anthropological character, see Demetrios Tselengidis, *I Theología tís Eikónas kaí i Anthropologikí Simasía tis* (Thessalonica, 1984), 77 and following. In addition, for the pedagogical aspect of the icon in the Eastern Church, where this is always understood as mystagogical guidance and direction, see K. Grigoriadis, *Ai Theologikaí Proypothéseis tís Didaktikís tón Thriskevtikón* (Athens, 1971), 124 and following.

[20]An example can be found in the story "The Dead Traveler" (*Ápanta*, vol. 4:342), where he provides a historical account of the finding of, as well as an analytical description of, the icon of the Panagia of Kounistras (or Knistriotissas) whose feast is the same day as the Entrance of the Theotokos into the Temple, November 21.

[21] *Ápanta*, vol. 2:524. [*The Boundless Garden*, 274.]

[22] Ibid. [*The Boundless Garden*, 274.]

[23] *Synodikon of Orthodoxy*.

[24] "My St. George!" *Ápanta*, vol. 5:188–189.

[25] "The Watchman at the Quarantine Colony," *Ápanta*, vol. 2:576.

[26] Ibid., 544–545.

[27] Ibid.

[28] John of Damascus, *On Icons*, 3, PG 94, 1332B.

[29] Ibid., 1, PG 94, 1268A, "I saw a God in human form and my soul was saved."

[30] *Exposition of the Orthodox Faith*, 4, PG 94, 1172B.

[31] Epistles 2, *To Eparchos Olympiodora*, 61, PG 79, 577D–580A.

[32] Herman of Constantinople, *Epistle to Thomas, Bishop of Klavdioupolis*, 4, PG 98, 172C.

[33] Kontakion of the Sunday of Orthodoxy.

[34] See doxastikon of Matins of the Sunday of the Holy Fathers.

[35] *Antirritikos*, 3, PG 99, 433A. Also see Archimandrite Vasilios (present abbot of the Monastery of Iveron), *Theologikó Schólio stis Toichographíes tis Ierás Monís Stavronikíta* (Athens: Domos Publications, 1987), 11–12.

[36] *Ápanta*, vol. 2:524. [*The Boundless Garden*, 274-275.]

[37] "*Aléxandros Papadiamántis*—Penínta Chrónia apó tó Thánató tou," from the journal, *O Tachydrómos*, 7 January 1961. Re-published in the volume *Aléxandros Papadiamántis*, Prologue and Epilogue by Nicholas D. Triandaphilopoulos (Athens, 1979), 224.

[38] See Nicholas D. Triandaphilopoulos, 177 and following.

[39] George Lampakis, *Katálogos tís en Zappeío Ekthéseos, ítoi agiographiká érga Theirsíou...*, (Athens, 1891). Compare the exhibition of his own works in *Deltíon Christianikís Archaiologikís Etaireías* (DCAE), 1st period (1892), vol. 1:89 and following; 116 and following. A bibliography of Theirsios is included in D. Papastamos's *I Epídrasi tís Nazarinís Sképsis stí Neoellinikí Ekklisiastikí Zographikí* (Athens, 1977), 71 and following. For the term "scuola bizantina migliorata," which was prior to the time of Theirsios, see A. Xyggopoulos, *Schedíasma tís Thriskevtikís Zographikís metá tín Álosin* (Athens, 1957), 278 and following. For all of this, see Demetrios Triandaphilopoulos, 193.

[40] See Demetrios Triandaphilopoulos, 193.

[41]Ibid., 184.

[42]"Easter Chanter," *Ápanta*, vol. 2:524. [*The Boundless Garden*, 275.] Also see Demetrios Triandaphilopoulos, 184.

[43]*Ápanta*, vol. 3:74.

[44]Ibid., 309.

[45]Demetrios Triandaphilopoulos, 179.

[46]Ibid.

[47]See *Ápanta*, vol. 5:155–158.

[48]Ibid.

[49]*Ápanta*, vol. 3:75.

[50]"At St. Anastasa's," *Ápanta*, vol. 2:353. [*The Boundless Garden*, 190.]

[51]"The Epitaphios and the Resurrection in the Villages," *Ápanta*, vol. 5:119.

[52]Thucydides, *Histories*, 2, 40, vi. 1–5.

[53]See, for example, John Chrysostom, *Commentary on the Gospel of Matthew. Sermon 50*, PG 58, 508: "not goldsmiths or silversmiths are the church, but the celebration of angels."

[54]"Excerpts of Thoughts," *Ápanta*, vol. 5:237.

[55]Ibid. It is worth noting that those then regarded as amateur poets were more interested in Nietzsche and Ibsen than "in their own rusty native things," 237–238.

[56]That is to say, through the daily use of Greek in the Church's liturgical texts. [Tr.] Ibid. See also, Archimandrite Sophrony (Sakharov), *We Shall See Him As He Is* (Essex, England: Holy Monastery of St. John the Forerunner, 1992), 373–376.

[57]Mark 16:15. When used, this way of enunciation is in the plagal of the fourth or grave mode.

[58]"Excerpts of Thoughts," *Ápanta*, vol. 5:238.

[59]"Great Week in Athens," *Ápanta*, vol. 5:170.

[60]It is unquestionable that if Kassiani's melody for the hymn "Lord, in many sins," was still preserved, that it would be the most perfect. Because such an original does not exist, the oldest existing composition, though not as old as the original melody, is preferable and regarded as more perfect than any newer melody. [Kassiani was one of the most celebrated Byzantine poets and hymnographers. She lived during the ninth century. (Tr.)]

[61]See *Laws*, 700a–701b.

[62]"Great Week in Athens," *Ápanta*, vol. 5:175–176.

[63]Psalm 150:4. The article was published in the newspaper, *Akrópoli*, on April 3, 1892.

[64]Cosmas Maïoumas, Canon for the Dormition of the Theotokos, See *Menaion*, August 15, canticle 7, troparion 2 [Translation: Mother Mary, Ware, 521.]

[65]See Daniel 3:5. Knowing that the voice of symbols contributes to the comprehension of the Church's truths more than theories or rhetoric, Papadiamandis asserts that "the Church has symbolism, and symbolism speaks more eloquently than rhetoric." "Great Week in Athens," *Ápanta*, vol. 5:176.

[66]"Excerpts of Thoughts," *Ápanta*, vol. 5:240.

[67]"The Epitaphios and the Resurrection in the Villages," *Ápanta*, vol. 5:119–120.

[68]"Priests of the Cities and Priests of the Villages," *Ápanta*, vol. 5:198.

[69]*The Republic*, 424b.

[70]Matthew 16:25.

[71]*Fount of Knowledge*, PG 94, 525A.

[72]See "Disenchantress," *Ápanta*, vol. 3:309.

[73]"Peter and Paul, the Foremost Among the Apostles," *Ápanta*, vol. 5:127.

Without a Wedding Crown

[1]1 Corinthians 1:27.

[2]See Matthew 21:9–10, Mark 11:9–10, John 12:13.

[3]Psalm 8:2.

[4]Psalm 12:5.

[5]Luke 23:42.

A Village Easter

[1]There are four fasting periods during the liturgical year: Advent, preceding Christmas, which lasts forty days; Great Lent, preceding Easter, which lasts six weeks; the Fast of the Holy Apostles, beginning on the moveable feast of All Saints and ending on 29 June; and the Fast of the Dormition of the Holy Theotokos, from 1 to 15 August. These fasts reflect the ascetical

practises of the Orthodox Church implying a restraint from the utilitarian exploitation of the natural world and its God-given resources through abstention, on the material level, from animal foods—meat, eggs and dairy products—and also from fish, wine and oil on certain other days, coupled with spiritual preparation and contemplation, prayer and confession of sins.

[2]At about 11 pm on the eve of Easter Sunday the faithful congregate at the church for the celebration of the resurrectional service, which commences with the *Pannychis* (vigil) beginning with the chanting of the canon "On the Waves of the Sea," following which the church is darkened and silence reigns. Then the Royal Doors are opened and the priest emerges clad in white robes and holding in his left hand the Gospel and in his right the lit Paschal candle, chanting the words, "Come, and receive the Light from the inextinguishable Light, and glorify Christ who has risen from the dead." The faithful rush to light their candles from the light offered by the priest, then all file outside, following the priest, for the reading of the Resurrection Gospel and the continuation of Matins.

[3]On Easter Sunday, the Vespers of the Second Resurrection, so called because the Resurrection gospel is read for the second time, in several languages to reflect its universal message, is celebrated. It is also known as the Vespers of Love because the kiss of love is exchanged between brethren amidst joyous exclamations of "Christ is risen!" It is sung earlier than a normal vesperal service, around noon, to allow the Easter day festivities to continue uninterrupted. This service is especially attended by children wearing bright garments and holding their decorated Easter candles.

[4]It is the Godfather, or Godmother, who represents the Church and brings the child within its fold, which includes the reality of the natural world, epitomized by his offerings of oil (the "oil of gladness"), with which he anoints the child during the sacrament of baptism, the cross, the pristine white clothes in which the child will be dressed after the sacrament, and the offerings of bread and wine for the subsequent liturgy when the child will receive its first communion. Traditionally the Godfather will also be the best man (*koumbaros*) at his Godchild's wedding when he will

crown the couple with wreaths. In ancient Greece the victors of athletic competitions received crowns of victory, wreathes made of olive branches; in a Christian context the martyrs, athletes fighting for the faith, received their crowns of martyrdom from God. The crowns received by the married couple are made from vine tendrils, reminding of the blood of Christ, an understanding reinforced by the fact they receive the cup of salvation, a cup of wine, immediately after their crowning.

[5]The correct rendering of the troparion is:

"Christ is risen from the dead
trampling down death by death
and upon those in the tombs
bestowing life."

[6]A hymn sung in the Supplication to the Theotokos; the full troparion is:

"Dumb are the lips of the impious
who are not venerating your holy icon, the Hodegetria,
the one painted by the Apostle,
Luke the most venerable."

[7]The *klephtiko* dance takes its name from the "*klephts*," or robbers, the legendary marauding bands of resistance fighters who circulated during the Ottoman period, living in the mountains and plundering village communities who collaborated with the Turks. The *syrto* and the *kamara* are traditional cyclical dances that commemorate events that have marked the life of the community. The week following Easter Sunday, called "*Diakainisimos*" – "Renewal or Bright Week," a festive week marking the eighth day of the new Creation, the new life that Christ brought into the fallen world by His Resurrection—is celebrated with daily liturgies in the chapels strewn throughout the countryside, followed by communal feasting, singing and dancing.

GLOSSARY

Agrypnía: The Greek word for "vigil." See "Vigil" below.

Canonarch: One who goes back and forth between the chanter on the left and the chanter on the right with an open liturgical book, reading the words of the hymns verse by verse before the chanters chant them.

Coenobitic: A term that literally means "common life" and refers to a monastery where monastic life is shared by all members of the community: in prayer, worship, and work. This is the most common form of monastic life.

Concelebrant: One that serves (celebrates) the Liturgy together with the priest.

Economy: The Church's use of this word derives from the "economy" of Jesus Christ, which was His condescension, as God, to become man in the Incarnation. Though man deserved death, God reached out to man in love, to save him. Economy involves the altering of a given rule, requirement, or practice in a specific concrete case so that the therapeutic aim of the rule can be fulfilled.

Epitaphios: A portable, physical representation of Christ's funeral bier, which is carried as in a funeral procession on the evening of Holy Friday. The term is used both for the funeral bier as well as for the image of Christ that is placed into it. The term is also used to refer to the hymns chanted by the faithful around the funeral bier of Christ on the evening of Holy Friday.

Hesychast: A monastic who undertakes the ascetic practice of *hesychia*, meaning "stillness." It is an ancient spiritual tradition that helps the ascetic remain constantly in prayer.

Hesychastírion: A place dedicated to the spiritual ascetic effort of the preservation of *hesychia* (stillness).

Holy Mountain: See "Mount Athos" below.

Katavasia: A liturgical term referring to the first troparion sung in a given ode of a canon. The rest of the troparions follow the katavasia.

Katharévousa: A form of Modern Greek based on the literary tradition. It is also sometimes called Purist Greek, which is how it is referred to in this text.

Kollyvádes Fathers: Monks from Mount Athos who were involved in the eighteenth century movement that inspired spiritual renewal and a return to more traditional liturgical and spiritual practices. The name *Kollyvádes* is derived from the Greek word *kóllyva*, the boiled wheat prepared by the faithful to be blessed in church, in memory of the reposed. The use of wheat as a Christian symbol for the soul is rooted in Christ's words in John 12:24. The name *Kollyvádes* was derisively given to this movement of spiritual renewal, because one of the issues that they addressed was the performance of memorial services for the reposed on Sundays. They were opposed to this innovation, as it was not in accordance with the traditional resurrectional character of Sunday.

Mount Athos: A monastic republic in northern Greece, on a peninsula surrounded by the Aegean Sea. Monks have inhabited the peninsula since the early Christian centuries. At present Mount Athos has over two thousand monks in twenty ruling monasteries as well as in smaller monastic establishments.

Mystery: The Greek word *mystírion* is translated throughout as "Mystery" rather than as "sacrament," because it corresponds more closely to the theological meaning of the word. It is also capitalized to differentiate it from the common meaning of the word.

Nous: The word nous has been translated elsewhere as "reason" or "intellect," but used in the patristic sense, as in this book, it refers to man's spiritual faculty rather than his logical ability.

Panagia: This is perhaps the most popular term of endearment for Mary the Mother of God in the Greek language.

Phanar: The section of Constantinople (Istanbul) where the Ecumenical Patriarchate is located.

Phrónima: Mindset or character. It also suggests one's upbringing and how this affects one's mindset and development of character.

Precision: Within ecclesiastical vocabulary, precision [*akríveia*] generally denotes the precise keeping of the Church's traditions (canonical, liturgical, etc.) as opposed to the use of economy (understood as a loosening of these traditions at a certain time, for a certain person (or persons), when precision obstructs the path to salvation).

Romyoí (or simply, Roman): Arguably the most precise way of referring to Orthodox Christians within the area and tradition of the Byzantine Empire. For more, see the works of Father John Romanidis.

Skete: A type of monastic organization somewhere between a coenobitic monastery and a hermitage. In a skete, a group of small monastic dwellings are located around a central church.

Stavropegic: A Stavropegic monastery is one that falls under the direct supervision of the most senior bishop in any given Church jurisdiction. In the case of Greece, a Stavropegic monastery would fall directly under the supervision of the Patriarch of Constantinople. The monasteries of Mount Athos are Stavropegic and enjoy a similar independence from the local bishop.

Símantron: Most commonly, a long and slender piece of wood struck rhythmically with a mallet. It is usually used in monasteries to call the community to services, although some parish churches also use them. According to a tradition of the Church, the use of the *símantron* dates from the time of Noah, who used the *símantron* to call the animals into the ark in pairs. Similarly, the *símantron* is used to call the "rational flock," that is, the faithful, into the ark of salvation, which is the Church.

Synaxarion: A collection of the lives of the Saints, arranged according to the day their memory is celebrated during the ecclesiastical year.

Typicon: In ecclesiastical terminology, typicon has a variety of meanings. It is used in this book, however, to mean the rules/ directions governing how a liturgical service is to be celebrated.

Vigil: The Greek word for vigil (*agrypnía*) refers both to one's own private vigil in prayer as well as to the long night services (particularly for Church feasts) celebrated in the Orthodox Church. It is the latter that is meant in this text. An Athonite monastery has about thirty-five vigils a year. A standard vigil lasts between nine and ten hours, while patronal vigils can last between twelve and seventeen hours.

TRANSLATED TITLES OF PAPADIAMANDIS'S STORIES

A Pilgrimage to the Kastro	Stó Christó stó Kástro
A Different Type	Állos Typos
A Drop of Water...	Stagóna Neroú...
A Roman Easter	Páscha Roméiko
A Village Easter	Exohikí Lamprí
Alone Among Strangers	Érmi stá Xéna
At Saint Anastasa's	Stín Agi-Anastasá
Athens as an Eastern City	Ai Athínai os Anatolikí Pólis
Biography of Al. Papadiamandis	Viographía Al. Papadiamánti
Black Scarf Rock	I Mavromantiloú
Bright Week	I Evdomás tís Diakainisímou
Burdened Bones	Fortoména Kókkala
Carnival Night	Apokriátiki Niktiá
Correspondence of Alex. Papadiamandis	Allilographía Alex. Papadiamánti
Delisiphero	Delisiphéro
Disenchantress	Pharmakolýtria
Easter Chanter	Lampriátikos Psáltis
Ecclesiastical Discourses and Studies	Lógoi Ekklisiastikoí kaí Melétai
Ecclesiastical Editions in Athens	Ekklisiastikaí Ekdóseis en Athínais
Ecclesiastical Rhetoricians and the Holy Synod	Ekklisiastikoí Rítores kaí Ierá Sýnodos
Eros-Hero	Éros-Íros
Excerpts of Thoughts	Apospásmata Sképseon
Father Dionysios	O Patír Dionýsios
Fey Folk	Oi Elaphroískiotoi
Final Response to The Word	Teleutaía Apántisis eis tón "Lógon"
For Pride	Giá tín Peripháneia

The Dead Traveler	Nekrós Taxidiótis
The Death Agony	T' Angéliasma
The Epidemics	Tá Kroúsmata
The Epitaphios and the Resurrection in the Villages	O Epitáphios kaí i Anástasis eis ta Horía
The Eternally Deluded One	O Aeiplánitos
The Fairy in the Tree	T' Aerikó stó Déndro
The Fallen Dervish	O Xepesménos Dervísis
The Furnace	Tó Kamíni
The Gleaner	Stahomazóchtra
The Godmother	I Sintéknissa
The Grumblers	Oi Paramponeménes
The Gypsy Girl	I Giphtopoúla
The Happenings at the Mill	Tá Symvánta stón Mýlo
The Hidden Wall	Tó Kryphó Mandráki
The House of Kokonas	Tís Kokkónas tó Spíti
The Hushing Up	Tó Koukoúloma
The Immigrant	I Metanástis
The Invalid	O Simademénos
The Lady Supporter of Makrakis	I Makrakistína
The Last One Baptized	I Teleutaía Vaptistikí
The Little Star	T' Asteráki
The Makrakian Episode in Skiathos	Tó Makrákeion Epeisódion en Skiátho
The Memorial Services and the Purgatorial Fire	Tá Mnimósina kaí tó Kathartírion
The Miracle of Kaisariani	Tó Thávma tís Kaisarianís
The Monk	O Kalógeros
The Murderess	I Phónissa
The Nine-Hundredth Anniversary of the Great Lavra	I Enneakosaetirís tís Pammegístis Lávras
The Orphan	O Pentárphanos
The Promiscuous One	O Anákatos
The Provisions of Grandeur	Megaleíon Opsónia
The Quintals	Oi Kantaraíoi
The Reverberation of the Mind	O Antíktypos toú Nou
The Richly Decorated Icon of the Mother of God	I Pepoikilméni
The Rose-Tinted Shores	Tá Ródin Akrogiália
The Stricken One	I Htypiméni
The Suicide	O Avtoktónos

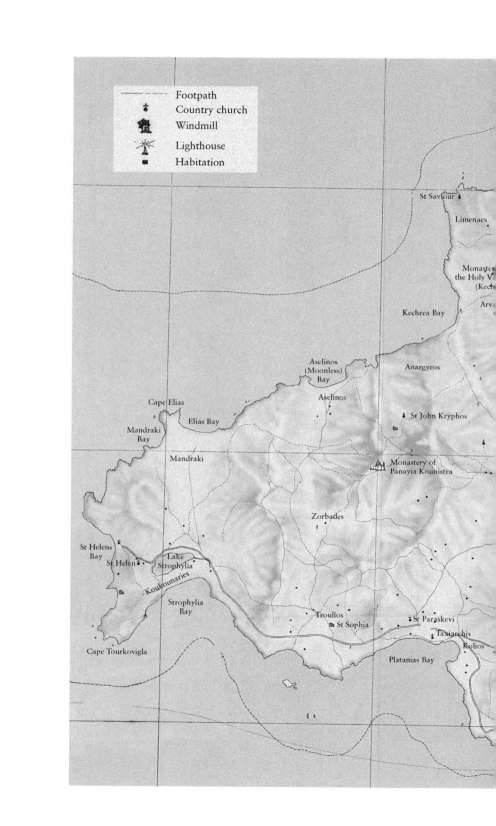

stro
ikros Yialos

Cape Kouroupi

Tripia Petra

ohn the Baptist   Klinias

Kambia   Kouroupi

Panayia Doman   Stivoto   Nikotsara Bay

Chairimona
Stream   Monastery of
                St Charalambos

Mygdali   Vigles

                                K'fandonis   Megalos
                                                    Yialos
Karafiltzanaka
                Monastery of
                the Annunciation   Xanemos

                            Deserted Village
                                            Kalivia   Cape Kephala
            Kanakis's Spring

  Three Crosses
is's   St George
        Cold Well   Christodoulitsa
            St Dimitris

St Athanasios   Stamelos's Spring
    Prophet Elias (Elijah)

Constantine

            Petralono

        Matarona

        Vourlidia

        Doctor's Vineyard   Lagoon

Livadia
    St Fanourios   St George

SKIATHOS
TOWN

                                        Pounda
raskevi

    Megali Ammos
                    Bourtzi   Daskalio
                               Island

                            Cape Pounda

lada
                    Maragos
                    Island   Arkas
                                            Island

sa
    Black Scarf Rock

alamaki   Tsoungria
                         Island

N

FORTHCOMING FROM PROTECTING VEIL

Further Up and Further In: The Theology of C.S. Lewis and the Church Fathers

An Eastern Orthodox bishop has referred to C. S. Lewis as an "Anonymous Orthodox," but as of yet there has been no full-length consideration of Lewis's theology in light of Orthodox patristic teachings.

What convictions were at the heart of Lewis's theology and how close was his teaching to that of the Christian Fathers of the East? *Further Up and Further In: The Theology of C.S. Lewis and the Church Fathers* addresses these questions to consider whether Lewis may be truly regarded as an "Anonymous Orthodox."

EDUCATIONAL DVDs

Collective Wisdom: Interviews With Contemporary Orthodox Thinkers

Volume 1: What is Orthodoxy? Answers for Enquirers

Volume 2: Orthodox Life in the Modern World

ALSO PUBLISHED BY
PROTECTING VEIL

Precious Vessels of the Holy Spirit: The Lives and Counsels of Contemporary Elders of Greece

In an age searching for solutions to its existential questions, the ancient ministry of the God-bearing elder is a gift to contemporary man. Termed the "golden chain" by St. Symeon the New Theologian, this life-giving ministry of the Church is a precious inheritance passed down from Christ, through the Apostles, from one generation to the next, to our own day. The lives and counsels contained in this volume attest to the continued vitality of this ancient ministry and its importance for the life of the Church today.

This volume includes a foreword by Dr. Georgios Mantzaridis, Professor Emeritus of the University of Thessalonica, extensive commentary providing the context for the lives and counsels, detailed maps, and a glossary of theological terms, making it an invaluable source of spiritual orientation and enlightenment for every seeker of Christian Orthodoxy.

In Peace Let Us Pray to the Lord: An Orthodox Interpretation of the Gifts of the Spirit

For many, the modern Pentecostal Movement can be a perplexing and mystifying world. In this masterful work, Fr. Alexis Trader provides one patristic answer to the questions that Pentecostalism raises, an answer fully grounded in Holy Scripture, and accessible through the spiritual life of stillness. Fr. Alexis deftly shows how the Church that experienced and was established at Pentecost, the Orthodox Church, can illumine our understanding of the history, experience, and teaching of Pentecostalism, while simultaneously providing a pathway to the gifts of the Spirit where seemingly confusing Biblical passages are placed in a context that brings clarity. Without a doubt, this is the best and fullest work dealing with this topic in the English language.

New translations of works by Alexandros Papadiamandis
THE BOUNDLESS GARDEN: SELECTED SHORT
STORIES, VOLUME I & *THE MURDERESS*

ALEXANDROS PAPADIAMANDIS lived in the midst of an uncertain age of transition for modern Greece. It was a period of post-Enlightenment turmoil when the traditional old ways were being undermined and were fast disappearing under the pressure of the indiscriminate adoption of western mores and ideas. His reflections on and observations of some of the most complex facets of Greek life in both his native island of Skiathos and in urban Athens during this time define the modern Greek experience in a way unattained by any of his now forgotten contemporaries.

The stories presented in Volume I of *The Boundless Garden* encompass the main and universal themes that best exemplify his work. In them he records and recreates that modern Greek experience as it was lived in its many perspectives — displacement, emigration, home-coming, estrangement, exile, attempts to reclaim lost innocence, visions of Paradise, the daily struggle for survival — and explores the souls of men and women as they succumbed to or struggled against the power of evil and dealt with life's ambiguities.

The Murderess, a novella, long considered to be Papadiamandis's masterpiece, tells the story of a country woman who has convinced herself that her mission is to rid the world from the unsolicited misery of female progeny. Papadiamandis charts the course of her life, its ambivalence and self-deception, faithfully and realistically recording events and the particular quality evil has of disguising itself as good, but never bringing judgment upon her person.

Within these themes Papadiamandis also embraced the mythic past as it survived through the Greek people's belief in supernatural wonders and that animated the countryside with haunted ruins, nymphs, and fairies, and the sea with mermaids and Tritons. His was an authentic expression of a reality that he saw as a seamless whole in which man, whether or not he was conscious of it, spirits, and the natural world all participate in a living liturgical now, ever moving towards their eternal source.

The Boundless Garden, Selected Short Stories, Vol. I
364 pages, 24.0 x 15.5 cm, sewn pages
ISBN 978-960-7120-22-9 (paper), 978-960-7120-21-2 (cloth)

The Murderess, translated by Liadain Sherrard
140 pages, 24.0 x 15.5 cm, sewn pages
ISBN 978-960-7120-28-1 (paper)

For more information and to order please visit:
www.DeniseHarveyPublisher.gr

Made in the USA
Monee, IL
04 August 2021